New Designs for
Teachers' Professional Learning

✓

The Bedford Way Papers Series

A full list of Bedford Way Papers, including earlier books in the series, may be found at www.ioe.ac.uk/publications

**Leading education
and social research**
Institute of Education
University of London

New Designs for Teachers' Professional Learning

Edited by
Jon Pickering, Caroline Daly and Norbert Pachler

Bedford Way Papers

First published in 2007 by the Institute of Education, University of London,
20 Bedford Way, London WC1H 0AL
www.ioe.ac.uk/publications

© Institute of Education, University of London 2007

British Library Cataloguing in Publication Data:
A catalogue record for this publication is available from the British Library

ISBN 978 0 85473 729 1

Design by River Design, Edinburgh
Typeset by Chapman Design Limited
Printed by Elanders Ltd

Contents

Contributors

Caroline Daly, Institute of Education, University of London

Elizabeth Gowing, Educational Consultant

John Hardcastle, Institute of Education, University of London

Louise Johns-Shepherd, Programme Director for Personalisation, Primary National Strategy

Hugh Kearns, Stranmillis University College, Belfast

Hilary Kemeny, National Institute of Education, Singapore

Jim O'Brien, Centre for Educational Leadership, University of Edinburgh

Norbert Pachler, Institute of Education, University of London

Jon Pickering, Institute of Education, University of London

Shirley Simon, Institute of Education, University of London

Maureen Thatcher, Stranmillis University College, Belfast

Karen Turner, Institute of Education, University of London

Anne Turvey, Institute of Education, University of London

Adam Unwin, Institute of Education, University of London

Introduction

Jon Pickering, Caroline Daly and Norbert Pachler
Institute of Education, University of London

Teachers' professional learning in the past 15 years has been increasingly shaped by global trends towards creating a 'modernised' and 're-professionalised' teaching workforce (Mahony and Hextall, 2000). Policy-making for teachers' continuing professional development (CPD) has focused on centralised ways of managing the development of teachers, and has seen an exponential growth in government intervention in CPD. The impact of these forces has been experienced differently by countries with distinct education systems within the United Kingdom. Here teachers work within differing policy-making environments, but within a shared context characterised by the development of new professionalism, shareholders' investment in teachers' CPD and the growth of interest in networks for teacher learning. At the same time, the role of universities in contributing to teachers' professional learning has been transformed within differing perceptions of what higher education (HE) can contribute to teachers' learning in practice, and the contested intellectual dimensions of teachers' knowledge.

In this book we bring together contributions from different parts of the UK in an attempt to provide insights into the different ways in which this agenda for change in CPD plays out within different policy contexts and its impact on teachers' experience of CPD. Therefore, whilst not international in the broader sense, this book certainly addresses the problematic from different national

1

perspectives. We do so deliberately in an attempt to recognise the diversity of educational context in the UK, a fact that is often at best overlooked and at worst ignored, as well as in a deliberate attempt to learn from each other as teacher educators. All the contributors are CPD practitioners with extensive experience of innovating teacher learning within networked, local authority and HE contexts.

By way of introduction and explanation, it is also necessary to discuss briefly one particular model of teachers' professional development, which underpins a number of chapters in this book. This is an award-bearing course at Master's level developed at the Institute of Education, University of London, which has since been adapted by other higher education institutions (HEIs) in the UK. The Master of Teaching is similar to other Master's-level provision in the field of education in that it aims to provide award-bearing professional development for teachers in line with the expectations of the relevant national qualifications framework level descriptors. It is quite different, though, in so far as it does not treat the students' engagement with education as the intellectual study of an academic discipline. Instead, it foregrounds critical reflection on professional practice as well as educational research literacy, i.e. the ability to read, interpret and implement educational policies in a critical and context-sensitive manner as well as to understand, apply and be able to produce educational research and enquiry.

The Master of Teaching (MTeach) also differs from traditional Master's-level courses in its emphasis on notions of knowledge construction by participants rather than knowledge transmission by university lecturers. In addition, it adopts a mixed-mode teaching pattern which uses computer-mediated communication between participants as its central pedagogic approach supported by some face-to-face encounters. Over the years the course team has developed and refined a course pedagogy, which uses a template-based approach to online discussion. Through this approach, debate is stimulated by think pieces posted by tutors to which participants are invited to engage with reference to their personal professional practice, as well as to carefully selected relevant professional and academic literature. Fundamental to the course are also innovative approaches to assessment, including the use of professional portfolios, reflective learner diaries and artefact creation and critique.

The MTeach at the Institute of Education was developed very much in an attempt to provide innovative CPD opportunities for teachers. Its central underpinning principle and feature remains the emphasis on the development of a sustained learning community supported by the use of new technology. The course team did not set out to add technology to traditional conceptualisations of CPD at Master's level. Instead, it developed a genuinely new model to meet the developing professional and personal needs of participants, attempting to accommodate the increasingly prevailing demands for anytime, anywhere and just-in-time, as well as to be able to reflect the ever-changing educational policy context in which they operate in real time. The focus on a learning community-based approach not only tries to accommodate the socio-political imperatives of the knowledge society, but it also attends to practitioners' needs and desire to work with peers in order to further their personal and professional growth and development. Informing the development of the course also was an acute awareness of the shortcomings of much traditional CPD, enumerated by Lock (2006: 665) as

> (a) one-shot and one-size-fits-all workshops; (b) use of the transmission model from experts to teachers; (c) failure to address school-specific differences; (d) just-in-case training; and (e) system-wide presentations that do not provide sufficient time to plan or to learn new strategies to meet the reality of their own classrooms.

The MTeach, rather than being a (series of) CPD event(s), is a sustained and intensive CPD experience that is situated both in the workplace and embedded in the work of a higher education institution. This provides ongoing opportunities for intensive, sustained and coherent individual and collaborative research-oriented learning, based on a notion of community of practice 'where enquiry is a stance, not a project or strategy' (Cochran-Smith and Lytle, 2001: 53). A key feature of the concept of CPD promoted through the MTeach is its focus on learning: 'Teachers need to be learners who engage in the learning process for themselves, are willing to refine their thinking and practice, to listen to each other as they formulate ideas and understandings, and are open to learn from errors' (Lock, 2006: 668–9).

Also characteristic of the MTeach is the model of teacher-learning communities developed by Lee and Judith Shulman (2004: 259), which defines an 'accomplished' teacher as follows:

> An accomplished teacher is a member of a professional community who is ready, willing and able to teach and to learn from his or her teaching experiences. Thus, the elements of the theory are: Ready (*possessing vision*), Willing (*having motivation*), Able (both *knowing* and *being able 'to do'*), Reflective (*learning from experience*), and Communal (*acting as a member of a professional community*).

With Shulman and Shulman we argue that each of these dimensions entails an aspect of personal and professional development, and the course team views the MTeach as instrumental in working towards such a notion of an 'accomplished teacher'.

Focus and principles

The book is organised into three parts, which deal with differing perspectives on key issues with regard to the nature and trajectory of CPD. However, the overall focus is a critique of the current government-driven training programmes and courses in the UK that seek to enhance teachers' professional development. The chapters debate the benefits of such programmes and courses for teachers, and, as a consequence, their pupils. The audience for this book will, hopefully, be as diverse as the chapters themselves and readers may wish to select chapters on the basis of the descriptive summaries at the end of the introduction. This diversity notwithstanding, the main thread in the book is a clear, yet contestable, argument that current CPD programmes and courses may well develop teachers. However, there are considerable inconsistencies within the UK regarding how they bring about the type of rounded and grounded learning that will lead to sustained benefits for individual teachers and the profession as a whole. This book combines investigations into, and judgements about, the current dominant forms of teachers' CPD and the benefits of formal and informal teachers' professional learning. These new designs for professional learning are exemplified by newly developed Master of Teaching courses in England, Northern Ireland and Scotland. Additionally there are the inductive approaches to CPD of the National College for School Leadership (NCSL), of the General Teaching Council for England (GTCE) to networked learning communities and of the Qualifications and Curriculum Authority (QCA), with the pilot curriculum groups that have come out of their *Futures* (2005) debate (pamphlet available at: www.qca.org.uk/11493.html).

There are two underpinning principles to the book, namely that collectively the authors are advocating a different approach to the current dominant discourse of CPD, and that they are advocating an approach that is innovative and new because of the potential of new technologies and collaborative approaches to CPD. These two principles mean that the authors are challenging overtly current orthodoxies, which position CPD, viewed as the delivery of teachers' professional learning, firmly in the arena of performance management and school improvement.

Instead a newly designed approach to CPD should focus on three key themes. These are:

- shared practice, i.e. more than just an exchange of practice but one that leads proactively into changes in practice. This contains the potential for all teachers to be agents for change, and is not best practice, 'delivered' as a top-down model by experts;

- collaborative CPD, which draws on the strengths of learning networks that are most effective when they are classroom-focused, and, where possible, cross-phase, cross-subject, cross-experience, i.e. not hierarchical; and

- scholarly reflection on practice, which regards the fusion of theory and practice as being what teaching is about, thus rejecting the prevalent skills-based approach to much CPD.

In practice this will mean that teachers, through their professional learning, will be encouraged to take a critical and independent stance towards 'best practice' and to challenge and contest constructively the perceived givens of evidence-informed policy and practice. This will be achieved through a collaborative orientation, characterised by shared practice and a focus on scholarly teaching in learning networks. The main processes and outcomes of the new designs will be a mixed-mode approach to CPD, and the foregrounding of collaborative online work and learning-focused portfolios. This is not to adopt an idealised view of what it is possible to achieve within contemporary contexts. However, it is to argue that we need new forms of professional learning (instruments) – and they are already becoming established – to enable teachers to be responsive and responsible in withstanding managerialist solutions to educating each new generation of pupils.

Context

Continuing professional development (CPD) is big business in the United Kingdom, especially in England. The government's Teachernet website provides a wealth of CPD guidance and opportunities (www.teachernet.gov.uk/professionaldevelopment/). Teachers can also access the websites of the General Teaching Council for England

(GTCE) (www.gtce.org.uk/cpd_home/) or that of the National College for School Leadership (NCSL) (www.ncsl.org.uk/programmes/index.cfm), to add to the wide choice of CPD opportunities. There is also a growing 'library' of research into CPD available, led by both the National Foundation for Educational Research (NFER) (at www.nfer.ac.uk) and the Evidence for Policy and Practice Information and Co-ordinating Centre based at the Institute of Education (see EPPI-Centre, 2003, 2005 and at www.eppi.ioe.ac.uk). There are also many professional and academic journals dedicated to the content and processes of CPD.

Key to an understanding of the context of this book on teachers' professional learning is the blurring by the Department for Education and Skills (DfES; previously the Department for Education and Employment, DfEE) in England and its associated agencies of professional development and professional learning. The government's *CPD Strategy* document (DfEE, 2001) and the more recent guidance on *Leading and Coordinating CPD in Secondary Schools* (DfES, 2005) sees professional development as primarily 'increasing teachers' skills, knowledge and understanding' (DfEE, 2001). Although both documents refer to professional learning, the distinction between development and learning is not made clear. Learning is not considered to be a personal, holistic process of professional development (Bolam, 1993; Day, 1999; Earley, 2005). Instead, according to the DfES, learning is seen, as noted above, specifically as the acquiring of knowledge, skills and understanding. This is a highly 'practical' view of teaching and a largely passive process, not an active, sharing, 'professional' one. The latter, akin to what Fielding *et al.* (2005) called 'joint practice development', would provide a model for CPD that considers learning as fundamental to development. By way of contrast, development does not in and of itself lead to the kind of deep and rich learning that many of the teachers[1] refer to in these chapters.

Just as the DfES's blurring of professional development and learning within CPD is seen as unproblematic, so there is a blurring of pupils' learning and performance. This is something that has been a strong and unfortunate feature of the standards debate in the last ten years or so in England. Unfortunate because it has created an emphasis on teachers' CPD that focuses almost exclusively on improving teaching, in order that teachers can improve pupils' learning. Or is it actually pupils' performance in public tests and assessments, an even more restricted and restricting view of learning? If it is learning, then there should be opportunities for CPD that is contesting and questioning, pushing the boundaries of teaching and learning through risk-taking. However, if CPD is about ensuring gains in pupil performance, then there have to be skills-based courses or training that help 'deliver' classroom practice. These, in turn, support the 'delivery' of national strategies, which are, in turn, assessed by national tests and assessments. The latter view of the purpose of CPD is a restricted one, not the more holistic one advocated by Bolam, Day and Earley (noted above). It is totally about teachers' professional development. It is not about teachers' learning. The real CPD focus in England is on courses such as the National Professional Qualification for Headship (NPQH) rather than professional doctorates, and on Leading from the Middle (LftM) rather than Master's courses. The latter are seen very much as a matter for personal choice; the former represent the professional choice. In the official discourse, CPD is about raising standards – performance standards. By contrast, the Chartered Teacher (CT) Scheme in Scotland includes 'Professional Actions' within its CT Standards, including 'Articulating a personal, independent and critical stance in relation to contrasting perspectives on educational issues, policies and developments' (PA9) and 'Ensuring that teaching is informed by reading and research' (PA6). The Professional Commitment (PC3) requires teachers to collaborate with and influence colleagues. Thus, there are considerable differences in the CPD priorities in Scotland and England concerning the development of teachers' professional identities with regard to their own learning and practice, and that of others notwithstanding invariable problems with the implementation of these standards in practice.

It is hard to argue against an emphasis on CPD that focuses on improving standards, i.e. pupil performance. However, if this means that most courses and INSET programmes are based on a generalised evidence base of 'what works', then there is an inevitability that the general nature of the advice offered will fail to speak to many teachers in their particular contexts. Moreover, if this general advice is 'delivered' in the sort of transmission mode that most teachers would be criticised for if they taught that way themselves, then the advice is likely to be seen as unwelcome and unhelpful. This is not to deny that there are elements of centrally organised CPD that stimulate teachers' learning through an approach that is active, collaborative and contextualised. One example of this is the NCSL approach in England to the development of serving headteachers, the Leadership Programme for Serving Headteachers (LPSH). Over time it has developed co-coaching groups as part of its programme. The agenda for these groups is very much self-directed and enables the headteachers to decide what, when, where and how they learn directly from their collective experience, much in the way that the groups of participants do on the three Master of Teaching courses described in this book. Similarly the professional learning networks of both the NCSL and the GTCE are described by previous members of both organisations in one of the chapters. These networks offer the possibility for teachers to decide what it is they want to get out of their networks, recognising the value of the 'clustered' approach to teacher and school development typical of some other countries (Bueler, 1998).

Given that we argue in this book for a new, more situated and contextualised design for teachers' professional learning, it might be expected that school-based CPD, including meetings, training and INSET, would be more highly prized and received. Whilst recognising the peril of generalising from a small sample, it would appear from the participants' feedback on the three MTeach courses on which chapters in this book are based, that much work-based learning for teachers, particularly the formally developed episodes, falls into the same trap as central provision. Regardless of whether the leaders of the CPD are senior leaders in the school, local authority advisers or external consultants, the dominant approach is characterised by a top-down, best practice orientation, delivered by a knowledge transmission model. There is little attention given to a collaborative orientation. There is rarely *authentic* group work, which draws on and values what all teachers have to offer and, crucially, creates knowledge about practice that can then be enacted. Finally, there is little scholarly, critical reflection on practice, which brings to bear on practice the fusion of local and (inter)national theory and deep reflections about teaching and learning.

The three models of teachers' professional learning – the Master of Teaching in England, Northern Ireland and Scotland[2] – have similarities and differences of approach and content that will become apparent from reading the different chapters. In general terms, however, it is possible to see that these three courses represent new designs for teachers' professional learning in as much as together they see teaching as a transformative profession, and learning as a transformative process. Teachers may, indeed do, need to see their learning in terms of developing skills, knowledge and understanding. However, there does need to be something more than the acquisition of these aspects of their learning, with professional learning that is not *solely* to improve pupils' performance in national tests and examinations. All three of the courses recognise the need for teachers to be critically informed about their practice and constructively contesting what they are asked to do, especially if it has little or no resonance in their context. Moreover, the contributors exemplify the other key feature of this book: the advocacy of the crucial role of higher education providers in offering a different perspective on teachers' professional learning, which enables and empowers teachers to think and work 'against the grain' of current CPD provision. It is through HE's pushing of the boundaries, especially through technology, and offering a new reality of how/what learning can take place, that the innovative approach to teachers' professional learning that is required can create different and new opportunities for teachers to share and improve their thinking and practice.

Structure

The structure of the book has a clear line of development. The contributors are teachers on, and active researchers of, the courses and programmes which they discuss, combining the development of innovative pedagogies and course design with an investigative stance towards their work in CPD. By this they seek to promote the way forward in developing new designs for professional learning, by establishing research and practitioner communities amongst CPD providers. The research approaches are eclectic, and reflect the multiple interests of those who are starting to provide new forms of CPD, but they are united by a commitment to reshaping the current learning experiences of teachers. As noted earlier, readers may wish to be selective about the chapters they read, as they intentionally include a wide range of practical and theoretical perspectives. Accordingly, the book is organised into three parts. The first part looks at the broad issues of teachers' professional learning in a twenty-first century context. The second part deals with a range of detailed and 'thick' descriptions of what teachers' professional learning can be like away from a dominant CPD discourse, and how this can benefit their engagement with and commitment to their practice. In the third part, two of the authors return to the benefits and challenges of moving the CPD agenda on in a way that acknowledges and benefits from what teachers can offer to CPD, not just receive.

Part 1 addresses two major features of change, which directly impact on the design and mediation of the CPD models that are presented in this book: the accreditation of high-level practice-based learning and the impact of new technologies on contemporary ways of learning. This is discussed within two contexts: the Master of Teaching in Northern Ireland and, then, the new opportunities afforded by constructivist approaches to learning in an online environment. Both Chapters 1 and 2 deal with contexts that we think are important, namely the broader UK themes and what we can learn from each other, and from the new technologies.

In Part 2, the contributors offer in six chapters rich descriptions of what the new designs for teachers' professional learning can look like. The focus of this section is the innovative use and outcomes of different networks for learning and the benefits to teachers of reflecting deeply and collaboratively on their practice.

Part 3 returns to the wider context, beginning with an examination of the way in which the Master of Teaching in a Scottish university relates to national policy considerations. The final chapter summarises the main outcomes and recommendations of the previous chapters, before engaging with the debate about desirable changes to the provision of initial and continuous teacher training.

Overview of the chapters

In the first of the two chapters in Part 1, Hugh Kearns and Maureen Thatcher from Stranmillis University College, Belfast, provide a rationale for redesigned pedagogies within a new professional Master's degree, giving a clear exposition of the role that a higher education institution can bring to teachers' CPD. In their chapter they evaluate a teaching strategy designed to support the accreditation of teacher CPD in Northern Ireland across a range of recently proposed stages of teacher professional registration. The authors draw upon an archive of online, shared and managed teacher discussion around critical incidents of learning at work, illustrated in the authors' action research. The authors consider the challenge to universities of gaining public funding for the refinement of pedagogies advancing both teacher activism and professional accountability within standards frameworks.

In Chapter 2, Caroline Daly and Norbert Pachler from the Institute of Education, University of London, look at the pedagogical possibilities offered through innovative use of new technologies. Constructivist approaches to knowledge-making underpin the design of the Institute of Education's Master of Teaching course. This is based on using computer-mediated communication to support teacher learning, and the course transposes social-constructivist approaches from face-to-face contexts to the online environment. The authors explore the individual and social perspectives on teacher narrative and learning, and what these perspectives suggest about the pedagogical role of technology in developing courses aimed at teachers' continuing professional development. The chapter examines the features of an online course design that aims to harness the potential of shared narratives as a professional learning tool, and which is based on the early years of course development in the Master of Teaching.

In Part 2, the focus is on the details of what happens on, and what innovations were developed by, the Institute of Education's Master of Teaching in particular and on learning networks in general. It begins with Karen Turner and Shirley Simon, from the Institute of Education, articulating a new approach to the use of portfolios as an aid to teachers' professional learning. The authors note that the literature on portfolio development emphasises the importance of providing teachers with the opportunity to reflect critically on their practice and to engage in a professional dialogue and collaboration with colleagues to develop understanding of teaching and learning. The research for this chapter focuses on an analysis of portfolio development experienced by four participants on the Master of Teaching: two have recently completed the course and two are embarking on their first year of study.

Chapter 4 is by Louise Johns-Shepherd, Programme Director for Personalisation for the Primary National Strategy, and Elizabeth Gowing, an educational consultant currently working in Kosovo. Until recently, Louise was a consultant headteacher for the National College for School Leadership, and Elizabeth was involved in the learning network programme of the General Teaching Council of England. They had previously worked together in an education action zone in south London. In their chapter they are writing in a personal capacity. They present professional learning networks as a way of empowering teachers to share the practice that they want to share. They assert the belief, held by all contributors to this book, that schools should not work in isolation and that they will never really make a difference to the lives of the children within them by closing their gates. Based on their experience in two national agencies, the authors posit that schools will not improve by simply implementing large box-files of government initiatives. Powerful, significant and long-lasting professional development happens, the authors' experience tells them, when teachers engage together in school-to-school networks, to solve real problems and make new meanings for application in real classrooms.

In chapter 5, Anne Turvey, from the Institute of Education, and Hilary Kemeny, from the National Institute of Education, Singapore, analyse in depth the engagement of new teachers with the process of reading and carrying out research. The authors take as their evidence base an online discussion on the Institute of Education's Master of Teaching 'Research and Professional Practice' module. In this example the participants on the course are taking part in an online discussion about educational research. Participants' responses and questions to each other are both timely and thought-provoking: 'Just what is teacher research? How do I turn what happens in my classroom into analysable data? What does "generalisable" mean?' These participants, all in their second year as qualified teachers, are just beginning to get to grips with the complexities of research. The authors consider how their discussions, collaborative and reflective, their progress as 'researchers' within different communities and the participation of their tutors, can illuminate aspects of educational research that concern all educators.

This collaborative reflection, leading to the co-construction of knowledge, is also evident in John Hardcastle's chapter, where he describes through the detailed case of an inner-city primary school teacher, how Master of Teaching participants learn to make sense of classroom talk as part of their module assessment. The author notes that teachers have always made sense of children's learning and development by drawing on both 'professional knowledge' as well as their 'life experiences'. This chapter looks at the way teachers present and interpret online incidents from classrooms where children's learning is complicated by urban issues – multi-ethnicity, multilingualism, poverty and power. In particular, it examines the way that a mixture of face-to-face contact and electronic communication creates distinct opportunities for teachers, and one teacher in particular, to develop professional understanding among their peers.

Much of the work described in this part of the book has emanated from the online discussions, formal and informal, which course participants engage in on the Master of Teaching course at the Institute of Education, University of London. In Chapter 7, Adam Unwin examines one of the 'tasks' undertaken by students on the course. This particular task is part of the first-year core module 'Understanding Teaching' taken by teachers in their Newly Qualified Teacher (NQT) year. The content, focus and timing of the online tasks have to be carefully designed to be relevant and pertinent to the issues that new teachers encounter in their classrooms in the busiest and most stressful year of their teaching career. The author's research demonstrates how much these 'first year' teachers benefit from the newness of cross-phase, cross-school, cross-subject, cross-location collaboration about their practice.

In the final chapter of Part 2, Jon Pickering draws on a study of teachers' experiences of professional learning. He examines what graduates from the Institute of Education's Master of Teaching course say about their professional learning. What they have to say reflects two of the key themes in this section. These are, first, the importance of learning that is networked, so that it is shared, participatory, engaging and relevant. And, second, teachers' professional learning also benefits from the very innovative approaches to teaching and learning that teachers themselves are encouraged to employ and develop. The model of transferring good practice, both external and school-based, is regarded by them in its current form as a disempowering model. The study suggests that the professional development of teachers in England needs to adopt a different conceptual model, if it is to meet the professional and personal learning needs of teachers in a rapidly changing teaching and learning context.

Part 3 returns to the wider context of CPD through the advocacy of a new design for teachers' professional learning in Scotland. Jim O'Brien from the University of Edinburgh considers whether the professional learning of Scottish teachers in the post-McCrone era can be characterised as control or empowerment. The post-devolution settlement in the UK has led to increasing divergence in educational policy and practice in the four home countries, although the control–empowerment tension is probably a common concern. The author argues in Chapter 9 that Scotland, in particular, with its long-established education system, appears determined to pursue different approaches to UK-wide issues and problems. The Scottish CPD Framework and the individual professionally endorsed standards have all been subject to research by the author. This research is drawn on to illuminate the process of policy development, how the standards have become accepted by Scottish teachers and the way in which programmes associated with various standards, including the Master of Teaching (Chartered Teacher Programme) at the University of Edinburgh, have been realised.

The concluding chapter in Part 3, by Norbert Pachler, explores the interrelationship between teachers' professional development and teacher professionalism and professionality. It does so with reference to the prevailing educational policy context and broader socio-political developments, such as the impact of neo-liberalism and managerialism on education. With reference to some examples from England, Pachler seeks to demonstrate that government-sponsored CPD initiatives are, at least to some extent, at odds with extended notions of teacher professionality, and he goes on to suggest some ways in which this shortcoming might be addressed. In particular, he foregrounds collaborative and enquiry-based approaches to teachers' CPD, namely the notions of productive pedagogy and enquiry as a stance on case-based learning, in an attempt to move conceptualisations of teacher professionalism from a restricted to an extended plane.

In the Conclusion, the editors reflect on the key themes of the book and propose ways forward, which focus on the benefits for the teaching profession of all stakeholders, including higher education, in working together to produce an energised, confident and informed teaching force, whose lifelong learning mirrors that, hopefully, of the pupils they teach.

The chapter structure of the book has developed a line of argument about new designs for teachers' professional learning from an overall rationale for innovation, through wider contexts into more detailed consideration of networks for learning and teachers' collaborative reflection on practice, and then makes suggestions for ways forward. The issues raised are the need for:

- a key part of professional learning to be the challenging of centralised orthodoxies; and

- a notion of newness – the new designs of the title of the book – to reflect the newness of developing technologies and the ways in which professionals learn in contemporary contexts.

What is clear is that professional learning experienced as a top-down event, characterised by an expert 'delivering' best practice advice, is not a satisfactory process. Nor are the outcomes productive. Also, delivering professional learning as a transmission process, using technology in old ways, does not explore new ways of teaching and learning, such as the development of narrative and sharing of practice. What is required is scholarly teaching and learning, embracing new technologies, with real consideration given to the relative merits of formal and informal, non-performance-based professional learning. Above all, the authors have focused on the need for teachers' professional learning to be an active, reflective and collaborative process, which relies far less on the current, individualistic, skills-focused, standards-driven approach.

Notes

1 All the teachers in the book have been anonymised.
2 The book does not deal with the Welsh context. The Furlong Report (2006) into university input to teacher education in Wales focused on initial teacher education as a main arena of change in the immediate future. Within a context of significant upheaval in the Welsh system, there are long-term implications for increased partnership and networking approaches, and it remains to be seen how these play out in the context of CPD.

Bibliography

Bentley, P. (2003) 'Continuous professional development: views from the front'. *Professional Development Today*, 6, 1, 57–62.

Bolam, R. (1993) 'Recent developments and emerging issues'. In *The Continuing Professional Development of Teachers*. London: General Teaching Council for England and Wales.

Bueler, X. (1998) 'Schulqualität und Schulwirksamkeit'. In H. Altrichter *et al.* (eds), *Handbuch zur Schulentwicklung*. Innsbruck: Studien Verlag.

Carnell, E. (1999) 'Understanding teachers' professional development: an investigation of teachers' learning and their learning contexts'. Unpublished PhD thesis, University of London.

Carnell, E. and Lodge, C. (2002) *Supporting Effective Learning*. London: Paul Chapman.

Cochran-Smith, M. and Lytle, S. (2001) 'Beyond certainty: taking an inquiry stance on practice'. In A. Lieberman and L. Miller (eds), *Teachers Caught in the Action: Professional development that matters*. New York: Teachers College Press, 45–58.

Craft, A. (2000) *Continuing Professional Development: A practical guide for teachers and schools*. London: RoutledgeFalmer.

Day, C. (1999) *Developing Teachers: The challenge of lifelong learning*. London: Falmer.

Day, C. and Sachs, J. (2004) *International Handbook on the Continuing Professional Development of Teachers*. Buckingham: Open University Press.

Department for Education and Employment (DfEE) (2001) *Learning and Teaching: a strategy for professional development*. London: DfES.

Department for Education and Skills (DfES) (2005) *Leading and Coordinating CPD in Secondary Schools*. London: DfES.

Earley, P. (2005) 'Continuing professional development: the learning community'. In M. Coleman and P. Earley (eds), *Leadership and Management in Education: Cultures, change and context*. Oxford: Oxford University Press.

Earley, P. and Bubb, S. (2004) *Leading and Managing Continuing Professional Development: Developing people, developing schools*. London: Paul Chapman.

EPPI-Centre (2003) *The Impact of Collaborative CPD on Classroom Teaching and Learning: How does collaborative CPD for the teachers aged 5–16 age range affect teaching and learning?* EPPI-Centre, Institute of Education, University of London.

EPPI-Centre (2005) *The Impact of Collaborative CPD on Classroom Teaching and Learning: How do collaborative and sustained CPD and sustained but not collaborative CPD affect teaching and learning?* EPPI-Centre, Institute of Education, University of London.

Fielding, M., Bragg, S., Craig, J., Cunningham, I., Eraut, M., Gillinson, S., Horne, M., Robinson, C. and Thorp, J. (2005) *Factors Influencing the Transfer of Good Practice.* Research Brief RB615. London: DfES.

Guskey, T. (2000) *Evaluating Professional Development.* New York: Corwin Press.

Guskey, T. (2002) 'Does it make a difference? Evaluating professional development'. *Educational Leadership*, March, 45–51.

Hargreaves, A. and Evans, R. (1997) 'Teachers and educational reform'. In A. Hargreaves and R. Evans (eds), *Beyond Education Reform: Bringing the teachers back.* Buckingham: Open University Press.

Harland, J. and Kinder, K. (1997) 'Teachers' continuing professional development: framing a model of outcomes'. *British Journal of In-service Education*, 23, 1, 71–84.

Harris, A., Mujis, D., Day, C. and Lindsay, G. (2004) 'Evaluating the impact of continuing professional development'. *Professional Development Today*, 7, 3, 7–11.

Jackson, D. (2002) 'Building schools' capacity as learning communities'. *Professional Development Today*, 5, 3, 17–24.

Lock, J (2006) 'A new image: online communities to facilitate teacher professional development'. *Journal of Technology and Teacher Education*, 14, 4, 663–78.

Mahony, P. and Hextall, I. (2000) *Reconstructing Teaching: Standards, performance and accountability.* London: RoutledgeFalmer.

Rosenholtz, S. (1989) *Teachers' Workplace: The social organization of schools.* New York: Longman.

Shulman, L. and Shulman, J. (2004) 'How and what teachers learn: a shifting perspective'. *Journal of Curriculum Studies*, 36, 2, 257–71.

Sullivan, J. (2000) 'Stand and deliver: the teacher's integrity?' In C. Watkins, C. Lodge and R. Best (eds), *Tomorrow's Schools: Towards integrity.* London: Routledge.

Watkins, C. (2004) *Building Learning Communities. What's in it for schools?* London: RoutledgeFalmer.

Part 1
Accreditation and impact of new technologies

1 Redesigning pedagogy for a modernised profession

A Master of Teaching for Northern Ireland
Hugh Kearns and Maureen Thatcher
Stranmillis University College, Belfast

Prospects for the MTeach in Northern Ireland

Career development for Northern Ireland (NI) teachers has traditionally been achieved individually and via a self-funded university Master's programme but these routes are gradually disappearing within the school context. This is not least because of an increase in mandatory professional development activities at work and also because of a general acknowledgement that academic and workplace learning practice can be mutually supportive (Hanson, 1996; Coben and Hull, 1994). Growing demand for accredited workplace learning has stimulated research into ways of building bridges from experience to learning, ensuring that teaching is reflective and experience is processed (Boud and Walker, 1990; Boud, 1993). For these historic reasons and in response to radical reform of the school curriculum, a major review of education administration and recent demands for more varied and flexible approaches to teacher continuing professional development (NITEC, 2001; NICCEA, 2004; GTCNI, 2005a), a Master of Teaching (MTeach) has been introduced and is being piloted at Stranmillis University College, Belfast. After two decades of direct rule and the failure of devolved government, the latest reforms of teacher education, commenced in 1993 (DENI, 1993) continue to follow the English example, with some notable differences. Since 1995 each NI school, local authority and university has been charged with participating in the integration of the initial, induction and early professional phases of teacher development, to achieve a closer working partnership and to locate professional growth within a developmental competence framework underpinning all programmes of teacher continuing professional development (CPD), teacher profiling, performance review and staff appraisal (DENI, 1995). The challenges of that enforced partnership in a system divided by religious affiliation, academic selection and fragmented training responsibilities has been well documented (Caul and McWilliams, 2002), but the inherent dilemmas remain those of integrating academic and workplace learning and reconciling the contrasting cultures of schools and universities. Developments in pedagogy, school curricula, teacher professionalism and in the public administration of education lead one to believe that significant improvements are now within our grasp.

Accrediting teacher learning at work: the challenge

The NI Teacher Education Competence Framework (NITEC, 2001) has been in place for over five years. Recently abbreviated and structured to map onto two new professional milestones (Chartered Teacher and Advanced Chartered Teacher status) (GTCNI, 2005b), the framework has formed the structure of initial teacher education, career profiling and non-award-bearing continuing professional development from the early professional development (EPD) programme (NITEC, 1998) to the Professional Qualification for Headship (NI). Following upon initial teacher qualification, competence-based training was exclusively the responsibility of five regional education and library boards, the Council for Catholic Maintained Schools and the Northern Ireland Regional Training Unit, until their abolition by ministerial edict in November 2005.

The EPD process introduced beginning teachers to mandatory portfolio templates for recording their critical reflection within a personally chosen action research project (NITEC, 1998: 91, 96). Universities, engaged wholly in initial teacher education, were called upon to accredit EPD portfolios at Master's level (accreditation to be at the teachers' own expense) but accorded no other function. University reluctance to grant direct credit to completed portfolios was attributed (Kearns 2001, 2003) to the shortcomings of portfolios in meeting standards for Master's level awards (QAA, 2001). Highly prescriptive templates were not considered conducive to personal, professional or systemic growth. Many beginning teachers were judged to respond instrumentally, engaging in short-term, technical self-appraisal rather than conducting principled enquiry or critically reflecting upon practice. Beginning teacher isolation by region, phase and subject, insufficient resources and lack of training capacity in schools were reported to be the source of shortcomings in teacher narrative, problem-solving or professional voice. Compliant demonstration and detailed reporting of specific framework competencies were seen as major obstacles which the reformed managers of EPD and CPD will need to address. The task is perhaps made easier by the more accommodating tone of the most recent recommendations (GTCNI, 2005a): that approaches to all teacher education should be varied and flexible, follow a revised competence framework, should encourage teacher choice and ownership, and promote enquiry-based and networked approaches to learning within wider professional communities.

A promised government White Paper describing the way ahead is widely expected to offer a greater partnership role to universities, expanding their current responsibility beyond initial teacher education into induction and EPD, a responsibility which may be cost-neutral given a demographic downturn and a predicted reduction in initial teacher education enrolments. Such extended responsibility will make greater demands on universities to agree, with their partners' systems for achieving and accrediting progression at initial and in-service levels, specifying progression in teaching competence, reflective practice and leadership across this extended range of teacher status and in response to major curriculum changes. The MTeach is being developed to explore ways of overcoming historical difficulties in the accreditation of reflective action for self-improvement on the part of beginning teachers. Its principal challenges are the sustainable development of systems of collegial regulation and of individual self-regulation in the quality management of teacher reflection, and action on issues of immediate and forthcoming national, community and professional concern.

Teacher preparation for professional grading

There are clear intentions in the review by the General Teaching Council for Northern Ireland (GTCNI) to develop a regional CPD framework whereby teachers may freely choose and access elements from a menu of development opportunities mapped to professional standards or advancing levels of teacher leadership. In NI the MTeach is not formalised as a career step but open to all teachers, in contrast to Scotland where it is restricted to those on higher salary grades who have maintained CPD portfolios. NI teacher promotion grades apply more to the efficient discharge of very specific functions defined differently in different schools (Kearns, 2005) rather than clear and generic standards for leadership or scholarship in teaching. The MTeach seeks to support and identify generic levels of progression in the scholarship of teaching for both change and improvement. In its review of teacher education, GTCNI (2005b) continues to emphasise, for both pre-service and in-service teachers, the preparatory nature of training in terms of its own constructions of what curriculum reform will mean. It draws attention to the future demands upon teacher education of a new curriculum based on lifelong learning, transformative skills, education for citizenship, comprehensive and inclusive forms of provision yet greater professional autonomy in curriculum decisions. The GTCNI emphasises the need for improved training capacity in schools, for greater collegiality and more collaborative approaches to education and training that remain principled while being contingent upon cost-efficiency and savings. Not least among these demands is the need to map course provision onto the two new 'milestones' of Chartered Teacher and Advanced Chartered Teacher status and to have these accredited. Teachers are predicted to achieve these milestones through critical reflective practice, improvements in teaching, participation in the creation of dynamic professional communities and competence at senior management level within schools (GTCNI 2005b: iv–v).

While arguing that acceptance of competence frameworks does not imply the reduction of teacher knowledge, skills and attributes to a discrete set of functional competences, the GTCNI hopes the framework will provide a language for dialogue and for the development of appropriate learning environments by partners. The province's major investment in information and communications technologies (ICT) is recommended as a means whereby partners may collaborate to meet the needs of the region's many small schools and extend opportunities for accreditation, connectivity and blended learning throughout schools and colleges. This is the environment within which the MTeach must seek to sustain an academic scholarship that has been considered under threat at pre-service level. The findings of Furlong *et al.* (1996) provide a warning that close partnerships with schools and excessive emphasis upon teacher preparation for teaching may undermine the academic role of universities. The MTeach stands astride this uneasy partnership and seeks to overcome traditional obstacles, while maintaining clear academic and professional standards. The fiscal separation of undergraduate and in-service teacher education has sustained a competence orientation in the former and a more traditional academic and research-led tradition in the latter. The separation has defied efforts to achieve creative forms of accreditation against a background of decline in student numbers on award-bearing CPD programmes and a growth in mandatory portfolio development in schools. In the face of perceived decline in professional status, intense speculation about the future of teacher professionalism and concerns about the growing politicisation of schooling, researchers (Sachs, 1997, 2003; Goodson, 2003; Hargreaves, 2003) have called for an activist professionalism mediating the influence of government, bureaucratic and managerialist prescription. Far from promoting revolution, Furlong and Maynard (1995) develop the notion of a listening, constructive and democratic professionalism. These voices urge us to consider more authentic pedagogies in teacher education at times when funding is under threat, standards are seen as obstructive rather than supportive and important members of the 'teacher education partnerships' feel driven rather than led to radical change.

A rationale for the MTeach

In the minds of its originators, the MTeach began very much as a pilot programme designed to provide support and accreditation for the Northern Ireland school-based early professional development programme. As the difficulties experienced by that programme became clearer, the MTeach sought to become a parallel programme for all teachers engaged in any structured periods of school-focused development being viewed, even loosely, as enquiry-based learning or critical reflective practice. With the intention that teachers will remain very much in control, the programme offers generic modules of very wide application so that individual teaching needs can gain expression in a regulated system for shared critical reflection and action research. In this context, the MTeach has become a strategy for sustaining institutional contacts with graduate teachers and advancing partnerships with placement schools.

The MTeach at the Institute of Education in the University of London (Pachler *et al.*, 2003; Pachler and Pickering, 2003; Pachler and Daly, 2006) continues to act as a model for the NI MTeach, with its online scaffolds for structuring evidence-based reflection and collegial presentations around practice and its strategies for managing shared critical commentaries by diverse teachers focused on action for school improvement. The NI programme still depends very much upon the refinement of pedagogies whereby diversity in teaching contexts becomes the springboard for dynamic reflection upon core aspects of professionalism, pedagogy, innovation, research and scholarship directed at the widest professional audience. Comprising four taught, single-semester modules and a one-year dissertation, this part-time programme, shortly to enter its third year, is managed increasingly online. Discussions are used largely to share information and to debate issues around selected areas of practice, with face-to-face meetings tending now to be reserved for housekeeping and theory-building. The taught modules are similar in title and content to the four core modules of the MTeach in Scotland, but the programme is intended mainly for beginning teachers and is currently funded by teachers themselves with no formalised school partnership arrangements. Upon application to the programme, teachers are required to provide testimonials regarding their own, and the school's, development plans. These have always been made available and have been useful for reference but there is a need for teachers to share and find common threads to their research. A single foundation module inducts teachers into the processes of critical reflection upon personal practice and the assessment of their professional development. Three intermediate modules then develop critical reflection in three areas: classroom pedagogy, student diversity and teacher leadership for learning. Each of the four taught modules systematically develops individual and shared teacher narratives (see Figure 1.1), using a range of learning tools designed to ensure Master's-level standards of critical reflection (see Table 1.1) and the planning of structured periods of research and development in learning and teaching.

Promoting a sustainable scholarship: getting to the heart of teaching and learning

The MTeach experiment is founded upon the twin beliefs that teachers in the twenty-first century will need the continuing support of universities for critical thinking and professional self-regulation in each of the areas described by these four modules, and that universities must support the process of moving teacher professionalism beyond compliance and techno-rationality. Sustaining effective teaching and learning during these times of radical change will require sustained and critical reflection upon beliefs and practices, and advanced understanding of the cognitive and motivational principles underpinning new forms of learning and teaching in schools. The changes taking place in NI education are, as elsewhere, based on very different assumptions about teaching and learning, students and schools. These changes challenge existing functionalist and prescriptive models of teacher and learner while not unambiguously leaving these models behind. In contrast to the continuing practice of training teachers and students to acquire fixed sets of skills, there have been growing demands (Paris and Winograd, 1998; Kremer-Hayon and Tillema, 1999; Boekaerts *et al.*, 2000) for a student and teacher education that corresponds to prevailing ideologies of lifelong learning. The meta-cognitive or self-regulatory dispositions required to sustain teachers and students as active participants in both individual and group teaching and learning cannot be authentically delivered as information or managed by bureaucratic means but must be gained in context through shared experience and active learning processes.

Self-regulated learning is characterised by an awareness of personal thinking, of one's conscious use of reflective strategies and of the authentic contexts that generate critical thinking. The restructuring of education for the demands of lifelong learning and a knowledge-based economy redefines teachers and teaching. The changes are so radical that they call for more authentic teaching problems, for more sustained and public reflection, for a tenacious determination to target and acquire deeper understanding with others and to test the results in practice. In the context of these changes, Katz argues for the cultivation in both teachers and learners of dispositions to exhibit behaviour that is goal- rather than performance-directed (Katz, 1993). If teachers are to be empowered to practise and teach higher-level thinking, then their own thinking and dispositions to thinking are critical subjects for sustained collegial support. Teachers need to be enabled to become self-regulated learners with knowledge about critical thinking, skills for critical thinking and appropriate dispositions towards the development of critical thinking in others. In this very challenging task we run counter to much traditional practice in teacher education. Traditional training pedagogies need not be abandoned but they must be rethought in the light of new and firmly held goals. This requires some radical deconstruction of the mindsets of teachers only recently trained to deliver prescribed curriculum content and develop phase-related teaching competencies.

Teacher narratives: developing audience and impact

In their education and at work, teachers traditionally write for a range of academic and bureaucratic audiences within frameworks of accountability that are restrictive and controlling. The pressures of performativity, marketisation, centralisation and standards in education and training (Tomlinson, 2001) demand that urgent efforts are made to ensure that individual teachers can argue their own decisions about teaching and assessment to a wide professional and public audience. With more authentic learning in view, the

MTeach must beware of being excessively focused on either the assimilation of reading in the research literature, in curriculum subject or in phase-specific knowledge. This has been a hard-learned lesson for the MTeach project team in its efforts to empower teachers. These forms of knowledge are already so well entrenched that considerable patience and experience are required if spontaneous teacher narratives are to be shaped into a sustainable, critically reflective and constructive scholarship. A real tension exists between the key goals of critical thinking and professional self-regulation and the powerful cultures represented by subject, phase or disciplinary bodies of knowledge, including their assumptions about teaching and learning. In spite of recent curriculum changes away from static content to transformative skills and from compliance to greater discretion and self-regulation, these traditional constructions remain powerful in the value judgements that tutors and teachers continue to make as they seek to understand the new realities. Consequently there is a struggle to write and reflect as a process of dynamic learning, with the need to self-regulate and obey conventions of citation, referencing and the scholarly presentation of findings to a professional readership. An important finding is that these challenges are best addressed in diverse collegial groups where there is a strong sense of a very mixed readership and expectation of diverse professional responses to one's work. This is, of course, an emerging feature of the daily professionalism of all teachers. Imposed changes in NI post-primary schools are now requiring trained subject specialists to teach a wider range of subjects to classes of more diverse students. The sudden move from selective to comprehensive schooling is requiring many teachers to gain more inclusive perspectives upon the whole curriculum and to seek a richer range of inputs into curriculum planning. Hence there is a need to bring diverse teachers and tutors together so that they find other communalities than specialist subject or phase knowledge.

Teacher empowerment through interdisciplinary thinking

A core belief of our MTeach philosophy is that teachers are weaker, and their ideas lack currency, within specialist groups. A central claim is that the criticality of reflection and the impact of scholarship are significantly improved by offering secondary-level specialists opportunities to describe their experiences and present their theories about important issues to a wider audience of primary teachers. Instrumental thinking is seen to become principled and strategic. Theory begins to exert greater influence upon the review of practice. In these encounters, specialists can be seen to mediate views emerging from other equally specialist perspectives as they seek, through critical questioning, more powerful common ground upon which they can support each other. Group reflection upon innovation in co-operative learning, assessment for learning or consulting pupils about their own learning can be restricted when viewed from a limited phase or subject perspective. Within these diverse MTeach groups of teachers, A-level subject specialists have genuinely asserted the argument that it is too late to attempt co-operative learning and nursery teachers the view that it is too early to introduce it. Each has identified or assisted the other to develop a wider range of strategies for change in very different schools.

Cross-phase and cross-subject group discussion can provide a more informed perspective upon the whole child, the developing child, diversity in classrooms and innovative pedagogies. Groups of teachers from a diverse range of schools offer more balanced perspectives upon professional realities, reveal a greater diversity of professional views and empower individual teachers to represent a range of perspectives upon critical issues. A more representative professional identity is achieved as the group provides a wider range of experience from which to draw. Managing these diverse groups requires similar change in tutors and a considerable broadening of the role of specialist teacher educators to that of learning resource, mentor, evaluator and organiser of deeper learning experiences.

Useful comparisons are made regarding classroom layout, the use of classroom space and pupil movement in class. Contrasting uses of time allocated to areas of curriculum content are generating new ideas about the use of time and about periodicity. Teachers are comparing systems of pupil grouping, pupil working patterns, and their differential emphases upon individuality, collaboration and conformity. Teachers are methodically gathering information on the range of classroom routines, rules and rituals, about classroom management styles and forms of assessment. Mentoring relationships and peer observation of teaching have become a focus, with developing views on teacher supervision, collaboration, independence, support and guidance.

Included among these new activities for learning about teaching to date are: modelling, scaffolding, study teams, project work in schools, classroom problem-focused learning, group presentations, managed discussions online and face-to-face, and increasingly focused questioning during the shared discussions. Some very general questions deserve vigorous investigation:

- Who am I as a teacher? How do I differ from others?
- Upon what occasions do I find that I am automatically appraising myself as a teacher?
- Who are the children I am teaching? How diverse are they? Do we really want to know?
- How often do I find myself asserting that there is something I really understand about my students or something I do not know enough about?
- What do I sometimes feel it is appropriate to reflect deeply upon?
- When and how do I observe and reflect upon my practice?
- In what ways do I find myself disciplining myself as I reflect? What steps do I take?

- Am I strategic or do I just have strategies? In what ways have I been strategic?

- What rules of practice, practical principles or images of practice guide me? (Elbaz, 1983)

- What educational dilemmas do I face and how do I deal with them?

- How often do I set myself the goal of mastering something?

- What comprises the school community? How am I part of it?

- Where is the curriculum in my understanding of myself, my students and my community?

Regulating academic and workplace learning

Shared regulatory mechanisms are required if academic learning and learning at work are to correspond. The recognition of progression in teaching needs to correspond with university recognition of progression in learning if teachers are to be assisted to claim credit for achievement and learning at work. Professional awards must respond to new models of teacher professionalism and new theories of professional learning. Theories of social constructivism (Vygotsky, 1978), post-structuralism (Foucault, 1978), post-modern theory (Lyotard, 1984), narrative theory (Bruner, 1986, 1990) and discourse analysis (Burman and Parker, 1993) are pertinent if teacher story, narrative enquiry, critical incident analysis and case-based reasoning are to be nurtured in ways that are consistent with the underpinning theories from which they have emerged. For this purpose, teacher professional knowledge needs to be respected as personal capital that can be gathered, shared, self-regulated and archived for the extension of knowledge and the improvement of practice. The regulatory mechanisms need to be agreed and increasing professional rigour identified if scholarship in teaching is to achieve appropriate levels of credit. Fenstermacher (1997: 123) has argued that teacher intentions and beliefs can only be known through deep regard for their narratives, but he cautions that narrators must be held accountable for any claims they make. University-led CPD can easily neglect to sustain or to raise teacher critical reflection upon immediate professional beliefs, intents and practices and focus instead upon educational debate around systemic issues and the grand narratives.

Continuous writing and the presentation of personal papers intimately connected to the practice of teaching have been widely used as tools for critical thinking on many pre-service courses (Broekman and Scott, 1999). Within in-service courses this may be absent entirely or included as part of summative assessment only. In spite of the theoretical benefits, the writing and rewriting of stories of practice are less likely to be sustained within postgraduate teacher education programmes. Teaching becomes more objective as writers make explicit their observations and beliefs, leaving these open for shared critical analysis and reflection. Individually and in teams, personal writing can be read, reread, rewritten from the first to the third person and re-evaluated. Progressively, position statements become adapted and a shared language emerges. Further possibilities for refining practice through action research appear, and self-regulatory mechanisms for its management and reporting can also be agreed. Within the Stranmillis MTeach programme, typologies of regulatory questions for critical reflection and for action research questions are currently being tested and are provided in Table 1.1. There is a danger that regulatory frameworks produce an instrumentalism in writing, but this is avoided by always asking the teacher to write freely, acknowledging the value of the content, then seeking the writer's comments upon questions raised within the typology.

Prompting shared reflections on practice

In the early stages, a range of tools is needed to evoke reflective writing for meta-cognitive understanding. These might be a teacher's daily or six-weekly plan, a class timetable, monthly notes, wall displays, samples of annotated pupil work, learning journals, student reports and letters to and from parents. Superficial language in these artefacts can be distinguished from analytic comment. Implicit meanings can be identified and questioned by other subject or key-stage specialists. Journal writing can become a vehicle for self-exploration, discovery and disclosure. Critical incident writing can be cued using models of such in the professional literature. These can be around a very extensive range of common teaching situations and critical reflections can be focused on: a period of teaching; a self-assessment of expertise; observations of a very different kind of teaching; rules of practice determining classroom interaction; patterns of classroom management; a special teaching intervention; a change in classroom layout; a class assessment; a pupil self-assessment; consultation with students about preferred learning or teaching strategies; a school policy document; a case of collegial conflict or co-operation; a staff meeting; a teacher with leadership qualities; parents, etc. These can be presented as online discussion tasks linked to key readings. Some examples are:

> Select a teaching unit you have recently completed. Briefly describe its aims, teaching strategies and intended outcomes. What stage of expertise do you feel you have achieved in the planning and teaching of this unit? How do you know? You may draw upon the work of David Berliner (2001) in considering this question.

> Select two critical incidents from which you have learned something as a teacher. Choose one positive and one negative event. Critically reflect upon one's ability to learn from positive and negative experiences. You may draw upon the work of Rollett (2001) in considering this question.

Identify and describe a teacher whose approach to practice can be readily contrasted with your own. Critically consider how you both differ at a visible surface and at a deeper level. Drawing upon the work of Maggie MacLure (2001), examine the view that teacher autobiographical accounts are attempts to make sense of their lives.

Identify and describe lessons you like and dislike teaching. Critically consider the reasons for your dislikes and preferences. Drawing upon the work of Banks, Leach and Moon (1999), identify the kinds of Teacher Professional Knowledge (School, Subject, Personal, and Pedagogic) that are needed if your concerns are to be addressed.

Table 1.1 A typology of questions for the regulation of reflections on practice

Domain	Typical question
Descriptive	What is happening?
Evaluation	Is it working? What are the goals? Are they being met? Who loses or benefits?
Evidence	How do I know? What evidence am I acting upon?
Affective	How am I feeling? How are others feeling?
Problematic	What am I content or concerned about?
Intellectual	What do I understand or not understand? What concepts have I difficulty with?
Critical/ comparative	What are the alternative perspectives? How do others describe or explain them? What does research tell me? What are the implications of the alternative perspectives?
Reading/research	How has reading informed my reflection, decision or action?
Intent	How can I improve matters?
Action/strategy	What are the alternative strategies? How have others managed these issues? Who has gained/not gained using different strategies?

Critical/decisive	Given the varying perspectives, my values and my school context, which approach is best?
Monitoring	How will I monitor actions, events and outcomes?
Professional relevance	How does this inform other professionals or relate to their concerns?

Source: adapted from Jay and Johnson (2002) and Lomax (1994).

Values development in teacher-shared critical reflection

The MTeach presents a developing structure for critical reflection upon practice, but the evidence is that, when first reflecting publicly upon practice, teachers will not immediately write following regulatory structures provided by typographies or standards. They are unsure of their audience and have little experience of writing for a readership. Accountability and self-advocacy dominate early reflections, even for teachers with five and ten years' experience.

In our analysis of teacher early postings, we detect a discourse which is rich in inference, in intentionality and emotion. The language is value intense, with many instances of 'I believe', 'I have tried' and 'It is important'. We see pedagogy at this early point as involving a development or a sophistication of the naive knowledge that teachers spontaneously bring. The tutor must act as advocate for the points being advanced by the teacher in these early efforts to articulate understandings about teaching. Tutor questioning can be metaphorically described as 'bringing to the surface' previously tacit and unexplored knowledge about teaching constraints and the potential for change. A teacher who asserts in a position paper 'I believe I have tried to accommodate a variety of learning styles' is asked by a tutor: 'Why do you believe that? Why do you say "tried"? Was it difficult? What's the problem? How have you failed? How did you overcome problems?' Another tutor queries: 'You say you "adopted whole-class teaching, small-group work and shared work to allow for different learning preferences". Tell us more about this. Can you describe pupils with clearly different learning preferences and how they succeed better under different styles?'

Teacher reflections upon personal change

In interviews, MTeach students have remarked upon changes in personal disposition over the course of the programme. For some there is a reduction in dogmatism and an increasing relativism: 'I tended to think of teaching quality as fixed and absolute, but talking to others about teaching has helped me to change my views.' For others there is a reduction in idealism and a growing pragmatism and perhaps even a growing eclecticism: 'We all have our own myths about what a good teacher looks like, at least I have … but really, in the end, quality is about the decisions you make and their consequences. Images don't matter. There are so many different viewpoints about quality teaching. I have been willing to try more things as I have heard them argued.' A growing confidence and a reduction in inferiority and neuroticism can also be identified in the comment: 'Some teachers don't feel they speak as significant members of the teaching profession and see "the good teacher" as something others tell them they should be. You are always conscious of criticism because your teaching is out of step. I think I can argue my own case better now.'

A key issue in the evaluation of online discussion around critical reflections upon practice is the extent to which comments made and questions raised in tutor and collegial responses to postings are seen by teachers as 'academic', 'bureaucratic', 'instrumental', diplomatic and merely 'considerate and polite', or whether fellow teachers, genuinely and for their own purposes, begin to express the same need for clarification and a desire to be systematic in their organisation of professional knowledge. If these are perceived as

Table 1.2 Observed changes in teacher critical reflection over time

From	To
Overemphasis upon self and personal opinions	Dynamic storytelling *Tutor comment: There are so many vivid portrayals of life in your class. You communicate teaching and learning as a living practice. You use humour to good effect.*
Reluctance to use objective information	
Focus upon difficulties in others	
Over-attention to certain individuals	A democratic professionalism *Tutor comment: You have done much to explain how you consult others in developing your practice.*
Inattention to groups as the target of change	
Self-destructiveness	Activism in the school and community *Tutor comment: You have done much to explain how your own investigations help you to interact constructively with others and how they also help others work for change with you.*
Resistance to autobiography	
Bureaucratic recording with little reflection	
Unexplained actions and judgements	Identifying the need for personal change
Speaking on behalf of others not fully consulted	Questioning personal motives and values
Excessive elaboration of personal hurt	Writing in the third person to gain some distance and objectivity
Unfocused discontent about teaching	Questioning grand theory and major policy initiatives
Claiming untested solutions to teaching problems	

academic questions rather than as the creative expressions of the natural curiosity of professional colleagues, the gap between university and workplace learning has not been bridged and the MTeach pedagogy fails. As fellow teachers begin to adopt standards in their commentaries, they begin to require less regulatory questioning. Common features of reflective difficulty are in evidence in the frequency of questions posed and comments made in online commentaries by tutors and colleagues.

Earliest attempts at online public reflection were often characterised by difficulty and vagueness within phrases such as 'It is difficult to explain', 'I cannot explain the reason but I do however feel', 'It is difficult to assess accurately' and 'It seems to me that maybe...'. The early voice is naive, well intentioned and value intense and there are numerous claims to commitment. Together, these persistent features appear as obstacles to the structured exploration and organisation of teacher knowledge. In these early stages, teachers appeared to tutors to need methods of gathering more objective information regarding the nature of problems. Tutors felt the need to act as advocates, helping the teachers to represent their experience through supportive typologies of questions. In response to such support, teachers might overuse these supportive prompts, answering these individually and discretely. Asked to report 'What is happening?', teachers' descriptions might tend to far exceed what was necessary to clarify any problems. Asked 'Is it working?', teachers might provide lengthy judgements of highly successful practice with little criticality. In response to 'How do I know?', teachers might indicate the source of evidence that had simply presented itself without being sought, providing little detail of the evidence itself, or of any conscious evidence-gathering.

In the early stages of reflection, beginners might routinely commence by describing a teaching problem, a point of conflict or realisation. They are encouraged to consider a range of appropriate responses, make tentative decisions about action and suggest strategies for monitoring processes and outcomes. Early actions appear largely interventionist and instrumental in nature. Gradually a greater variety of reflection emerges, centred around action that is principled and more likely to inform learning and teaching. In the context of a recurrent difficulty, a range of successful preventive practices might be analysed and their combination planned within a structured teaching project. Three developmental processes can be identified: a developing awareness of standards in reflection; a greater willingness to share evaluations of teaching and learning processes; and a greater confidence in advancing novel perspectives with fellow professionals. Teachers are gradually showing greater appreciation of questioning as a refining process rather than as the final gesture in a failed reflection. The reframing of questions is now enjoyed and perhaps, at times, even preferred to the simple solution, which has become increasingly suspect. Indeed there is increasing interest in finding questions that uncover thought processes underlying success and failure. More recently, teachers are challenging impulsive colleagues who advance innovations (co-operative learning, self-assessment or the use of ICT) as being of intrinsic value in themselves. In this way teachers are becoming self-regulatory, moving away from compliant instrumentalism and naive techno-rationality ('In that lesson I should have used a stuffed dog rather than a real one') to collegial support for more informed speculation and a professional balance ('We need time to discover what different groups do with the problem and why').

In preparation for their dissertations, teachers are revealing a democratic and ethical professionalism that engages those previously marginalised and are gaining greater support for structured initiatives promoting social justice. Others remain unsure and return to archived discussion, to their practice or to their schools for ideas and support. A tentative developmental model defining a diversity of individual learning pathways from teacher critical intents and incidents towards their plans for structured workplace learning and scholarship is offered in Figure 1.1. From their earliest encounters, some critical incidents become pivotal in focusing discussion around a network of previously unexplored controversial issues. In the face of adverse commentaries and selected readings, the narratives may be revised and refined. Narrative becomes more critical, balanced, less polarised and increasingly qualified. Archived teacher narratives become reusable learning objects, revisited for further enquiry, and for some teachers the design of narrative discourse is identified. For others, this is not so. According to McIntyre (1992) these later stages of critical reflection upon political, ethical and social issues are rarely practised even amongst experienced teachers. At this point in reflection, the wider political, ethical and social significance of teaching questions may become intimately known and valued to such a degree that they must be strategically explored in structured periods of personal action or among fellow professionals at work. For some teachers this point is not one of a new departure but of exit and return to the points of conflict and the pivotal incidents that sent others on their way to independent study and classroom research. The alternative is to follow and to model instrumentally the principled intent of others. For example, one teacher wishes to know how her colleagues learn and collaborate at work in order to consider the inferences and the implications for teachers' professional lives. A second does the same but as a precursor to the more instrumental purpose of designing a staff development policy in her school. Their development needs are very different, as is the significance of narrative in their work. Figure 1.1 seeks to explain graphically how different teachers may progress, how some move easily from personal teaching concerns to activism in their professional lives, while others require more time to reflect and yet others go on regardless to achieve more for their schools than for themselves.

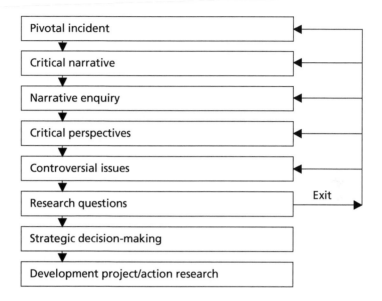

Figure 1.1 Individual pathways in community enquiry: a predictive model

Conclusion

In advance of the implementation of the latest raft of reforms, Northern Ireland teacher education remains divided by phase of schooling, phase of training, curricular specialisms and school leadership functions. Against this background, regional curricular reforms designed to accommodate diversity and promote equality remain customised for discrete professional groupings, each with their part to play. Similarly, responsibility for support, accreditation, accountability and quality assurance of teacher professional learning is held separately by a curriculum council, five education boards, three universities, schools, government departments and training agencies. In sharp contrast, unifying features of contemporary thinking are present in a developmental framework of teacher competencies, a belief in the teacher as critically reflective practitioner, a respect for evidence, communities of practice and for technology and the e-portfolio as a force for centralisation and uniformity amid the increasing diversity of the post-modern world.

The MTeach project seeks to develop a process whereby teachers can invest their knowledge and may experience its growth within supportive frameworks that integrate action at work and reflective practice in universities, bringing together diverse teaching professionals and separate phases of teacher education around contemporary themes and situated practices. It seeks to advance, for teachers and their students, learning that is sustainable, transformative, contextualised and self-regulated within a set of academic standards and ethical controls. A major force for division remains in the commonly held view that the competence approach is an alternative paradigm to precursor models based on teacher personality and classroom enquiry. At the centre of the MTeach idea is a determination to be eclectic in approach, developing professional identity through a pedagogy that closely relates individual functioning, personal development, socio-cultural processes and school contexts. Together, teachers are exploring for their underlying public significance the practices of teaching as these relate to their own personal meanings and moving on. As managed by MTeach tutors, this exploration is purposefully constructive, directed to the sharing of classroom research and to the development of meaningful action in practice.

References

Banks, F., Leach, J. and Moon, B. (1999) 'New understandings of teachers' pedagogic knowledge'. In J. Leach and B. Moon (eds), *Learners and Pedagogy*. London: Paul Chapman.

Berliner, D. (2001) 'Teacher expertise'. In F. Banks and A.S. Mayes (eds), *Early Professional Development for Teachers*. London: David Fulton.

Boekaerts, M., Pintrich, P.R. and Zeidner, M. (eds) (2000) *Handbook on Self-Regulation*. San Diego, CA: Academic Press.

Boud, D. (1993) 'Experience as the base for learning'. *Higher Education Research and Development*, 12, 1, 33–44.

Boud, D. and Walker, D. (1990) 'Making the most of experience'. *Studies in Continuing Education*, 12, 2, 61–80.

Broekman, H. and Scott, H. (1999) 'Teacher development by using writing as a tool'. *Teacher Development*, 3, 2, 233–48.

Bruner, J. (1986) *Actual Minds, Possible Worlds*. Cambridge, MA: Harvard University Press.

Bruner, J. (1990) *Acts of Meaning*. Cambridge, MA: Harvard University Press.

Burman, E. and Parker, I. (eds) (1993) *Discourse Analytic Research: Repertoires and readings of texts in action*. London: Routledge.

Caul, L. and McWilliams, S. (2002) 'Accountability in partnership or partnership in accountability: initial teacher education in Northern Ireland'. *European Journal of Teacher Education*, 25, 2/3, 187–98.

Coben, D. and Hull, C. (1994) 'Professional training or academic education: a continuing problem'. *Journal of Interprofessional Care*, 5, 1, 45–55.

DENI (Department of Education for Northern Ireland) (1993) *Teachers for the 21st Century: A review of initial teacher training*. Bangor: Rathgael House.

DENI (Department of Education for Northern Ireland) (1995) *Initial Teacher Education Guidance for the 1995/96 Development Year*. Bangor: Rathgael House.

Elbaz, F. (1983) *Teacher Thinking: A study of practical knowledge*. London: Croom Helm.

Fenstermacher, G. (1997) 'On narrative'. *Teaching and Teacher Education*, 13, 1, 119–24.

Foucault, M. (1978) *Discipline and Punish*, trans. Alan Sheridan. New York: Vintage Books.

Furlong, J. and Maynard, T. (1995) *Mentoring Student Teachers: The growth of professional knowledge.* London: Routledge.

Furlong, J., Whitty, G., Whiting, C., Miles, S., Barton, L. and Barrett, E. (1996) 'Redefining partnership: revolution or reform in initial teacher education?' *Journal of Education for Teaching*, 22, 39–55.

Goodson, I.F. (2003) *Professional Knowledge, Professional Lives: Studies in education and change.* Maidenhead: Open University Press.

GTCNI (General Teaching Council for Northern Ireland) (2005a) *Corporate Plan 2004–7.* Available at: www.gtcni.org.uk/publications

GTCNI (General Teaching Council for Northern Ireland) (2005b) *Reviews of Teacher Competences and Continuing Professional Development.* Available at: www.gtcni.org.uk/

Hanson, A. (1996) 'The search for a separate theory of adult learning: does anyone really need andragogy?' In R. Edwards, A. Hanson and P. Raggatt (eds), *Boundaries of Adult Learning.* London: Routledge.

Hargreaves, A. (2003) *Teaching in the Knowledge Society: Education in the age of insecurity.* Maidenhead: Open University Press.

Jay, J.K. and Johnson, K.L. (2002) 'Capturing complexity: a typology of reflective practice for teacher education'. *Teaching and Teacher Education*, 18, 73–85.

Katz, L.G. (1993) *Dispositions as Educational Goals.* ERIC Digest. Urbana, IL: ERIC Clearinghouse on Elementary and Early Childhood Education. ED363454.

Kearns, H. (2001) 'Competence-based early professional development: first impressions of the Northern Ireland programme'. *Journal of In-service Education*, 27, 1, 65–83.

Kearns, H. (2003) 'University accreditation of professional development in schools: can professional development serve two masters?' *Journal of In-Service Education*, 29, 1, 11–29.

Kearns, H. (2005) 'Exploring the experiential learning of special educational needs coordinators'. *Journal of In-service Education*, 31, 1, 131–49.

Kremer-Hayon, L. and Tillema, H.H. (1999) 'Self-regulated learning in the context of teacher education'. *Teacher and Teacher Education*, 15, 5, 507–22.

Lomax, P. (1994) 'Standards, criteria and the problematic of action research within an award bearing course'. *Educational Action Research*, 2, 1, 113–26.

Lyotard, J.F. (1984) *The Postmodern Condition: A report on knowledge.* Manchester: Manchester University Press.

McIntyre, D. (1992) 'Theory, theorising and reflection in initial teacher education'. In J. Calderhead (ed.), *Conceptualising Reflection in Teacher Development.* London: Falmer.

MacLure, M. (2001) 'Arguing for your self: identity as an organising principle in teachers' jobs and lives'. In J. Soler, A. Craft and H. Burgess (eds), *Teacher Development: Exploring our own practice.* London: Paul Chapman.

NICCEA (Northern Ireland Council for Curriculum Examinations and Assessment) (2004) *The Way Ahead.* Available at: www.ccea.org.uk/

NITEC (Northern Ireland Teacher Education Committee and Committee for Early Professional Development) (1998) *The Teacher Education Partnership Handbook.* Bangor: Rathgael House.

NITEC (Northern Ireland Teacher Education Committee and Committee for Early Professional Development) (2001) *The Teacher Education Partnership Handbook.* Bangor: Rathgael House. Available at: www.nine.org.uk/index.asp

Pachler, N. and Pickering, J. (2003) '"Talking teaching"– the master of teaching'. *Change*, 6, 2, 38–45.

Pachler, C. and Daly, C. (2006) 'Professional teacher learning in virtual environments'. *European Education Research Journal*, 3, 1, 62–74.

Pachler, N., Daly, C. and Lambert, D. (2003) 'Teacher learning: reconceptualising the relationship between theory and practical teaching in Master's level course development'. In J.J. Güther (ed.), *Quality Assurance in Distance-Learning and E-learning.* Krems: European Association of Telematic Applications.

Paris, S.G. and Winograd, P. (1998) *The role of self-regulated learning in contextual teaching: principles and practices for teacher preparation.* Available at: www.ciera.org/library/archive/2001-04/0104prwn.pdf

QAA (Quality Assurance Agency for Higher Education) (2001) *Descriptors for Qualifications at Master's Level.* Available at: www.qaa.ac.uk/ academicinfrastructure/benchmark/masters/default.asp (April 2005)

Rollett, B.A. (2001) 'How do expert teachers view themselves?' In F. Banks and A.S. Mayes (eds), *Early Professional Development for Teachers.* London: David Fulton.

Sachs, J. (1997) 'The challenge of school–university partnerships: walking the tightrope between theory and practice'. Keynote address presented at the Australian Curriculum Studies Association Biennial Conference, University of Sydney.

Sachs, J. (2003) *The Activist Teaching Profession.* Maidenhead: Open University Press.

Tomlinson, S. (2001) *Education in a Post-Welfare Society.* Buckingham: Open University Press.

Vygotsky, L. (1978) *Mind in Society: The development of higher psychological processes.* Boston: Harvard University Press.

2 Learning with others in mind

Caroline Daly and Norbert Pachler
Institute of Education, University of London

Introduction

In this chapter we draw on our research into the online writing of a group of teachers who are studying for the mixed-mode Master of Teaching (MTeach) degree at the Institute of Education, University of London, to argue for the catalytic role in professional learning of collaborative online discussion. Our interest in how teachers can learn with others in mind draws on both meanings of the term 'learning' – to do with the effects on teachers of learning as a literate activity undertaken with a high degree of peer presence; and to do with conceptual transformations which occur as a result of 'joint thinking' (Mercer, 1995) within the environment of an online teachers' forum. We consider the following key questions:

- What are the processes of professional learning in a computer-supported, mixed-mode environment? How do the course design, and to a lesser extent the characteristics of the online learning environment, influence these processes?

- How are the individual cognitive processes of participants influenced by social interaction and how does learning take place in the computer-mediated interaction between participants? Do cognitive phenomena exist transpersonally? Can learning be distributed across people and artefacts? (See Suthers, 2005: 665.)

51

- How can we understand knowledge as a shared narrated practice in a computer-supported environment?

- What constitutes appropriate research methods in the field of online professional learning?

The MTeach is based on the notion of shared knowledge construction at a distance through computer-mediated communication (CMC), which is conceived of as both a literacy and social practice. The course is mixed-mode, in that the collaborative online activity is regular and compulsory, and is the main learning context for the first two core modules for all cohorts of participants. For the first year of the course, therefore, the online forum is in fact what Harasim (2000) calls the 'primary environment' for participation and interaction, and this environment plays a central role in the programme towards the development of criticality as an intrinsic component of professional development.

We propose an approach to identifying professional learning in online discussion which is based on a qualitative content analysis model, by which the online writing of teachers is investigated by coding for themes related to critical and reflexive concepts of professional knowledge within what Suthers (2005) has called an 'intersubjective epistemology' of computer-supported collaborative learning. We do so in order to explore what kinds of learning take place within an online teachers' forum at Master's level, and what possibilities exist for developing collaborative frameworks for CPD by harnessing the potential of CMC for the joint interpretation and co-construction of professional knowledge by participants. The online discussion we examine here was generated by members of a tutor group consisting of 11 London secondary school teachers during their first term on the course. The participants are all in the first five years of teaching (most beginning their second year). In their discussion, entitled 'Understanding Learning', they were asked to recount an episode from their own experience of professional

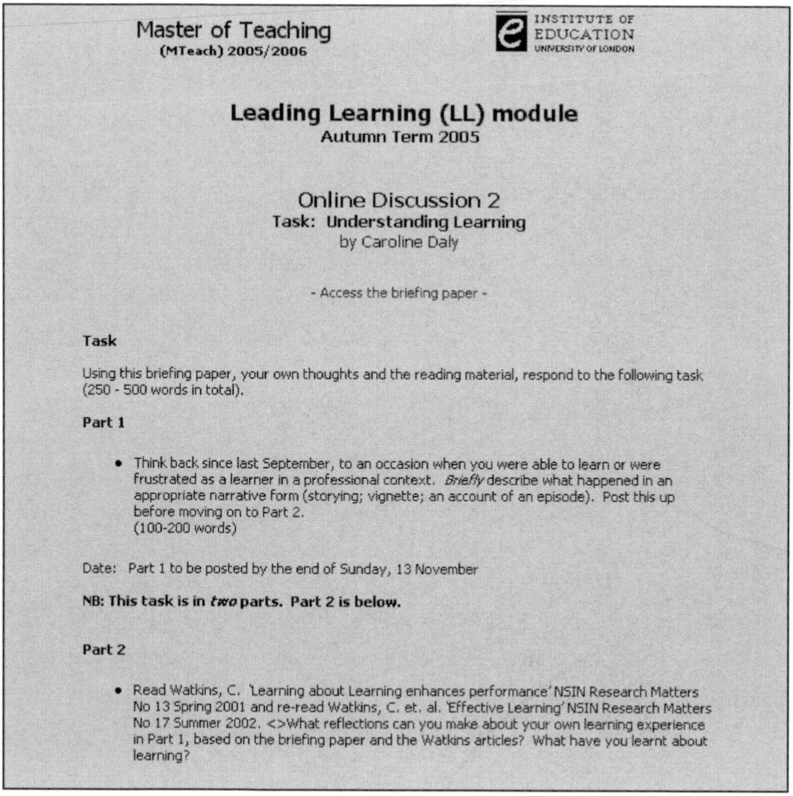

Master of Teaching
(MTeach) 2005/2006

INSTITUTE OF EDUCATION
UNIVERSITY OF LONDON

Leading Learning (LL) module
Autumn Term 2005

Online Discussion 2
Task: Understanding Learning
by Caroline Daly

- Access the briefing paper -

Task

Using this briefing paper, your own thoughts and the reading material, respond to the following task (250 - 500 words in total).

Part 1

- Think back since last September, to an occasion when you were able to learn or were frustrated as a learner in a professional context. *Briefly* describe what happened in an appropriate narrative form (storying; vignette; an account of an episode). Post this up before moving on to Part 2.
(100-200 words)

Date: Part 1 to be posted by the end of Sunday, 13 November

NB: This task is in *two* parts. Part 2 is below.

Part 2

- Read Watkins, C. 'Learning about Learning enhances performance' NSIN Research Matters No 13 Spring 2001 and re-read Watkins, C. et. al. 'Effective Learning' NSIN Research Matters No 17 Summer 2002. <>What reflections can you make about your own learning experience in Part 1, based on the briefing paper and the Watkins articles? What have you learnt about learning?

Figure 2.1 Task template for Leading Learning module discussion 2

learning, and then critically reflect upon it. By offering an analysis of both the surface (manifest) and sub-textual (latent) features of their online discussion, we argue that CMC enables teachers to develop critical and agentive ways of thinking through collaborative practices involving the sharing of electronic writing.

Twinned with this qualitative study of their online writing is an analysis of narrative as a collaborative learning tool for teachers, in which participants recount their experiences from their practice intersubjectively through CMC. There is an autobiographical dimension that is central to the ways in which the teachers engage with online discussion, in that they are encouraged to narrate their experiences using task templates (see Ruthoff and Ritter, 2001), which require them to relate episodes from their practice (see Figure 2.1).

The core aim of our study has been to understand the effects of the practice of CMC on the professional and pedagogic ideas which emerge. This is achieved first by identifying the *manifest* (or readily observable) content that is discernible in participants' online writing, and second by interpreting this content within a theoretical framework for agentive and reflexive paradigms of teachers' professional learning (drawing on Sachs, 2003; Lingard *et al.*, 2003; Moore, 2004; Furlong, 2000). This allows a further stage of investigation to identify the *latent* features which lie beneath the surface of the online text, and which indicate how the teachers' writing reflects more complex themes which may be operating at a less conscious level, but which reveal further dimensions of professional learning. We have been particularly interested in the potential of CMC to support the development of agentive identities through constructivist practices, to better understand the interrelation between joint professional written activity and individual cognition.

Collaboration within a community of practice

The nature of what Garrison and Anderson (2003) call the 'educational transaction' is at the centre of any query into the impact of CMC within a constructivist theory of learning, and helps to conceptualise the interplay which takes place around online interaction between teachers:

> an educational experience has a dual purpose. The first is to construct meaning (reconstruction of experience) from a personal perspective. The second is to refine and confirm this understanding

collaboratively within a community of learners ... the transaction
reveals the inseparability of teaching and learning roles.

(Garrison and Anderson, 2003:13)

The relationship between the individual and the social dimensions
of learning, particularly located within recent theories of community
and practice-based learning, provides a theoretical focus for an
interpretation of the interrelatedness of individual conceptual
change and social interaction in the online discussions within the
teachers' forum. Communities of practice (COPs) have been
examined for their potential in fostering learning through 'talking
within practice' (Wenger, 1998), and there is widespread interest in
the potential of online communities to facilitate constructivist
approaches to learning (see Rovai, 2002; Lapadat, 2000, 2002). Both
the personal and social perspectives are essential to cognition, but
for teachers' professional learning, participation in a social
transaction of learning must be related to practice. Within what
Wenger defines as a 'social theory of learning' (1998: 3), he sees
learning as a process of social participation, one that places learning
'in the context of our lived experience of participation in the world'
(1998: 3). The belief is that 'communities of practice can be thought
of as shared histories of learning' (1998: 86). For this to be the case
in online discussion, there must be an effective environment for
participants' 'histories' to be realised by being narrated – in fact only
a *shared* history can constitute learning in this context. Participation
through narration affects the identities of participants, shaping 'not
only what we do, but also who we are and how we interpret what
we do' (1998: 86). It is the emergent *collaborative* rendering of
meaning that is central to teachers being able to participate in new
ways of thinking – or 'counter-thinking' – in order to act according
to critically informed understandings of teaching and learning.

Teacher narration and professional meanings

Teachers' knowledge is constantly evolving from their daily experiences both inside and outside their classrooms. Clandinin and Connelly (1995) describe this as engaging within the narrative planes of 'professional landscapes' which are both inward and outward looking, and have a past and future perspective. The nature of that knowledge is particular, complex and shaped by the multiple forms of interactions teachers experience within practice. It is further complicated by potential conflicts between the stories they live out in the different 'landscapes' which they talk about online, as they move between varying agendas which constantly determine aspects of what it is they do as teachers. Such ideas are founded on the argument that narrative is the 'primary form' by which human experience is made meaningful (Bruner, 1985). Polkinghorne's (1988) adaptation to the field of social sciences of Bruner's (1985) theory of narrative as a 'mode of thought' enables us to examine the role of narrative in learning in the online discourse of the MTeach. In particular, Polkinghorne's notion of the 'realm of meaning' to describe the convergence of matter, life and consciousness has applicability to the professional domain. It explains why teachers are able to discuss the matter of their professional everyday lives within a broader framework which gives it political and social significance beyond the events themselves. What emerges as 'meaning' is a construction of knowledge that is collaboratively forged and modified by interaction:

> Narrative meaning is created by the notion that something is a part of some whole and that something is the cause of something else.... It is the connections or relationships among events that is their meaning.... Narrative creates its meaning by noting the contributions that actions and events make to a particular outcome and then configures these parts into a whole episode.
>
> (Polkinghorne, 1988: 6)

Narrative, defined as a way of understanding, organising and communicating experience as 'stories', is viewed by some, including us, as an alternative way of engaging with certain aspects of learning about teaching which cannot be uncovered with the traditional approaches such as logical exposition (see Heo, 2004: 374). The literature on narrative and learning distinguishes different approaches; the most significant for our current purposes seem to be cognitive/constructivist and socio-cultural in nature (see Bamberg, 1997: 90). These different approaches are characterised by different definitional bases, conceptualisations of the learner and the narrator, and perceptions of the role of technology. The main distinction to be made here is that between an emphasis on the individual and the social, i.e. the individual experience versus the social sharing of practices.

Bamberg (2004: 213) bemoans the preponderance of cognitive approaches in narratology, which he polemically calls the 'cognition-über-alles' position. He refers to Ochs and Capps (2001), who note a number of practical implications of this preponderance. These include the privileging of 'one active teller' in contrast to 'multiple active co-tellers', the over-exploration of high 'tellability' (i.e. of high potential narrative appeal such as unsuccessful actions, broken promises, violated interdictions, mistaken interpretations, and deception (see Ryan, 1991)), an underemphasis on contextual and situational 'embeddedness', and a relative focus on a closed temporal, causal and spatial ordering. This also chimes with Klerfelt (2005: 14), who stresses the importance of narrative as a tool in the exchange of culturally constituted knowledge. The relevance to teaching, and learning about teaching – viewed as a cultural activity following cultural scripts, i.e. representations of cultural norms, for example about role expectations in learning, which are widely held in a given societal context – is self-evident to us (see Stigler and Hiebert, 1998). Like children learning about the world they live in through stories and storying, teachers can (attempt to) understand the world around them through narrative, appropriate its (meta)language, participate in relevant discursive contexts and develop autobiographical professional memory (see Klerfelt, 2005: 14). 'Through appropriation of knowledge, values and moral identity processes that lead to a "cultural self" are shaped' (Klerfelt, 2005: 14) and, we would add, teachers can develop professional intersubjectivity.

In the context of the MTeach we are interested in narrative that goes beyond individual cognition and becomes a vehicle of meaning-making, reality construction and the giving of meaning to experience with others in a social and interpersonal context (see Nicolopoulou, 1997: 208), in particular professional identity formation through online narrative, a focus we deem aptly described by Bamberg's notion of 'narrative-in-interaction' (2004: 214). Like Bamberg's, our interest in narratives lies not primarily in their form and content but mainly, if not exclusively, in what he calls 'identity negotiation' or 'identity confrontations'. These negotiations or confrontations 'are events in which conversationalists encounter interaction-trouble and need to manage and fine-tune their resources in order to come across in alignment with institutional and interpersonal demands' (pp. 220–1). In this discursive approach, narratives perform the function of navigating one's way through challenging circumstances and the analytical focus is on 'identifying the rhetorical and argumentative organization of discourse the way it is used to fashion self- and identity-claims' (p. 221).

> Analyzing narratives-in-interaction operates in close proximity to discursive approaches that examine evaluative expressions as parts of interactive, social, and cultural practices, which implies the close scrutiny of how such expressions are put to use, as opposed to speculating about the mental or attitudinal objects that they putatively reflect.
>
> (Bamberg, 2004: 222)

Bamberg (2004: 223) posits that great care needs to be taken not to conflate the self as character in the narrative and the self as author as 'constructing a self as a character in the story world and entering this construction as a claim for the self of the speaker, requires "additional" rhetorical work in order to be heard "correctly"' (p. 224). How interactants establish a sense of self, in his view, is through 'additional rhetorical work ... that elevates "personal narratives" into the realm of interesting data, and not the fact that speakers are revealing something that counts as more intimate or "personal"' (p. 224). This perspective has been crucial to the approach we adopt in interrogating the online writing of teachers, by which we disaggregate the individual authors from their textual output, and develop methods to elicit the inter-textual evidence of learning by identifying prevalent themes and processes of professional redefinition and transformation of ideas within the discourse as a whole.

Computer-supported collaborative learning

Following Koschmann (2002), we define computer-supported collaborative learning (CSCL) as 'practices of meaning-making in the context of joint activity mediated through designed artefacts'.

Drawing on a range of sources, Suthers (2005: 662–3) distinguishes the following epistemologies, i.e. theoretical perspectives, underlying the concept of 'collaborative learning':

- a knowledge-communication epistemology: how can the acquisition of knowledge be caused/supported by communications?

- a constructivist epistemology, which emphasises the agency of the individual in the learning process rather than as just receiving knowledge from others; collaborative forms locate the meaning-making in a group context;

- an interactional epistemology, which examines how interactions between people lead to learning;

- intersubjective learning, our preferred concept, which goes beyond a notion of information-sharing to include the sharing of interpretations and the joint creation of interpretations through interaction; it includes disagreement; learning is not only brought about through interactions of participants but also consists of those interactions; the process of meaning-making is constituted of social interaction;

- knowledge building, by which he means a collective version of intentional learning.

This list of perspectives sets out what Suthers calls a 'thematic agenda' for the future exploration of CSCL, and he suggests possible research foci in the context of intersubjective learning to do with participants' methods of problematisation, interpretation, argumentation, negotiation and achieving a working consensus (Suthers, 2005: 665). In taking up such an agenda in the context of electronic teachers' forums, there is a need to develop appropriate methods, and some fundamental questions and issues arise in examining how teachers learn with others in mind:

- What are appropriate units of analysis? The online environment we use on the MTeach is deliberately not interaction-based in the narrow sense and it is difficult to obtain 'process data'. We require participants to produce 'outcome data', i.e. teacher narratives.

- What coding categories are most appropriate? There is a need to move 'from coding and counting' to 'exploring and understanding'. Numerical and statistical data are often merely 'proxies' for the phenomenon of interest rather than those phenomena themselves, e.g. counting how often a student makes a posting in and of itself says nothing about quality and extent of participation and learning taking place (see Suthers, 2005: 665). Accepting the need to move to a more interpretative approach implies the use of a descriptive rather than an experimental research methodology, i.e. 'the analysis must examine the structure and intention of specific cases of interaction rather than count and aggregate behavioral categories' (p. 666). There is an imperative for the study of electronic texts to uncover the methods by which participants accomplish learning and there is a need for the process to be data-driven, i.e. for researchers to seek to discover patterns in the data rather than impose theoretical categories. Analysis in this research paradigm, by implication, needs to be 'microanalytic', i.e. to examine brief episodes in great detail. Matters are further complicated by the fact that online discussions are collaborative texts and, therefore, an accumulation of interpretative acts. For this reason the analysis also needs to focus on 'uptake events', 'in which one participant takes up another's contribution and does something further with it' (Suthers, 2005: 668). Once uptake events have been identified, it needs to be determined what participants have jointly accomplished through (sequences of) uptake.

- What are the limitations of such an approach? Suthers (2005: 667) rightly points out that by focusing on finding examples of how participants accomplish learning, we may miss examples of how they fail to do so. To counteract this potential shortcoming, there is a need to analyse examples of unsuccessful collaboration with a view to determining what strategies for successful collaboration identified elsewhere are missing and why.

Methodological issues

We have developed a methodology for researching teachers' online discussions in order to identify how, as a community of practitioners, teachers talk about their professional activities and thereby develop meanings about their practice which can be identified at a collaborative and inter-textual level. This is to draw on what Wenger (1998) calls the dual processes of *participation* and *reification* by which the meanings of professional phenomena are made. The meanings enable a community to encode its practices and share recognition and understandings of core phenomena and the political implications for how individuals can act or 'be' within that world. Our methodology is based on the need to build an analysis of teachers' online writing from an agentive theoretical basis, allowing us to bring a critical epistemological stance to our interpretation of what it contains. In their online narration, MTeach participants exhibit many indications that they are experiencing doubts in the educational purpose which shapes their practice and their identities as teachers: 'schemes of work, time restraints and a lack of resources seem to prevent me from being the inspirational teacher I would like to be' (Message 27R).

If teachers are to be able to work with the 'counter-pessimism' which is demanded by Sachs's (2003) call for a 'new professionalism' based on agentive professional identities, they need professional learning instruments by which to re-establish the relationship between themselves as teachers, with histories and knowledge rooted in their experience, and the types of knowledge which are available through external forces – both educational theory and government policy and standards frameworks. Key to this link between the teacher-self and these contexts of knowledge production is the role of narration, by which teachers are enabled to locate themselves as learners within a historicised view of their own practice, both in school and in the world.

This connection between the teacher-self and teacher-learning is central to Moore's (2004) conceptualisation of the historicised teacher, whose agency is rooted in the capacity for reflexivity. The notion of the teacher-self has been eroded by the performative agenda which is one feature of the globalised context for learning in the twenty-first century, and reflects the pressure on governments to function on a global scale, to produce an economically viable workforce with the requisite skills to perform competitively. Learning has been conceived as a commodity in this context. Agency becomes highly problematic in a context where teachers' professional learning is to a large extent driven by the pressure to achieve ever-improving performance from their pupils.

Developing a methodology

As has already been noted, most research into computer-mediated communication has had a narrow focus on counting or categorising patterns of participant interaction, linguistic features, discourse features, language functions and motivation in ways which are easily quantifiable (for example Garrison *et al.*, 2001; Bradshaw *et al.*, 2002; Fahy, 2003). These features are relatively straightforward to identify, but such positivist approaches offer little in-depth analysis of the complex psychological phenomenon of learning in a social-interactive context. There have been difficulties in finding analytical tools that tell us about what conceptual transformations are occurring (Kern *et al.*, 2004). In order to engage with the complexities involved, we have adapted the content analysis model of Garrison and Anderson (2003). Despite its origins in quantitative research design, content analysis offers helpful organisational principles to a qualitative study of online learning, providing an effective way of organising a collection of online texts in order to analyse them, and to distinguish the nature of the material which is of hermeneutical interest.

This study uses the message as the unit of analysis. The reasons for this lie within the conceptualisation of 'text', and the need for a relevant way of identifying what constitutes the 'texts' to be examined. Professional learning, as the construct being examined, has been conceptualised as complex and located in narrative ways of knowing. Because of the highly complex nature of teachers' professional learning, the unit of analysis is irreducible to single words or sentences within messages as a consistent and reliable way of affording an examination of the construct in its observable form. It may be that on some occasions a meaning can be observed within an altered use of a word within a collection of messages written by one or more participants. But it may be observable only within the message as a whole, in terms of how it works within text-level analysis that is based on the linguistic concept of cohesion, which links parts of a single text towards a consistent purpose or meaning.

The asynchronous online discussions within the MTeach take place mostly through a set of initial postings based on a task, and at least one response. The postings are relatively long (250–300 words) and there is little response beyond the primary level. Thus, the main opportunity for interpretation lies in the ways in which ideas are constructed over the length of the message. There is little dialogue to and fro between participants, but the messages reveal the presence of others online, and particular features of writing for fellow learners over time. 'As participants strive to put their thoughts into writing clearly, they will take their time, reflect, consider their audience's perspectives, and use critical and higher order thinking skills' (Lapadat, 2002: n.p.). Participants take time to compose these messages, and our knowledge of the context of the text production informs the choice of the message as the unit of analysis. The text in itself is a 'bounded instance of something else' (Brown and Dowling, 1998) and each participant's text is to be read and understood within the context of the community in which it is made. Whilst acknowledging that there are complexities in viewing electronic writing as a hybrid between spoken and written communicative forms, there is mileage in viewing online writing as a form of 'speech utterance' (Hymes, 1994), by which meanings are located within the community in which it was produced and for whom it is intended. Professional learning in online writing is therefore extremely complex, and has a dual possibility of interpretation, embedded at the individual level of each person's text and in the interplay between texts by which fragments are echoed, appropriated and augmented in order for further collaborative thinking to develop through further writing.

Categories and indicators are used to provide a framework in which to search the text in a systematic way, by rigorously reading for items which display pre-selected features. Anderson and Kanuka (2003) explain that content analysis does not have to be rigidly quantitative, despite its main use within computer-aided methodology. It is a 'crossover technique' because of the need for critical interpretative skills for the researcher to identify the significant features within the text by rigorous reading, searching for themes or categories which have been derived from a theoretical perspective on teachers' learning. Thus, it involves the researchers in taking a stance, in our case one which is coherent with the MTeach course philosophy.

We identified five categories of teachers' professional learning which are derived from literature offering critical and reflexive theoretical perspectives on teacher learning, from which activist identities can evolve: *knowledge construction*, *community*, *metalearning*, *autobiography* and *cognition*. The five categories are not hierarchical, and apply across the spectrum of individual and social learning. In our view, there is a lack of explicitness about the theoretical underpinnings of the selection of categories and indicators for coding in current accounts of qualitative content analysis, and we include the derivation in Appendix 2.1.

The indicators to be searched for in the text under each category are based on a reading of the literature and our experience of reading teachers' online discussion. A typology of indicators is derived from an analysis of theoretical perspectives on knowledge construction in CMC and teachers' professional learning, which incorporates perspectives on learning as a matter of both social engagement and individual cognition. The typology consists of 20 indicators and provides the framework for the initial coding of the transcripts (see Table 2.1).

Table 2.1 Categories and indicators of professional learning through participation in CMC

Category	Indicators
Knowledge construction	Reassessments New ideas/proposals Questions/enquiries Endorsements/verified ideas Modified ideas
Community	Shared values/goals Seeking/giving support Statements expressing mutuality Practice-based exchanges
Metalearning	Verbalising the learning process Verbalising understanding Verbalising difficulties
Autobiography	Critical incidents Personal reflection Teacher identity Learner identity
Cognition	Statements of understanding: – theoretical – critical – practical References to personal learning

There were 30 messages in the whole discussion, sent by a total of 11 participants. The task required an initial posting in two parts, followed by a response:

Initial task posting (part 1)	11
Follow-up posting (part 2)	10
Responses	9
Total messages	30

An initial reading of the messages made it clear that only the responses were of relevance to the content of interest, since the initial task postings were highly individualised and self-contained forms of text, which did not reveal a sufficient mass of data to indicate any effects of the interactive environment (and that is not their intention). The responses (n=9) revealed the richest data, with a total of 89 examples of the five categories.

The sample texts were then scrutinised to identify examples of the indicators for the five categories, producing what Garrison and Anderson (2003) call manifest and latent variables. Manifest variables consist of readily observable features of the discourse which occur at declarative level, i.e. what the participants say they are thinking, how they report on their actions and learning episodes, how they use language to establish community and purpose and relationships with their peers. This is the first stage of coding. For example, the statement 'it is a big relief to find out that other people are also concerned with this issue' is a manifest variable of the category 'community', identified by the indicator 'shared values/goals'. Table 2.2 shows examples of the manifest variables for each of the categories which are drawn from the sample.

Table 2.2 Professional learning categories and indicators, adapted from the "practical enquiry model" of research into computer-mediated communication

Category	Indicators	Examples
Knowledge construction	Reassessments	'Reading your posting made me realise that …'
	New ideas/ proposals	'I think it's also our job to provide a learning orientation within the classroom …'
	Questions/ enquiries	'Do we ever reach the stage where we as teachers have run out of ways of …?'
	Endorsements/ verified ideas	'One idea that definitely struck a chord was … this was brought clearly home to me …'
	Modified ideas	'Maybe her preferred learning style was not being considered?'
Community	Shared values/goals	'It is a big relief to find out that other people are also concerned with this issue'
	Seeking/giving support	'not entirely sure if my response is appropriate … but have tried my best to …'
	Statements of mutuality	'having read through your contributions I felt like I am reading my own thoughts'
	Practice-based exchanges	'I agree that in several instances within class … Today a year 7 class were busily …'
Metalearning	Verbalising the learning process	'Reading the personal responses from L and S made me think about myself and my learning in a way that the academic papers didn't'
	Verbalising understanding	'Going back over what has been discussed so far … I can see more and more clearly how important and valuable narratives could be as a knowledge base for teachers'

Category	Indicators	Examples
	Verbalising difficulties	'I found this task more difficult'
Autobiography	Critical incidents	'He couldn't understand why I couldn't understand ...'
	Personal reflection	'Reflecting on my related learning experience I can see that ...'
	Teacher identity	'schemes of work, time restraints ... prevent me from being the teacher I would like to be'
	Learner identity	'they learnt it was the taking part that counted ... it is more important to know how we learn'
Cognition	Statements of understanding: – theoretical – critical – practical	'I have changed my mind ... learning is more complex ...' 'The performance-based nature of teaching in my opinion has to change' 'Untangl[ing] the reasons why some of us can and cannot learn ... is entirely transferable to students'
	References to personal learning	'the discussion made me see, perhaps for the first time ...'

Source: Garrison and Anderson (2003)

Once the manifest variables have been identified, an analysis is made of the prevalent features of the teachers' thinking. It is at this inter-textual level that the effect of collaborative processes on teacher meanings can be traced. For reasons of space in this chapter, a worked example is shown of the data for only one of these categories: Autobiography (Table 2.3).

Table 2.3 Autobiography classification and indicators

Critical incidents	• 'He couldn't understand why I couldn't understand ...' (25R) • 'I can think of numerous moments in my career where I have had to stop and think' (25R) • 'We recently had a very interesting INSET evening where ...' (27R) • 'This was brought clearly home to me today when I had 9D1. Suddenly Z was not in his usual "I hate geography" mode' (28R) • 'Today a year 7 class were busily completing ...' (29R)
Personal reflection	• 'Reflecting on my related learning experience I can see that ...' (25R) • 'The types of learners, learning experiences, motivation and methods vary and make for a fascinating catalogue of narratives of experiences' (27R) • 'The introduction of a computer produced the most amazing ... It is clear that by using different learning styles students can learn by the methods that suit them best. It must be our job to provide these different styles ... Every lesson in geography cannot include computers but if I can instil a learning orientation within students they can learn ...' (28R) • '[Today a year 7 class were ...] It became clear that it didn't matter if they got the answers right, there was a much more useful activity going on ... they did learn a fair amount about ... but more importantly they learnt that it was the taking part that counted' (29R) • 'Maybe the student [subject of narration] will understand the concept he was trying to explain tomorrow, perhaps, like you experienced, it was the way [the teacher] was explaining the concept that she just "didn't get"' (26R)

Teacher identity	• 'schemes of work, time restraints ... prevent me from being the teacher I would like to be' (29R)
	• 'Part of my motivation for doing this MTeach is because I want to become a better teacher ... not just better than I was before but better than other teachers who have chosen not to' (21R)
	• '[The discussion ... made me see] ... so much of my feelings of self-worth are tied up with my performance as a teacher and as a learner' (21R)
	• 'Don't get me wrong, I am not a rebel and have not refused to teach my subject's syllabus' (26R)
	• 'I have also had experiences where I have had to think of alternative teaching approaches ... Sometimes this still fails and, as a colleague said to me just today ...' (26R)
Learner identity	• 'they learnt it was the taking part that counted ... it is more important to know how we learn' (29R)

Analysis of the manifest variables

From this classification, we can begin to distinguish emergent patterns in the declarations of teachers along two clear thematic strands:

1 declarations that show teachers are contributing as practitioners; and

2 declarations that show teachers' reflections on their practice, which involve statements about their professional identities.

Declarations showing that teachers' contributions are embedded in practice include a variety of workplace contexts and incidents which constitute the broader narrative world of the teacher, in which meanings about practice can be located:

71

'a very interesting INSET evening'
'when I had 9D1'
'the introduction of a computer produced'
'Today a Year 7 class were'
'schemes of work, time restraints'
'the way [the teacher] was explaining the concept'

Declarations that offer reflection on practice and professional identities include both individual and shared perspectives:

'I want to become a better teacher ... not just better than I was before but better than other teachers'
'so much of my feelings of self-worth are tied up with my performance as a teacher and as a learner'
'I am not a rebel'
'prevent me from being the teacher I would like to be'
'moments in my career where I have had to stop and think'
'I have had to think of alternative teaching approaches'
'It must be our job to provide'

Wenger's (1998) theory of COPs encourages us to look at these together as constituting the 'politics' of meaning-making at work, via the process of reification. By reification, professional phenomena are rendered meaningful by the ways in which people talk about them, and thus constitute their practice. There is a relationship here between the 'things' which constitute daily practice – INSET, teaching Year 7, using a computer, explaining a concept, etc. – and the meanings which can be negotiated around them which bring about professional knowledge involving a high degree of impact on 'feelings of self-worth'. By this, participants learn what it is to be a teacher, by narrating what Bamberg called 'interaction-trouble' (2004) as they articulate the 'duality' of institutional and interpersonal demands. This duality demands further analysis to identify what lies behind a statement like 'I am not a rebel', where face-value meanings are inadequate to explain all that is significant in such a claim (or denial), and where authorial intention is not helpful as an indicator of its potential meanings.

Latent variables – projecting a theory

It is the latent variables, therefore, within the teachers' messages, which are especially relevant to examining their learning, and are difficult to observe. In the context of CMC, higher order learning has been described as 'covert processes' (Garrison and Anderson, 2003: 140) but it is worth 'struggling with the important (though hidden) facets of individual and social cognition rather than assessing that which is most easily measured'.

Identification and analysis of latent variables is necessary to reveal a:

> hidden 'interior being'.... Latent variables ... include important concepts such as evidence of creative or critical thinking ... [they] must be inferred from manifest content and this inferential procedure inevitably provides opportunities for inconsistencies and error on the one hand and insight and interpretation on the other. The nature of the latent variable influences the manner in which it is identified and described.
>
> (Anderson and Kanuka, 2003: 175)

This approach has been developed by a continuing refinement in qualitative adaptations of a content analysis model (Garrison *et al.*, 2001; Anderson *et al.*, 2001; Anderson and Kanuka, 2003; Garrison and Anderson, 2003). Hermeneutic understanding uses processes such as analogy and pattern recognition to draw conclusions about the meaning content of linguistic messages. This stage of the content analysis proposes an 'inferential procedure to recognise variables in a pattern that is consistent across the textual content. The more difficult inferential procedure involves the recognition of 'latent projective variables' which are identified by judgements 'based on a "projection" of an abstract concept by the researcher' (Garrison and Anderson, 2003: 140).

The teachers narrate a range of professional situations here, which are both practically and critically situated within the dominant discourses of teaching. Their narratives contain a large number of references to their own identities as teachers, both explicitly – 'the teacher I would like to be' – and implicitly by describing their actions within the dominant discourses (Moore, 2004) of 'good teaching': 'It is clear that by using different learning styles ... It must be our job to provide these'. There is, however, a concurrent discomfort with the discourses they draw on, and they struggle to find a language which articulates different values and indicators of learning which are individual-focused and have a perspective of change over time according to personal contexts and goals. There is resistance to the managerialist discourse, to 'schemes of work, time restraints' which are seen as inhibiting self-aware professional practices and creativity, but at the same time teachers inhabit the language of target-driven performativity. The teacher's comment 'It must be our job to provide these different [learning] styles' reflects the duality of the teacher's position, anxious to implement a recent government initiative on learning styles to support individual student differences, but missing the point completely by inhabiting the language of 'delivery' by aiming to *provide* the students with them. The coexistence of these conflicting concepts of professional practice is a source of confusion. In the comment 'Don't get me wrong, I am not a rebel' the idea of resistance disconcerts, and yet the texts include ample examples of 'rebelliousness', but lack an appropriate discourse that may be legitimately occupied by a teacher. Being 'a rebel' is absolutely not seen as a possible role of the contemporary teacher. This duality is a source of considerable professional dissatisfaction for some, or proficient compromise for others who appropriate the discourse of the 'competent craftsperson' (Moore, 2004). They write about themselves as practitioners in a way frequently marked by this duality, so that an almost (unarticulated as yet) 'schizophrenic' professional identity emerges (Strauss, 1995).

It is not a matter of teachers inventing a new discourse in their online writing, but rather of the individuals revealing how differently they negotiate the discourses which are available to frame their professional actions. There is outright critique from some. Others, though, take authenticity from their experiences and use this to challenge orthodoxies: 'they learnt it was the taking part that counted … it is more important to know how we learn'. Whatever the difficulties, there is a sense of mutuality in their struggle for a coherent professional identity which must be practised in order to 'be' a teacher, and a strong sense of shared professional ethics centred on a concern for the value of students' learning experiences. There is certainly reflection, but more than a self-referential concern to perform better.

In summary, therefore, the latent variables which emerge from an analysis of the category of 'autobiography' in teachers' professional learning are each related to an aspect of transformation and struggle through engaging with *dominant discourses, professional redefinition* and *growing reflexivity.*

- Early career teachers can be seen to be inhabiting *dominant discourses* within their recount – in particular, the 'competent craftsperson' and the 'reflective practitioner'. Writing online involves drawing on the available discourses to describe their practice to others. At the same time, the ways they appropriate the language of the discourses shows they do not fully own the practices they enact, and this leads to difficulty in accommodating their views of themselves within the language available.

- The problems they experience in so doing form a process of *professional redefinition*, involving the articulation of ethical uncertainties about the actions demanded by these discourses. This is disconcerting, and we see a desire to establish identity within a professional community in which there is a shared sense of struggle.

- There are the beginnings of *growing reflexivity* – detected in the recourse to the teacher-self as complex and historicised, as located in personal histories of learning which are embedded in culture and over time, and where narrative is a key to the development of complex teacher identities which are capable of agency and generating knowledge based on critical examination of experience.

Conclusion

The production through computer-mediated communication of a permanent written manuscript has implications for professional learning, as it facilitates a conscious engagement with language that can be subjected to interpretation and reinterpretation, thus extending the levels of further meaning-making by participants and interpretation by researchers. The fact that participants can appropriate and adapt material from the textual archive into their own narrations means that traditional notions of individual authorship and intellectual possession become less fixed. The resultant dominant reading experience can be of the overall articulation of ideas, both manifest and latent, and a considerable degree of semantic cohesion exists within a multiple-authored online manuscript. We believe there is under-explored potential in understanding the benefits for teachers of learning with others in mind within online forums of this type.

The participants in our study are moving towards collaborative notions of reflexivity in their discussions about their practice, but this is a complex process. This is the first term of their course, and the teachers are mostly beginning their second year of teaching, therefore, with very recent experience of the standards which have relentlessly regulated their professional development for the preceding two years of initial and newly qualified teacher (NQT) training. The roles of teachers, what they can tell and how they conceive of learning, are vital to the formulation of what Lingard has referred to as a 'positive thesis' (Lingard *et al.*, 2003: 5) for

76

professional learning in contexts of continual change. Snyder's analysis of the impact of new technologies on education is uncompromising on this: 'The world for which schools were formed no longer exists' (2002: 179), and within this context our analysis of online interaction indicates that electronic teacher forums can contribute to the co-construction of evolving professional knowledge. The potential for online discussion in contributing to this reflexive process deserves further exploration in the design of university CPD programmes.

References

Anderson, T. and Kanuka, H. (2003) *E-Research: Methods, strategies and issues.* Boston: Allyn and Bacon.

Anderson, T., Rourke, L., Garrison, D. and Archer, W. (2001) 'Assessing teaching presence in a computer conferencing context'. *Journal of Asynchronous Learning Networks,* 5, 2, 2–17.

Bamberg, M. (1997) 'A constructivist approach to narrative development'. In M. Bamberg (ed.), *Narrative Development: Six approaches.* Mahwah, NJ: Lawrence Erlbaum, 89–132.

Bamberg, M. (2004) 'Narrative discourse and identities'. In J. Meister, T. Kindt, W. Schernus and M. Stein (eds), *Narratology Beyond Literary Criticism.* Berlin and New York: Walter de Gruyter, 213–37.

Bradshaw, P., Chapman, C. and Gee, A. (2002) *A Report on the ULTRALAB's Development of Online Components in NCSL Programmes.* Chelmsford: Ultralab.

Brown, A. and Dowling, P. (1998) *Doing Research/Reading Research: A mode of interrogation for education.* London: Falmer Press.

Bruner, J. (1985) 'Narrative and paradigmatic modes of thought'. In E. Eisner (ed.), *Learning and Teaching the Ways of Knowing.* Chicago: University of Chicago Press.

Clandinin, D.J and Connelly, F.M. (1995) *Teachers' Professional Knowledge Landscapes.* New York: Teachers College Press.

Clandinin, D.J. and Connelly, F.M. (2000) *Narrative Inquiry*. San Francisco: Jossey-Bass.

Fahy, P. (2003) 'Indicators of support in online interaction'. *International Review of Research in Open and Distance Learning*, 4, 1. Available at: www.irrodl.org/content/v4.1/fahy.html

Furlong, J. (2000) *Higher Education and the New Professionalism for Teachers. Realising the potential of partnership*. London: Universities UK.

Garrison, D. and Anderson, T. (2003) *E-Learning in the 21st Century: A framework for research and practice*. London: RoutledgeFalmer.

Garrison, D., Anderson, T. and Archer, W. (2001) 'Critical thinking, cognitive presence and computer conferencing in distance education'. *American Journal of Distance Education*, 15, 1, 7–23. Available at: www.atl.ualberta.ca/cmc/CTinTextEnvFinal.pdf

Harasim, L. (2000) 'Shift happens. Online education as a new paradigm in learning'. *Internet and Higher Education*, 3, 41–61.

Heo, H. (2004) 'Story telling and retelling as narrative inquiry in cyber learning environments'. In R. Atkinson, C. McBeath, D. Jonas-Dwyer and R. Phillips (eds), *Beyond the Comfort Zone: Proceedings of the 21st ASCILITE Conference*, Perth, 5–8 December, 374–8. Available at: www.ascilite.org.au/conferences/perth04/procs/pdf/heo.pdf

Hymes, D. (1994) 'Towards ethnographies of communication'. In J. Maybin (ed.), *Language and Literacy in Social Practice*. Clevedon: Multilingual Matters/Open University.

Kern, R., Ware, P. and Warschauer, M. (2004) 'Crossing frontiers: New directions in online pedagogy and research'. *Annual Review of Applied Linguistics*, 24, 243–60.

Klerfelt, A. (2005) 'Narratives and their significance for children's communication about their world'. In K. Steffens (ed.), *Guide for the Implementation of Narrative Learning Environments*. Version 1. Köln: Kaleidoscope, 5–16. Available at: www.noe-kaleidoscope.org

Koschmann, T. (2002) 'Dewey's contribution to the foundations of CSCL research'. In *Proc. Computer Supported Collaborative Learning 2002*, Boulder, 7–11 January, 17–22.

Koschmann, T. (2003) 'CSCL, argumentation and Deweyan inquiry'. In J. Andriessen, M. Baker and D. Suthers (eds), *Confronting Cognitions in*

Computer-supported Collaborative Learning Environments. Amsterdam: Kluwer Academic Publishers.

Lapadat, J. (2000) 'Tracking conceptual change: an indicator of online learning'. Paper presented at *International Online Conference on Teaching Online in Higher Education.*

Lapadat, J. (2002) 'Written interaction: a key component in online learning'. *Journal of Computer-mediated Communication,* 7, 4.
Available at: www.ascusc.org/jcmc/vol7/issue4/lapadat.html

Laurillard, D. (2002) *Rethinking University Teaching: A conversational framework for the effective use of learning technologies.* London: Routledge Falmer.

Lave, J. and Wenger, E. (1991) *Situated Learning: Legitimate peripheral participation.* Cambridge: Cambridge University Press.

Lingard, B., Hayes, D., Mills, M. and Christie, P. (2003) *Leading Learning.* Maidenhead: Open University Press.

Mercer, N. (1995) *The Guided Construction of Knowledge.* Clevedon: Multilingual Matters.

Moore, A. (2004) *The Good Teacher.* London: RoutledgeFalmer.

Nicolopoulou, A. (1997) 'Children and narratives: toward an interpretative and sociocultural approach'. In M. Bamberg (ed.), *Narrative Development: Six approaches.* Mahwah, NJ: Lawrence Erlbaum, 179–215.

Ochs, E. and Capps, L. (2001) *Living Narrative. Creating lives in everyday storytelling.* Cambridge, MA: Harvard University Press.

Polkinghorne, D. (1988) *Narrative Knowing and the Human Sciences.* New York: State University of New York Press.

Preece, J. and Maloney-Krichmar, D. (2005) 'A multilevel analysis of sociability, usability, and community dynamics in an online health community'. *ACM Transactions on Computer–Human Interaction (TOCHI),* 12, 2, 201–32.

Ravenscroft, A. (2003) 'The influence of educational best practice in ICT in teaching and learning'. Round table at Beyond Theory, one-day conference, Oxford Union Debating Chamber, 11 April. Available at: www.oucs.ox.ac.uk/ltg/events/beyondnew/transcripts.html#ravenscroft

Rovai, A. (2002) 'Building a sense of community at a distance'. *International Review of Research in Open and Distance Learning,* 3, 1.

Rüschoff, B. and Ritter, M. (2001) 'Technology-enhanced language learning: construction of knowledge and template-based learning in the foreign language classroom'. *Computer Assisted Language Learning*, 14, 3/4, 219–32.

Ryan, M.-L. (1991) 'Virtuality and tellability'. In *Possible Worlds, Artificial Intelligence and Narrative Theory*. Bloomington: Indiana University Press, 148–74.

Sachs, J. (2003) *The Activist Teaching Profession*. Buckingham: Open University Press.

Snyder, I. (2002) *Silicon Literacies: Communication, innovation and education in the electronic age*. London: Routledge.

Stigler, J. and Hiebert, J. (1998) 'Teaching is a cultural activity'. *American Educator*, Winter, 1–10.

Strauss, P. (1995) 'No easy answers: the dilemmas and challenges of teacher research'. In *Educational Action Research*, 3, 1, 29–39.

Suthers, D. (2005) 'Technology affordances for intersubjective learning: a thematic agenda for CSCL'. In T. Koschmann, D. Suthers and T. Chan (eds), *Computer Supported Collaborative Learning 005: The next 10 years!* Mahwah, NJ: Lawrence Erlbaum, 662–71.

Tripp, D. (1983) *Critical Incidents in Teaching*. London: Routledge.

Vygotsky, L.S. (1986) *Thought and Language*, revised edition, revised and edited by Alex Kozulin. Boston: MIT Press.

Wenger, E. (1998) *Communities of Practice: Learning, meaning and identity*. Cambridge: Cambridge University Press.

Appendix 2.1

Theoretical derivation of categories of professional learning for content analysis

Knowledge construction

Learning is viewed both as a product of cognitive activity and at the same time as the process by which meaning is made in communion with others. A socio-cultural version of constructivism, most frequently adopted within CMC pedagogical design, posits knowledge as a social construct (Laurillard, 2002). That which is 'known' is that which carries a shared orientation towards its meaning, arrived at through collaborative processes which are conducted through language. Vygotskian views on concept formation centre on the 'significative use' of language, which is prompted 'not from within but from without, by the social milieu' (Vygotsky, 1986: 108). Theories of knowledge construction have taken as a premise that coming to 'know' something is not an act of individual cognition alone, but is a process of engaging in the social world and mediating the sense that is made of it through some form of sign which is communicable to others. Discourse is analysed for its role as catalyst in the interplay between the individual and the social, the private world and the public, as a means of constructing knowledge. In the text-based asynchronous environment, narrative is the means by which teachers account for their professional actions, and present themselves as actors within a peer context. Literate behaviours for learning centre around participation in textual 'thinking' through: augmentation, peer learning, adaptation and modification of expressed ideas. Lapadat (2002) has based her arguments for the constructivist properties of asynchronous CMC on such literate behaviours being facilitated by the online environment, describing the participants as

81

'conversationalists'. Her argument is that writing online is the participatory core of CMC, as it facilitates constructivist approaches to meaning-making (2000, 2002). Indicators of knowledge construction through social interactive processes are derived from Mercer's 'sketch' of the nature of learning through language interaction in constructivist contexts: 'This is a social, historical process ... so that the knowledge that is created carries with it echoes of the conversations in which it was generated' (1995: 84).

The indicators for the category of 'knowledge construction' include 'echoing' properties: reassessments, new ideas/proposals, questions, endorsements/verified ideas and modified ideas.

Community

Wenger (1998) makes it clear that a *community* does not necessarily imply a shared *practice*, and it is in the relations with practice that the core relevance to teachers' learning lies. Wenger's concept of a community of practice (COP) links the aspects of 'community' with 'practice' as a collaborative learning enterprise, offering a way of understanding professional learning from the 'inside out', as an alternative to the reductive frameworks for learning about practice in which teachers currently operate. The COP emphasises 'a way of talking', a communicative function of community which establishes the meaning of what people do, and enables them to take future actions. Researchers now consider the nature of relationships between individuals to be more indicative of the existence of community than physical proximity (Preece and Maloney-Krichmar, 2005: n.p.). The distinguishing point about a COP as a metaphor for an electronic discourse community lies in the potential of CMC to support the possibilities of agency brought about by individuals engaging in constructivist approaches to learning about practice. Within Wenger's conceptualisation, learning is premised on constructivist ideas which have become marginalised within discourses of teaching in recent years. Teachers do not ordinarily engage in collaborative approaches to knowledge construction in their professional learning. For community to be relevant as a core element of learning as participatory narrative, there needs to be a sense of common purpose and satisfaction of needs through active participation (Rovai, 2002). One of Rovai's criteria for a 'sense of community' is having common expectations of learning, citing Lave and Wenger's (1991: 31) assertion that within communities of practice, learning is considered 'an integral and inseparable aspect of social practice'.

The indicators for the category of 'community' are: shared values/goals, giving/seeking support, mutuality and practice-based exchanges.

Metalearning

Agentive and reflexive paradigms of teachers' professional learning draw on the development of metalearning capabilities in teachers (Sachs, 2003; Lingard *et al.*, 2003; Furlong, 2000). The notion of the 'activist professional' depends on metalearning which enables teacher-identity to be complex and multiple. Ways of becoming reflexive are based on teachers narrating, historicising and critically deconstructing at a meta-level how they act in order to understand themselves and their practice within the social and political conditions which bear on those actions. Moore's analysis (2004) of dominant discourses of teaching suggests that the potential for agency (and thus 'hope') lies where teachers engage in an alternative way of constructing the professional self, by adopting the 'reflexive turn' (p. 141). The reflexive turn is an agentive factor in teacher learning, where it develops the discourse of the 'reflective practitioner' away from its self-referring and inward-looking solo-performative connotations, and takes reflection to another level. Reflexive practice should be 'authentically and constructively critical

... challenging rather than confirmatory' (p. 142). It is rooted in the construction of continually evolving identities that are based on understanding the teacher as a person whose practice is continually developing, and grounded in their history as a social and intellectual being.

The indicators for the category of 'metalearning' are: verbalising the learning process, verbalising consciousness of understanding and verbalising consciousness of difficulties.

Autobiography

Shared narrative as a cognitive process that organises human experiences into 'temporarily meaningful episodes' (Polkinghorne, 1988: 1) has informed the view of teacher narrative as arising from and constituting 'critical episodes' (Tripp, 1993) and having a vital role in enabling teachers to challenge orthodox, universal 'truths' which govern their practice (Clandinin and Connelly, 2000). Narrative *function* contributes to teachers' learning by the ways in which subjectivities are constructed through the 'telling' of experience from professional life. Our interest lies in the 'verisimilitude' of such narratives of experience, which cognitive psychologist Bruner argues are constructed by individuals to organise their experiences in order to make sense of them (Bruner, 1985). This function of narrative we see as supported by peer interaction online over time. CMC in the MTeach helps participants to develop deeper professional meanings, which are co-constructed, based on a range of narratives which they tell online. In these they recount critical episodes, offer personal retrospectives and reflection and 'story' their teacher and learner identities within the contexts of the actions which have helped to shaped them.

These form the indicators for the category of 'autobiography': critical incidents, personal reflection, teacher identity and learner identity.

Cognition

A central issue is the relationship between individual meanings and the shared social contexts within which knowledge is situated: 'While knowledge is a social artefact, in an educational context, it is the individual learner who must grasp its meaning or offer an improved understanding' (Garrison and Anderson, 2003: 12–13). Alternative emphasis is made by Koschmann (2003), who asserts that there needs to be a theory of learning through CMC that embraces cognition as rooted in various forms of social relations, which he terms 'social conflict', 'social practice' and 'distributed cognition'.

An emphasis on indicators of 'cognitive presence' highlights 'phases' in cognition (see Garrison *et al.*, 2001: 11), by which the online learning process can be described in relation to sequential phases of critical thinking. Such a linear process model of cognitive growth, however, does not address the possibility of multiple and coexisting *forms* of cognition, which for teachers' professional learning seem characteristic of the complex relations between what they know and how they identify themselves as teachers.

Some constructivist theories of learning within new technologies have emphasised 'epistemic conflict' or the clash of differing opinions and ideas as a core element (Harasim, 2000; Ravenscroft, 2003; Koschmann, 2003). In this 'social conflict' view, interaction based on conflict is posited as having a causal effect on cognition, although the link between the conflict model of social relations and cognitive transformation is not clear, but implies an accommodation or adaptation by the individual brought about by the social relations of conflict. In the transcripts analysed in this study, there was no manifest evidence of conflict like this, and so this variable has not been included in the coding. The reasons for this absence are unclear, but it may be that the mutuality of the teachers may be conditioned by common notions of professionality to a greater extent than other types of online learning communities. The indicators for the category 'cognition' are drawn from analyses of professional teacher learning, Moore's analysis (2004) of the development of the 'reflective turn' and Lingard's concept (Lingard *et al.*, 2003) of what teachers need to learn in order to enact 'productive pedagogies', which have an agentive dimension and counter-reductivist orientation.

The indicators for the category of 'cognition' are therefore the following: developing understanding – theoretical, critical and practical – and learning from others.

Part 2
New designs for
teachers' professional learning

3 Portfolios for learning

*Teachers' professional development through
M-level portfolios*
Karen Turner and Shirley Simon
Institute of Education, University of London

Introduction: portfolios for learning and portfolios for assessment

A portfolio is often defined as a 'collection of work' or a 'collection of evidence' (Paulson *et al.*, 1991; Snadden and Thomas, 1998; Hoel and Haugalokken, 2004). Just as the collection of any artefact is varied and built up gradually, implicit in the term 'collection' is the idea that the material presented shows change and development in different contexts over time and is not a product of the moment. Portfolios as a showcase for an individual's work have a long-established history in the world of art, design and photography. In these portfolios, a practitioner collects examples of work of particular personal importance to illustrate practical skills and the development of ideas.

Since the early 1990s, portfolios have been used in the United Kingdom to showcase professional skills and knowledge in other fields such as medicine and education. In teacher education, portfolios have served two purposes: assessing performance and supporting professional learning. In a portfolio designed to assess performance, the collection of evidence must demonstrate (that is, prove) the achievement of professional standards prescribed by external agencies such as the Training and Development Agency (e.g. TDA, 2006). Such evidence could, on the one hand, include improved results in national assessments or curriculum materials which demonstrate the application of government strategy, but it would not include any sort of critical review of centrally imposed systems and initiatives. On the other hand, in a portfolio designed to support professional learning, the ability to question, analyse and reflect on that evidence is seen as fundamental to understanding 'the complex, messy, multiple dimensions of teaching and of teacher learning' (Lyons, 1998b: 15). A learning portfolio allows teachers to 'engage in professional dialogue with colleagues', and 'to collaborate and develop understanding and ideas on teaching and learning' (Klenowski, 2002: 25).

Herein lies a major difference between a competence portfolio and a learning portfolio. In the former, teachers must show they have acquired a set of generic 'context-free' teaching skills considered necessary for all those who seek recognition for a particular level of teaching expertise. In contrast, a learning portfolio is personalised and richly contextualised; it acknowledges the teacher as an individual with a personal philosophy of education, working in a particular context with specific challenges. A learning portfolio involves thinking, talking and knowing about teaching; it is self-directed and involves a process of discovery (Grant and Huebner, 1998). The process of coming to understand better the complexities of teaching involves asking questions, sometimes difficult ones which challenge the status quo and which query why things are the way they are. For some of these questions, there may be no easy answers. Scott (2000: 126) refers to this as 'taking up a position of reflective scepticism' and it includes identifying and challenging assumptions and imagining and exploring alternatives. Underlying the two types of portfolio are very different perspectives on teacher professionalism. The competence portfolio reflects a view of the teacher as 'technician whose primary function is to develop the skills to put into practice a set of behaviours determined by policy-makers' (Scott, 2000: 4). Advocates of the learning portfolio would see the teacher as an autonomous professional, theoretically informed and able to make independent judgements about effective practice (Furlong *et al.*, 2000).

When portfolios are used for both assessment of performance and professional learning, there are tensions (Klenowski, 2002) which can lead to the neglect of learning in favour of tick-lists of standards. Such tensions are inherent in our own portfolios on the Master of Teaching (MTeach) at the Institute of Education.

The MTeach portfolios

Two portfolios form a compulsory part of the assessment process in the MTeach, making up one-third of the total credits. They were designed to serve the dual purpose of assessment and scaffold for professional learning. This dual role is part of the history of the MTeach, which was created to engage teachers in continuous professional development through higher-level scholarly reflection and the evaluation and analysis of their classroom teaching. In this context, assessment is not concerned with the demonstration of standards but with understanding of the academic literature and engagement with theory in relation to practice in school and learning on the core modules of the MTeach.

The definition of a portfolio is shaped by the purpose it serves and by the philosophy of the course to which it belongs (Hoel and Haugalokken, 2004; Dollase, 1998). The philosophy informing the MTeach at the Institute of Education is that of teaching as an act of enquiry, in which classroom experiences are interrogated and complex issues identified. Learning is seen as an act of co-construction and participants are part of a dialogic community of learners who teach in different cultural settings, which provide the context for their professional development during the course. This philosophy is clearly evident in the definition of the portfolio as it appears in our course documentation: 'A portfolio is a structured collection of evidence of a teacher's best work that is selective, reflective and collaborative and demonstrates a teacher's accomplishments over time and across a variety of contexts.' Reflection and collaboration, then, are fundamental to both the course as a whole and the portfolios.

The first portfolio, Professional Development Portfolio 1 (PDP1), is submitted during the early part of the first term of the course and is the first piece of assessed work. Professional Development Portfolio 2 (PDP2) is submitted at the end of the first or second year of the course, depending on the sequence of modules taken. The first portfolio, therefore, is concerned with accreditation of prior learning. As our teachers begin the course with varying amounts of professional experience, the first portfolio might involve looking back over the recent past (the training year or the induction year) or a much longer period of time. The second portfolio focuses on learning during the MTeach course and requires a review of theoretical and practical learning. In between the two portfolios, teachers have been involved in online modules where they have read background papers and the related academic literature, contributed to online discussions and worked with response partners. They have attended face-to-face sessions, presented drafts for peer review and written coursework assignments. These are the experiences that form the basis of PDP2, which also includes evidence studies that draw on both literature work and practical teaching.

Each portfolio requires the teacher to write a philosophical statement. This is concerned with personal and professional values and the wider role of the teacher as educator. When teachers write the second philosophical statement, they begin by returning to their first statement written one or two years earlier. Some teachers may go further back to a statement produced during the initial training year. This returning to a particular point in time is an invitation to see whether, amidst all the changes, the initiatives and strategies, and fundamental beliefs about the purposes of education, remain the same. This can be a transforming or a reconfirming process. The philosophical statement involves looking back over time and looking beyond the confines of a particular subject or phase specialism. Both looking 'long' and looking 'wide' are considered to be key elements in critical reflection.

For the purposes of consistency in assessment, the contents of the portfolio are prescribed, but within the prescriptions there is choice and flexibility and we believe teachers have scope and discretion to demonstrate individual capability and achievement (Dinham and Scott, 2003). The essential components of the two portfolios are:

Professional Development Portfolio 1:
In addition to the philosophical statement, teachers must include:
- A critical appraisal of an article from a professional or academic journal
- A piece of reflective writing related to an oral presentation by applicants to peers at the course interview
- Three pieces of evidence showing professional development prefaced by reflections on the way the evidence contributes to development. These pieces might include schemes of work, lesson observations, projects.

Professional Development Portfolio 2:
In addition to the philosophical statement, teachers must include:
- A review of their online learning as part of an electronic tutor group
- An evidence study which is carried out in school and reviewed critically. The study might relate to development as a subject or phase specialist, to development as a researcher, to the study of pupil progression, to the use of teacher narrative in understanding professional development.

These two elements forge strong links between school and university, between practice and theory, because they require critical review of practice in the light of understandings of the academic literature.
- Finally, the second portfolio requires a summary of achievements and evidence of engagement in research and scholarship.

The requirements of the portfolios are such that teachers must engage with those intellectual activities identified earlier as being essential to professional learning. Moreover, such activities are the very essence of 'M-ness'. At Master's level, teachers are assessed, amongst other things, on their capacity to 'refine professional knowledge through scholarship and critical reflection, to analyse pedagogy within immediate and wider professional contexts' and on their 'ability to draw from appropriate intellectual perspectives through their knowledge of the related academic literature' (Grade-related criteria for Master's degrees, Institute of Education, University of London, 2005).

There is, then, a degree of synergy between the requirements of the portfolio as a vehicle for assessment at Master's level and as a vehicle for professional learning. Nevertheless, as new module leaders conscious of inherent tensions in the dual purpose of our portfolios, we were concerned that teachers might feel constrained in their construction of the portfolio. It was possible that teachers would be more focused on trying to compile a quantity of documentation that would address assessment requirements, rather than concentrating on critical reflection and analysis.

Our empirical investigation

With the graduation of our first major cohort of teachers in September 2004, the moment seemed right to review portfolio work. We wanted to know whether the portfolios were playing the dual role they were designed for and we wanted to understand more about the construction of the portfolio from the learner perspective. Our research was, therefore, both evaluative and exploratory. Mindful that many teachers' experience of professional development focuses on the demonstration of skills and evidence of performance, because this is what is required for promotion, we wanted to explore their perceptions of portfolios and determine whether they had assimilated the professional learning purpose.

An initial review of the literature related to portfolio construction (Lyons, 1998a, 2002; Klenowksi, 2002) confirmed that, in theory, our portfolios included three important tenets fundamental to learning, namely:

- selection of material by the learners (albeit within limited ways);
- collaboration with others; and
- critical reflection.

In practice, we did not know how MTeach participants constructed their portfolios around these elements and the value they gave to each. The research aimed to explore our teachers' perceptions of the portfolio with respect to these elements in the context of the portfolio they had most recently constructed. Our understanding of the importance of the three aspects outlined above shaped our investigation and the questions we asked our teachers. We were interested to explore how our teachers:

- selected their material for the portfolio and what critical analysis was evident in the decisions they made about what to include;
- collaborated with others and what kinds of collaboration had been helpful in the reflective process; and
- perceived what it meant to be critically reflective.

Our investigations began with a review of the literature related to the three key elements we were interested in so that we had a better understanding of each. We report first on this before providing details of the interview study.

Selection of materials

A final portfolio is often a judicious selection from a much larger number of entries and artefacts that have been gathered over time. Selecting from all that might be available those pieces that best reflect one's work – whether to prove competence or to demonstrate learning – requires critical evaluation and an awareness of what learning has taken place and how. It requires a degree of autonomy and self-awareness (Klenowski, 2002). The final portfolio 'tells a story' of a teacher's teaching and learning experiences over a particular period of time. Yet, to tell an interesting story, the different artefacts that are chosen need to cohere in some way. Narration is concerned with interpretation and the construction of meaning; it is a way of knowing, which can capture the complexities of teaching (Lyons, 2002). It is this meta-understanding of how knowledge of teaching and learning has developed over the year that enables a teacher to make a whole out of a number of disparate pieces. Such artefacts might include work by pupils, audio or video recordings, lesson evaluations, lesson observations as well as the more academic pieces. For this reason, definitions of 'portfolio' often qualify 'collection of work' with the word 'purposeful' and writers talk of 'constructing' or 'creating' a portfolio.

Collaboration with others

When thinking and learning are viewed as social as well as intellectual activities (Cochran-Smith, 1991), we expect collaborative practice to be fundamental to pedagogy. Moreover, working together, talking about issues, advising and mentoring are important aspects of belonging to a profession (Shulman, 1998). Collaborative working affirms the value of one's experiences and invites other perspectives (Orland-Barak, 2005), and supports higher levels of thinking and leads to improved grades (Hoel and Haugalokken, 2004). Collaborative reflection, a process which involves articulating one's own ideas and listening to the views of others (Glazer *et al.*, 2004), scaffolds understanding of personal practice and opens the mind to different perspectives. Glazer *et al.* see this as fundamental to the formation of a personal philosophy of teaching and learning.

Critical reflection

Reflection is 'a purposeful, systematic enquiry into practice' (Schön, 1983) with a view to its improvement and which allows for doubt and perplexity (Hatton and Smith, 1995; Pedro, 2005). According to Furlong *et al.* (2000), it is a way of coming to know by capturing practical experience in order to learn from it. Reflection involves both doing and thinking, looking back and looking forward and is concerned with learning in order to be a better practitioner. 'Critical' when used with reference to academic writing, might be defined as careful and well informed and it includes healthy scepticism and a personal standpoint (Wellington *et al.*, 2005).

When critical and reflection are put together, 'critical' has other specific meanings. Critical reflection is placed in contrast to lay reflection (Furlong *et al.*, 2000) or technical, descriptive and dialogic reflection (Hatton and Smith, 1995). These lower levels of reflection are characterised by recounts of personal experience. They do not go beyond the self, or they focus on the effectiveness of skills without any broader critique, or they simply provide some reasons for action. However, they are limited to personal judgement. Critical reflection, by contrast, is wider and longer term. It goes beyond the personal to review experiences in the light of other forms of professional knowledge, such as the findings of research and theoretical insights derived from the foundation disciplines (Furlong *et al.*, 2000).

For some writers, critical reflection extends to a consideration of the socio-political context and includes moral and ethical issues in teaching (Hatton and Smith, 1995; Scott; 2000; Pedro, 2005). Lyons

(1998c: 116) uses the metaphor of weaving and threading to illustrate how critical thinking can connect different experiences to bring into consciousness teachers' beliefs and values. This aspect of critical thinking might involve going beyond the conventional to challenge 'taken for granted notions about education' and developing 'alternative modes of practice to those intended by policy-makers' (Scott, 2000: 126). In these ways, critical reflection is 'transformational' (Barnett, 1997) and involves becoming 'a critical being' rather than being critical (Askew *et al.*, 2006).

The interview study

We conducted an interview study involving five teachers; two teachers (Angela and Nathalie) had completed their PDP2 18 months prior to the interview and had graduated from the MTeach course. Both Angela and Nathalie had entered the course as newly qualified teachers (NQTs), having just completed their Postgraduate Certificate in Education (PGCE). They had submitted their PDP1 at the very beginning of the course and the PDP2 at the end of the first year, so they had experience of working on two MTeach portfolios at the time of the interviews. Three teachers (Ellen, Jane and Valerie) were coming to the end of their first year of the course and had submitted their PDP1 during the first term. These are more experienced teachers: Ellen has worked for many years in post-16 education, Jane has had one year's teaching experience in a secondary school and Valerie has worked for a number of years with adults in further education. These five teachers were chosen as they represented a range of experience, both of teaching and of the MTeach course, as we wanted different perspectives of the MTeach portfolios.

The interview questions were similar for both sets of teachers (see Appendix 3.1). We focused on the purpose of the portfolio, as we wanted to establish whether the teachers perceived a learning purpose beyond the need to submit the portfolio for summative assessment. The interview also elicited the kind of learning the teachers experienced from constructing the various components of the portfolios and whether they worked collaboratively, in any way co-operating, sharing or co-constructing their portfolios with others. The teachers were asked about their understanding of what it meant to critically reflect, and what the portfolio demonstrated about their professional development.

All five interviews were audio-recorded and fully transcribed. We then undertook a thematic analysis, as did Pedro (2005) in her study of pre-service teachers' meanings of reflective practice. Each of us read and coded the transcripts independently, focusing on teachers' overall perceptions of the portfolio and the themes identified above. We then compared and discussed our coding, and wrote an interpretative account that captured the essence of the data, particularly addressing each theme.

Interpretations and discussion

The opening questions of the interview were phrased to stimulate responses that captured each teacher's overall perception of what the portfolio was about. This was an important step for us in seeing whether each participant had assimilated the learning purpose of the portfolio within the context of the assessment requirement. We begin here by identifying these overall perceptions, focusing on whether teachers emphasised the portfolio as a process or talked about it as a product. Setting the scene in this way, we go on to discuss each theme, namely selection of materials, collaboration and critical reflection. Finally we report on how the teachers perceived their professional learning through the portfolio and how they envisaged its influence on future activity.

Perceptions of the portfolio: process and product

We found that all of our teachers made a clear distinction between the assessment and learning functions of the portfolio. They had slightly different perspectives, but experienced few tensions of the sort that we envisaged might be problematic. Angela perceived the portfolio as a means of professional development as well as assessment. Not only did she talk about collecting and showing evidence, but also about reflecting on how the evidence demonstrated development, including explaining the choice of evidence. She also valued the portfolio as a record of professional development that subsequently enabled her to reflect and analyse how she had changed and developed as a teacher. She could see the extent to which she had changed and developed professionally. In contrast, Nathalie viewed the MTeach portfolio as a showcase of her work for the year, as a record of what had been achieved. Her main emphasis was on the portfolio as a product. However, as she looked back through her philosophical statements, she was able to see how she had changed and so the portfolio enabled her to identify her progress. She, like Angela, valued the portfolio as a record, or landmark, of her professional knowledge at that time. For these two teachers there was clearly a difference in interpretation as to the purpose of the portfolio. Yet this difference does not seem to have hampered their learning from the portfolio.

Jane perceived two purposes for the portfolio: first as a means of reviewing progress and seeing changes in practice or development; second as: 'a way of working that we've used again and again on the MTeach, that sort of reflective style of learning and going back over evidence that you've gathered over a period of time and examining it, summarising it and saying what you've learned from it and how you've changed.' She referred to other MTeach modules where she had exercised the same kind of reflective process. She saw the construction of the MTeach portfolio as an important process, as distinct from the PGCE portfolio, in which reflection was tokenistic, and which was produced to get through the course assessment. For Jane, constructing the portfolio led her to question the rationale for DfES requirements. It also enabled her to consider how she would mentor an NQT in her department and support her portfolio, reflecting together on the reasons for carrying out different practices. Initially, the assessment aspect of the MTeach portfolio had driven Jane to believe she had to 'prove' everything through the portfolio. However, once she became engaged in the 'Leading Learning' module, she understood the value of reflection and its role in the portfolio became clearer.

Like Jane, Valerie viewed the portfolio in professional development terms, as she saw it as a means of 'reflecting on reflection' in the sense that she had to organise her thoughts and put these in a written form for others. Through reviewing past experiences she had been able to think more about how to do things in the future, so the portfolio provided a means for future planning. Like Angela and Nathalie, the portfolio also provided Valerie with a 'picture' of where she was at the start of her Master's course. For Valerie, the assessment aspect of the portfolio was not uppermost. She wanted to present her portfolio well for someone else to look at, but in terms of the content she was more concerned with thinking about her practice rather than the fact that it was assessed. She saw the MTeach portfolio as very different from the PGCE portfolio, which was a collection of artefacts that showed what you are doing, rather than being reflective.

Ellen also perceived the portfolio process as a vehicle for reflection, not only on past experiences, but also on reasons for teaching. The need to produce reflective writing and a philosophical statement acted like triggers that encouraged Ellen to ask herself fundamental questions about her reasons for teaching, going beyond the recent past to her original childhood desires. She reflected on all her work experiences and how they influenced her current practice as a teacher. On completing the portfolio, she realised how much she had achieved and it was good for her morale to have completed the process. Ellen also saw the benefits of the portfolio for assessment and recording progress. She planned to introduce the use of portfolios to her students as a means of 'moving away from exams'. Though she intends to use the student portfolio for assessment purposes, she will also expect them to reflect on their learning.

These perceptions of the portfolio served to demonstrate that the dual purpose we had been concerned with was not too critical for our teachers, and that four of them clearly perceived the portfolio as a means of professional development through being reflective.

Selection of materials

We were concerned that teachers would feel constrained by the prescriptive nature of most of the contents of the two portfolios but this was not borne out in the interview findings. Opinions varied about the degree of structure in the latter sections of the portfolios. Ellen liked the open-endedness of the last section of the portfolio, which she organised first and then used to shape the earlier sections, whereas Nathalie did not like the more unstructured nature of the last two sections. She preferred the guidance of the more directed earlier sections and so provided 'pretty things' like photographs and classroom displays in the second section. All the teachers reported being involved in a process of collecting widely from a range of sources, of sifting and sorting, of deciding on a personal criterion by which to shape the final selection.

Angela and Nathalie archived the discussions from the online modules for the first section of the portfolio and made final selections based on different criteria. Angela, for example, selected conversations that illustrated how others had responded to or learned from her postings. Nathalie, on the other hand, chose examples of extended, threaded online conversations, which showed how ideas had developed. We learned from these teachers that they regretted not annotating their online discussions at the time they were taking place. Annotations at the time would have supported retrospective evaluations and helped them to see more clearly how thinking and ideas had developed and changed.

Ellen and Jane looked back through a large collection of artefacts and chose those which were personally significant. This evaluative process supported the tracing of change over time and was a self-affirming activity, which brought to mind good things that had been forgotten and a realisation of just how much had been achieved. Valerie focused on the recent past and used the portfolio as a catalyst to review management responsibilities that she had only recently taken on. Through reflecting on new experiences for the portfolio, Valerie hoped to deepen her understanding of them. Making sense of them in order to write about them in the portfolio required her to go beyond her own experiences to the background literature.

Our conclusion is that, from the responses to questions about how materials were selected, the act of portfolio construction is a learning experience in itself. It requires a stepping back and a review over time. This is a powerful process, which appears to have had a profound effect on those interviewed.

Collaboration with others

We wanted to know whether teachers had shared their portfolio work with others as a matter of course and whether they felt this had been beneficial. We found that all the interviewees had shared some aspects of their portfolio work with others. Angela and Nathalie had worked with each other, and found that discussion had helped them to make the final selections for the portfolio.

Jane talked to her PGCE mentor about the task of constructing her portfolio, and received advice about how to create a dialogue about her artefacts. Jane also found it valuable to talk to another MTeach student. Valerie was able to share her portfolio process with a teacher friend who discussed different aspects with her and who also read the portfolio before it was handed in. Valerie found these discussions very helpful, because through exchanging ideas with her friend, it was like 'seeing yourself in the mirror, your practice reflected in somebody else'. This statement really demonstrates the power of sharing in reflective analysis. Ellen felt the need to share her MTeach experience with someone and so shared her work with her partner, who had trained as a teacher. He read her work and made suggestions, pointing out her strengths as a writer of resources materials for non-specialists. She thought it was useful to share her portfolio with 'someone who knows me well'.

Thus the interviews demonstrated that some form of collaboration was important to all our interviewees.

Critical reflection

In this section we report not only on the ways in which teachers talked about 'critical reflection', which demonstrate varying perspectives on what this term means, but also about how they viewed the philosophical statements written for their portfolios, as these demonstrate how they reflected through the portfolio process. Teachers did not refer to those longer, wider elements of critical reflection found in the literature in their answers to the question about critical reflection, but in talking about their philosophical statements they did.

Angela's understanding of what it meant to 'critically reflect' on her practice involved looking back over what she had done, evaluating what went well, getting information about how to improve, then reviewing the process again. She emphasised that critical reflection focused on the purpose of the improvement, examining how and why the change was valuable. For Nathalie, critical reflection meant looking back and thinking about what happened in a lesson, analysing moments from the lesson. She used video recordings of herself to reflect in this way, thinking about how she could have improved different aspects of her practice.

These different views do not seem to encompass the wider notion of critical reflection that we have seen in the literature (Hatton and Smith, 1995). Rather, they are couched in terms of what is identified as descriptive or dialogic reflection.

In defining critical reflection, Jane, Valerie and Ellen also demonstrated an understanding that is more akin to descriptive or dialogic reflection, but with some essential differences. Jane's account of what it means to critically reflect is similar to Nathalie's in that she looked back at instances within a lesson and examined what went well and what went badly. However, she also questioned why things happened the way they did. For Jane, the process of critical reflection involved thinking about ways of changing things and why. This view of critical reflection again does not include reference to wider structures (Hatton and Smith, 1995), but is more than an individual's internal dialogue. It is linked to collaborative acts of reflection, identified as important in the process of developing more advanced forms of reflection.

Critical reflection, according to Valerie, meant thinking deeply about something, asking herself questions about what she was doing and thinking further about what had happened after the event. Such thinking has helped her to understand whether something was working and to identify gaps and problems. For Ellen, critical reflection was a personal, introspective act of asking oneself 'why I do things the way I do them ... what made me do things in this way?' She made little reference to other perspectives.

The philosophical statement made all the teachers think more widely and required them to look back long term. Engagement with the readings enabled Angela to apply ideas from the literature to her practice. She was aware that she could gain more from revisiting some of the course readings and interpreting them again in the light of her experience. Nathalie found that having to construct a philosophical statement enabled her to clarify her own reasons for being a teacher and what she would want to 'concentrate on'. She found that engaging with the readings was daunting at first, but appreciated that it 'gets you into the mindset of thinking critically'. Her experience of thinking in this way has enabled her to take a critical view of recent developments in her school that she perceives as simply 'glossy and pretty'. She has continued to engage in the literature, extending her understanding of recent developments in her subject area and theories of learning.

Jane liked engaging in critical analysis of research and considering its value to her own practice. She found it interesting to review a philosophical statement from her PGCE year, realising how much she had changed and that she was now more concerned with 'big questions' about practice. She found the practice of presenting her own critical commentary useful, and further study on the MTeach module enabled her to link classroom learning experiences to research.

Writing the philosophical statement was new to Valerie and enabled her to think deeply about her reasons for teaching: 'It made me analyse who I am actually as a teacher and why I am doing this job and the positive aspects ... I don't think many teachers get the chance to deeply think about why they are where they are.' Valerie's engagement with scholarly reading and writing for the portfolio was also a new experience and helped her with forward thinking and planning in preparation for her research approach for the second module. Ellen, who writes widely about her subject specialism, found the portfolio provided a stimulus for engaging in more scholarly reading about education than she had been used to.

Our conclusions from these responses are that the incorporation of readings into the MTeach and the construction of a philosophical statement that encourages a reflective analysis drawing on the readings help to achieve that fusion of theory and practice that characterises the MTeach. In doing so, we begin to see what critical reflection means within the MTeach.

Professional learning, future activity, and the value of the portfolio

In response to questions about the professional learning gained from the portfolio, teachers were able to identify their learning and also express how they would take the experience forward. Angela and Nathalie had more to say in this regard, as they were now looking back over 18 months of practice since the completion of their last portfolio, and were able to analyse the learning from that distance in time. They expressed their learning in connection with the PDP2 evidence study, which included observation of their practice by others and also of others by themselves. Angela identified personal change and development by reviewing how her analysis of other people's lessons changed over the year: 'I had to think about how I'd changed and what evidence there was about how I changed.' Nathalie also realised the value of this evidence study, as she had been recently engaged in carrying out observations of colleagues. She felt she had become much more 'advanced' in her ability to observe, critically analyse and feed back on practice with junior colleagues.

The portfolio provided Jane with a sense of professional development, and Valerie found that the process of constructing the portfolio made her realise how much she had developed in the five years she had been teaching. The reflective elements, such as the philosophical statement, indicated her development as a teacher, but essentially the portfolio product served to show 'a picture of a certain time'. She was already looking forward to the process of constructing the second portfolio. Ellen was also looking forward to constructing the second portfolio, as she wanted to begin thinking about where she 'was going' well in advance. She was already working on the next portfolio 'in my head', showing that the portfolio process had become a way of life because it was perceived to have value.

Conclusions and implications

This small-scale study set out to explore the perceptions of portfolios held by some of our MTeach participants, our concern being that the tensions between assessment and learning purposes that are identified in the literature would be apparent for our teachers. Yet the synergy between requirements for M-level assessment and a portfolio for learning means that both can be successfully achieved. That is why the teachers we interviewed do not experience conflict between the dual role played by the portfolio. However, it is possible that not all the teachers undertaking the Master's course would find unproblematic the concept of a learning portfolio that is also assessed. We should continue to be aware of possible tensions in this regard.

Our research showed that teachers considered the first portfolio as both a review of the past and a critical evaluation of their experiences and beliefs at a particular point in time, a sort of 'landmark', as they set out on a course of study for a higher degree. This landmark is the point to which they return when constructing the second portfolio, which focuses on learning during the MTeach course and requires a review of theoretical and practical learning. This includes experiences directly related to the MTeach and those outside it related to school-based experience. The notion of a landmark that serves to locate change over time is one we had not explicitly foreseen, and provides us with better knowledge of how to relate the second portfolio to the first. We now encourage our teachers more forcefully to review the first portfolio when moving on to the second, to appreciate their own developmental process.

Our interviews and analysis were influenced by three tenets of portfolios identified in the literature: selection of materials, collaboration with others and critical reflection. We have found that selection of materials was purposeful according to each teacher's perception of what the portfolio was for. To some extent all perceived a learning purpose, which guided their selection of materials. Moreover, they had continued to collect evidence for possible inclusion in a future portfolio even if, as one of the graduates pointed out, she was not sure how she would use it. The PDP1 teachers had begun to collect materials for the second portfolio but two of them had also extended portfolio work to other aspects of their professional lives. Other teachers on the course may have difficulties perceiving the learning purpose behind selection of materials and we need to be aware of ways of ensuring that their selection does not result in a glossy showcase with little reflective analysis.

In pursuing our teachers' experiences of collaborating with others, we concluded that portfolio construction is not a lone activity but currently possibilities for sharing are dependent upon circumstances. All our interviewees needed someone to talk to. The two graduates in particular were dependent on each other for support and for bouncing off ideas. The need to collaborate at some level is an important message, and, as we currently rely on the online participation as the main mode for discussion, participation is important. We were able to distinguish between three different kinds of collaborative working, which will inform our future guidance within the portfolio modules. MTeach participants are involved in *co-construction* in the work they do in the online modules (see Chapter 2), where they read background papers and academic literature to which they respond in their online discussion groups. An analysis of this co-construction of meaning is a required element of the portfolio. They *co-operate* with university tutors by submitting draft entries of the portfolio for comment. For organisational reasons, we do not currently have formalised procedures for teachers to *share* draft elements from their portfolios with MTeach peers even though this is established practice in other parts of the course. Hoel and Haugalokken (2004) attributed improved grades in portfolio work on the 'Art of Teaching Norwegian' course to peer response groups. Their student portfolios contained both response texts to peers and response texts from peers on which individuals had to comment. The process involved therefore both individual and collective reflection. An implication of our findings for course development is that we make formal arrangements for peer review, so that the collaboration needed for enhancing reflective processes (Glazer *et al.*, 2004) is encouraged.

In developing the portfolio within the MTeach, we were asking our teachers to be critically reflective about their practice. Reflection is fundamental to the two portfolios and in setting out on this research we wanted to consider in particular the meaning of 'critical' reflection in a portfolio at Master's level. Much of the literature reported on portfolio work in the field of education refers to pre-service teachers but critical reflection seems to us to be an aspect of the MTeach portfolio that plays a significant role in the 'M-ness' of the work. Our guidance notes use the term 'critical reflection' – for example in PDP1: 'a portfolio is a working document which records work in progress and critical reflection on it'; and in PDP2: 'the portfolio contains evidence and critical reflections of that evidence' – but we do not specifically define the term. When we asked our teachers what they understood by 'critical reflection', they made reference to looking back, thinking deeply or introspecting so as to evaluate good and bad to improve practice. The process involved asking *why* questions and seeing change, and it was bound up with reflective scepticism. For some, reflective scepticism was a *result* of analytical reflection, so that having been reflective for their MTeach work, they took a critical stance on recent developments in school. They were able to identify some initiatives as being 'glossy and pretty' and take a more analytical approach to initiatives like accelerated learning that may be promoted unquestioningly in school. There is some evidence here of the transformational effect of critical reflection, with teachers starting to move from being critical to becoming critical beings (Barnett, 1997; Askew *et al.*, 2006).

When we embarked on this enterprise, our own understanding of critical reflection was less informed by the literature, and has developed in the light of our work. We emphasised that teachers' reflections on practice should be informed by their scholarly activity, but had not made explicit what 'critical reflection' meant. We now have a somewhat better understanding of what we mean by 'critical reflection' in the portfolio to share with our teachers. Now we plan to extend our research to looking at the documents themselves in order to clarify our understanding further. Also, we have to think about how to nurture and develop powers of critical reflection which are not innate. We believe this issue is relevant to the whole course, not just to our portfolio modules. Jane's response clearly shows that her perception of the portfolio was influenced by the emphasis on reflective practice she experienced in her first MTeach module. The message for us is that all teachers need such an experience, and that beginning modules have a role to play in helping teachers to understand what reflective practice means.

References

Askew, S., Carnell, E. and Klenowski, V. (2006) 'Students' conceptions of critical writing in higher education: from being critical to critical being?' Unpublished paper presented at the Institute of Education, University of London, 17 November 2005.

Barnett, R. (1997) *Higher Education: A critical business*. Buckingham: SRHE/Open University Press.

Cochran-Smith, M. (1991) 'Learning to teach against the grain'. *Harvard Educational Review*, 61, 3, 279–310.

Dinham, S. and Scott, C. (2003) 'Benefits to teachers of the professional learning portfolio: a case study'. *Teacher Development*, 7, 2, 229–44.

Dollase, R.H. (1998) 'When the state mandates portfolios: the Vermont experience'. In N. Lyons (ed.), *With Portfolio in Hand: Validating the new teacher professionalism*. New York: Teachers College Press.

Furlong, J., Barton, L., Miles, S., Whiting, C. and Whitty, G. (2000) *Teacher Education in Transition: Re-forming professionalism?* Buckingham: Open University Press.

Glazer, C., Abbot, L. and Harris, J. (2004) 'A teacher-developed process for collaborative professional reflection'. *Reflective Practice*, 5, 1, 33–46.

Grant, G.E. and Huebner, T.A. (1998) 'The portfolio question: the power of self-directed inquiry'. In N. Lyons (ed.), *With Portfolio in Hand: Validating the new teacher professionalism*. New York: Teachers College Press.

Hatton, N. and Smith, D. (1995) 'Reflection in teacher education: towards definition and implementation'. *Teaching and Teacher Education*, 11, 1, 33–49.

Hoel, T.L. and Haugalokken, O.K. (2004) 'Response groups as learning resources when working with portfolios'. *Journal of Education for Teaching*, 30, 3, 225–41.

Institute of Education, University of London (2005) Grade-related Criteria for Master's Degrees.

Klenowski, V. (2002) *Developing Portfolios for Learning and Assessment: Processes and principles.* Abingdon: RoutledgeFalmer.

Lyons, N. (ed.) (1998a) *With Portfolio in Hand: Validating the new teacher professionalism*. New York: Teachers College Press.

Lyons, N. (1998b) 'Portfolio possibilities: validating a new teacher professionalism'. In N. Lyons (ed.), *With Portfolio in Hand: Validating the new teacher professionalism.* New York: Teachers College Press.

Lyons, N. (1998c) 'Constructing narratives for understanding: using portfolio interviews to scaffold teaching reflection'. In N. Lyons (ed.), *With Portfolio in Hand: Validating the new teacher professionalism.* New York: Teachers College Press.

Lyons, N. (2002) 'The personal self in a public story: the portfolio presentation narrative'. In N. Lyons and V.A. LaBoskey (eds), *Narrative Inquiry in Practice: Advancing the knowledge of teaching.* New York: Teachers College Press.

Orland-Barak, L. (2005) 'Portfolios as evidence of reflective practice: what remains "untold"'. *Educational Research*, 47, 1, 25–44.

Paulson, F.L., Paulson, P.R. and Meyer, C.A. (1991) 'What makes a portfolio a portfolio?' *Educational Leadership*, 45, 5, 60–3.

Pedro, J. (2005) 'Reflection in teacher education: exploring pre-service teachers' meaning of reflective practice'. *Reflective Practice*, 6, 1, 49–66.

Schön, D. (1983) *The Reflective Practitioner: How professionals think in action*. New York: Basic Books.

Scott, D. (2000) *Reading Educational Research and Policy.* London: RoutledgeFalmer.

Shulman, L. (1998) 'Teacher portfolios: a theoretical activity'. In N. Lyons (ed.), *With Portfolio in Hand: Validating the new teacher professionalism.* New York: Teachers College Press.

Snadden, D. and Thomas, M. (1998) 'The use of portfolio learning in medical education'. *Medical Teacher,* 20, 3, 192–9.

Training and Development Agency (2006) *Professional Standards for Classroom Teachers*. Available at: www.tda.gov.uk

Wellington, J., Bathmaker, A.-M., Hunt, C., McCulloch, G. and Sikes, P. (2005) *Succeeding with your Doctorate*. London: Sage Publications.

Appendix 3.1

Interview study questions

What purpose do you think the portfolio serves?

- Does the portfolio have value?
- What did you gain from producing a portfolio?
- Have there been any positive consequences?
- Has there been a pay-off beyond the actual completion of the document?

What have you learnt from constructing the different components of the portfolio?

- Philosophical statement
- Reporting online tasks
- Critical writing/evidence studies
- Review of an article
- Selecting and documenting personal evidence

How did you go about constructing your portfolio?

Did you work with or talk to anyone else about the pieces you selected or your reflections on them?

What does the portfolio show about your professional development?

The portfolio requires you to reflect critically on your teaching.

What do you understand by 'reflection'? What do you do when you critically reflect?

Were there problems in producing a portfolio?

How did the knowledge that it would be assessed influence your portfolio?

Have you constructed a portfolio for any other reasons? Was the process the same?

4   Beyond the classroom door, beyond the school gates

The imperative for school-to-school networks for professional learning
Louise Johns-Shepherd, Programme Director for Personalisation, Primary National Strategy, and Elizabeth Gowing, educational consultant

> When you are on playground duty at Nightingale Primary School, you can hear from the school across the road an echo of the squeals and shouts of your own children's games. You can tell when it's the other school's Year Six's turn for dinner, and on a calm afternoon you can even hear the plaintive whistle of another teacher leading outdoor games. But until recently, teachers in the neighbouring schools knew nothing at all of each other's approaches to teaching Year Six, and shared none of their training on strategies for improving the quality of outdoor play. They were too busy – on their separate sides of the street – working through the same cycles of trial and improvement to address the same challenges.

What can we do to ensure that the best practice in our classrooms and playgrounds travels more widely – across the road and far beyond – and develops, and impacts upon the learning of both teachers and pupils? In our work we have looked into this question as school leaders, working for partnership in an Education Action Zone (EAZ) across secondary and primary schools. Since then we have worked separately with national initiatives to research and develop networks, including the National College for School Leadership's (NCSL's) Networked Learning Group, the National

Strategy's Primary Learning Networks and the General Teaching Council for England's (GTCE's) professional networks.

This chapter presents our personal vision of professional learning in education based on school-to-school networks. It identifies what makes learning networks a powerful and democratic form of relevant professional development, and it outlines what have been identified as some of the features of successful learning networks. We will also analyse the extent to which the current policy context provides fertile ground for this model of professional development, which acknowledges the power of learning 'with, from and on behalf of' others in the teaching profession (NCSL, 2005a).

Learning together: the pedigree

Most teachers can tell a story about a significant event that changed or developed their individual classroom practice. Most of these stories will be about another inspirational teacher, a wonderful classroom, a working relationship or an external event that gave them workable ideas that changed what they did in their classrooms: someone else's method, or lesson, organising principle or a piece of research that spoke to them and helped them to make the learning experience for children in their classrooms different and better (MORI, 2004). Those of us who have worked in schools have known for a long time that the best teachers are learners, that they learn best from one another, in one another's classrooms and by modifying or 'stealing' ideas that they have seen work well. We know that to make plans together, to solve problems collaboratively and to enquire into learning is what makes a difference to teaching, to learning and to children. Powerful, significant and long-lasting professional development happens when teachers engage together to solve real problems and make new meanings for application in real classrooms (CUREE, 2003).

Over the last ten years in education, the importance of schools working collaboratively has become a truth universally acknowledged. Schools can now be part of Education Improvement Partnerships, Specialist School Networks, Primary Learning Networks, Networked Learning Communities, Foundation Partnerships, to name but a few (GTCE, 2005). The latest White Paper advocates collaborative opportunities as a way of schools tackling everything from falling rolls, to behaviour and truancy, to the delivery of the 14–19 curriculum (DfES, 2005). *Every Child Matters* (HMSO, 2004) provides a legislative framework which articulates requirements and expectations for all those involved in services which include children, acknowledging that schools need to work with their surrounding communities to meet both the social and educational needs of children. Policy-makers and practitioners are united in the belief that schools no longer work best in isolation, that they do not make a difference to the lives of the children within them by closing their gates, keeping their teachers inside, and focusing on single-institution outcomes above all else.

So does the current policy context simply offer the teaching profession something they already have? We would argue that this new legislative and policy context is one that gives us a structure within which we can maximise collaborative advantage for all children; the opportunity to work in a way we have always felt is best for children. There have long been opportunities to use formal and informal networks to further teachers' professional learning and an enthusiasm for learning from proven good practice, but the use of them has been rather ad hoc and unco-ordinated.

It's rather like the development of eBay. For a long time you knew that there must be people who wanted or needed the things that were in your loft, and you knew that there must be people who had that book/album/vintage handbag that you were looking for. But until recently the only way to arrange a mutually beneficial sale or exchange was by scouring junk shops, trekking to car boot sales or by taking out an advertisement in a local newspaper. Then eBay provided a mechanism by which you could do it from the comfort of your own home. Combine the structure eBay provides with increased computer ownership and access to the internet and suddenly it's not just a few people on a wet Sunday. It's many, at all hours of the day and night. And as more people have used eBay, the system has become increasingly self-regulating and reliable – members of the community have developed their profiles, building their reputations for trustworthiness (or otherwise), and new arrivals have learned from the experiences of others.

In the same way, learning networks offer opportunities for people who are initially strangers to exchange their professional wisdom, to advertise their latest innovation for others to use themselves and to offer their practice for peer review. In doing so, they create trust and new professional relationships for themselves, their colleagues and their institutions, and build a community. And because such networks are based around a common focus, and those who take part in them have invested time and reputation in them, they are efficient and relevant to the needs of those who use them. They are no loose coalition of junk-shop browsers.

With such deep and deeply useful connections between the members of a network, the networks are also enduring. People acknowledge and develop the shared values with partners to whom they turned for one transaction, and build on this not just for ongoing trading but for research and development. Once you have your eBay log-in and have seen the array of handbags available there, you are tempted to return again and again to the site.

We have a policy structure now which recognises the power of collaborative learning as a means of school improvement. We have a bank of research and best practice from the UK and abroad which evidences this way of learning as productive (NCSL and CUREE, 2006; NCSL, 2005d). We have a profession whose members have direct experience of joint planning, peer coaching and mentoring, collaborative enquiry and of working in a variety of networks. So we are in a position to be able to utilise the body of research to develop and extend the knowledge and experience each of us brings to our work. Together, using a variety of network forms, we will be able to create new knowledge about children, about their learning and about teaching practices – networked learning. To do this, we need both the enthusiasm of the profession and a policy structure that is enabling; as Charles Leadbetter says: 'Effective collaboration requires a mix of top-down and bottom-up. Without commitment from the participants there will not be the culture of trust needed to make collaboration work. Without a sense of strategic ambition to take on bigger challenges, collaboration will often fall short of its full potential' (Leadbetter, 2005).

Learning networks – why and how?

So what is it that you can do in a group of schools that can't be done in a school or classroom by yourself? There are, of course, the economic benefits that come with schools working together in professional learning networks. Many Networked Learning Communities (NLCs) have found that they are able to pool and share their professional development costs and that expertise is shared between a number of schools, as are resources – human and material. A secondary school shared the skills and time of its IT technician with a number of feeder primary schools by co-funding his salary. Schools across Poole set their Inset dates to coincide with others local to them and used the time for workshops they developed together and for inspirational speakers whose ideas they built on in context together.

It is possible to define six further broad areas where a network structure really adds value to professional learning: shared responsibility; building commonalities; ownership; innovation; developed leaders; and recognising and transferring effective practice. These six elements are drawn from studies in the UK and abroad and, in particular, from the work of the NCSL's NLCs.

NCSL's NLC programme was launched in 2002. It is a coordinated reform initiative involving over 130 school-to-school networks drawn from over 1,500 schools. Each NLC comprises a group or cluster of schools working collaboratively in partnership with local authorities, higher education institutions and the wider community to improve opportunities and raise standards for their pupils (NCSL, 2005a).

Shared responsibility

Networks offer opportunities for people to take responsibility together for the well-being, beyond education, of those in their communities. For example, one secondary NLC has been involved in auditing health issues and counselling. Accessing funding through the Children's Fund has enabled the network to gather expertise and to work with a multi-agency focus. The network is also part of a group investigating the local authority approach to developing emotional intelligence and literate schools at both primary and secondary level; one of the co-leaders is advancing this initiative as part of a multi-agency steering group within the borough.

More specifically, in a learning network the members take a shared responsibility for enquiring into practice. Following up what one teacher had heard about encouraging pupils' free, unmonitored use of a personal writing journal, a group of teachers from across networked primary schools in South London decided to investigate what the impact of this approach might be on standards and attitudes in writing. There were no predefined solutions, so there was the opportunity to investigate, discuss and try out ideas that challenge current orthodoxies; to be accountable to a peer group rather than a hierarchy (Lieberman, 1999). The notion that the development of one teacher's practice can improve the learning experience for more than one class of children is unique to the learning network. The notion that different practice from five schools can combine to benefit one child is unique to the learning network.

Building on commonalities

Learning networks enable practitioners to unite around the things they have in common. This may be a shared geographical context, a curriculum area or a cross-curricular theme such as support for gifted and talented pupils. The first stage is therefore for teachers to acknowledge their commonalities, as well as respecting their differences. A teacher from an urban school in the South-East of England with a high asylum-seeker population visited a school in an ex-mining village in the North-East to share ways of working. She commented:

> it would have been easy to say that because their school was built with pit props and filled with white faces it had nothing in common with mine. But when they told me about the approaches they'd used for school self-evaluation I realised they'd been grappling with exactly the same issues that we had, and that we'd be able to use their format for consultation with our parents and other stakeholders.

Similarly, primary and secondary teachers who work together often comment that the deepest learning that emerges from their collaboration is recognition of the elements of their professional lives, which are the same, despite superficial differences.

Once these cross-country, cross-phase, cross-curricular commonalities have been recognised, networks also enable teachers to use their shared knowledge bases to create customised, relevant approaches to their classroom practice. What matters is that the experience and knowledge of the practitioners is relevant to the problem they are trying to investigate.

Ownership

A review of successful networks identified that ownership of the network's goals and processes is an important element in sustaining collaborative activity. Similarly, we know that teachers who are enabled to take ownership of their learning goals and processes are more likely to learn and to develop an important sense of self-efficacy (CUREE, 2003). Teachers who are members of a Primary Learning Network say that the volunteerism of the scheme was an important factor in this initiative's effectiveness. By being given an opportunity to define an issue themselves, they were able to create locally relevant and context-specific approaches which work for their children and their schools.

Innovation

NCSL's Networked Learning Group identifies three fields of knowledge: 'what is known' (the knowledge from theory, research and best practice); 'what we know' (what practitioners know); and – most important here – 'new knowledge' (the knowledge that people can create together through collaborative work) (NCSL, 2005a). These three fields of knowledge are mutually dependent, which means that it is only when the knowledge from theory, research and best practice is brought together with what practitioners know that new knowledge can be created. Learning networks therefore offer an ideal opportunity for this new knowledge to be generated, based on evidence, focused on classroom processes and supporting educational improvement and innovation (Hopkins in NCSL, 2005c).

Networks have the potential to develop what David Hargreaves (2003) calls a process of 'disciplined innovation'. We saw an example of this when a secondary girls' school designed a new way of working with its underachieving Year 9 pupils. These students still had an average reading age of only just over 7 years, and were getting further behind their peers with every year in the school, despite having been offered a range of intervention and support strategies targeted at reading. The school tried a new tack, focusing on building the girls' confidence and enthusiasm for reading by coaching them as 'reading mentors' for Year 1 pupils. They drew from existing literacy support programmes for the structure of the sessions that the reading mentors would lead with their primary partners. The project was an enormous success (girls made an average of one year's progress in reading age in the six months of the project) and the school wanted to share its innovation with others. They designed a briefing session and invited schools through the DfES 'EAZnet'/'clusternet' listserv. Schools from around the country attended, and the innovation was replicated and refined in a number of different contexts, such as different year groups, people with different roles in school delivering it and mixed gender groups. Each refinement that was fed back to the originators of the scheme reinforced or deepened their understanding of the factors at play in the project's success.

Developing leaders

We know from the extensive research into the NLC programme how important networks are for developing and distributing leadership. Networks encourage a broad base of leadership, which allows those without formal positions of authority to learn, practise and develop leadership skills (NCSL, 2005c). Leadership of a network:

> is not the kind of leadership that one person can do. It is leadership that requires many people – a 'leader-full' organisation. In a network one person cannot control the system, nor can one person fully understand it. Therefore models of collaborative, shared or multi-level leadership become more important and critical. Developing the capacities of others becomes essential in building a 'leader-full' organisation.
>
> (NCSL, 2005c)

Recognising and transferring effective practice

Networks also provide a mechanism for transferring new ideas and ways of working from teacher to teacher, school to school and network to network. Schools need to be able to work together to ensure that the best practice is transferred between schools, to help all schools benefit from the talent within them. Learning Networks give schools the capacity to do this.

A school in Bristol shared its transformational work on peer mentoring with other members of the General Teaching Council's Connect network (for those who support the professional learning of others) through a website case study. This enabled the deputy head of a school in Nottingham to adopt the same approaches – and even some of the exact proformas for planning and recording the learning that took place through this way of working.

NCSL identifies six levels of networked learning:

1 the pupil learning which gives a network its purpose and urgency;

2 the adult learning which gives additional motivation for those who take part;

3 the leadership learning which we have already seen as a powerful dimension to the opportunities which networks offer;

4 school-wide learning;

5 school-to-school learning; and

6 network-to-network learning.

Thus the importance of transfer – at the level of the pupils, the adults and the leaders in a school, and at the level of the institutions and networks themselves – is seen as fundamental to the purpose of the network. Schools applying to become NLCs had to demonstrate at that stage, and beyond, how they had taken into account all of the potential means of transfer that their network offered (NCSL, 2005a).

Through NCSL and others there is now a body of knowledge

about the components that go to make up a successful learning network. There is no blueprint for an effective network. No one set of arrangements or one particular type of organisation is necessarily better than another. In fact, one of the most important things to acknowledge when working as a network is that the schools, staff and children will be the guides that will provide the shape of activity. More specifically, local context, histories of collaboration, individual school strengths and needs will all influence the design of a network and its activities. However, it is possible to identify factors that enable networks to be successful in what they set out to do (Johns-Shepherd in NCSL, 2005c).

Effective networks are designed around a compelling idea or vision statement and have an appropriate form and structure

Successful networks are those which manage to unite all their school communities around a purpose that is relevant and compelling, whatever the school contexts or current circumstances. These networks also consider how best to structure their network themselves to ensure that all the schools can get involved in real activity around this focus. They provide an opportunity to 'work smarter together, not harder alone' and also to generate knowledge together that can have a direct impact on children in classrooms across the network.

Effective school-to-school networks make a difference to pupils by allowing staff to investigate practice

The real benefit of being part of a network is the impact a group of schools can have on children and their learning. Research has shown that people in networks do unite around those things that they can see will develop and enhance children's learning around things that would not be possible if they worked in isolation.

A shared pupil learning focus is really important to the effectiveness of any network. If all members of the network can answer the question: 'What difference is what we are doing likely to make to children in our schools?', then network activity has the greatest chance of success. The DfES/GTC/NCSL research on Effective Professional Learning Communities identified as the first of its key findings that, 'pupil learning was the foremost concern of people working in a school operating as a professional learning community (PLC) and the more developed the PLC appeared to be, the more positive was the association with ... pupil achievement and professional learning' (Stoll *et al.*, 2006).

Effective school-to-school networks create new opportunities for adult learning

Whilst a pupil learning focus will give network activity a unifying purpose, what is likely to make it sustainable and a real force for improvement is the engagement of the adults in schools in purposeful, focused and informed learning of their own. Ultimately, it is through teachers and other adults doing things differently (or doing different things) in classrooms that pupils' learning is positively affected.

It helps to be clear about what is different and additional about what the adults in a network are going to do. Network activity is a means of studying and learning what is happening in schools and a way of improving learning opportunities for pupils. We know that when teachers are engaged in actively researching and enquiring about existing practice, processes and outcomes with teachers from other schools, they are more likely to improve their own analytical thinking and be more prepared to take risks.

Effective networks require planning and dedicated leadership and management

For learning networks to add value to the existing connections between teachers and schools, they need a structure that allows these kinds of 'sporadic contacts and idiosyncratic affiliations to [develop into] joint work of a more rigorous and enduring sort' (Warren Little, 1982: 86).

The leadership and management of a network are crucial to its development. Research (NCSL, 2005d) has shown that the success of a network (particularly in its early stages) is almost uniquely dependent upon the vision, energy and effort of those who take on a leadership role. The leadership of a network will sort and shape the activity, guiding reflection and adaptation and helping to re-focus activity to make sure it remains purposeful.

However, this, as one of the most powerful aspects of being a network, is also the most difficult to plan for. The knowledge about schools generated by network activity will not just come from senior managers in the schools but from all those working and learning within the network. It is vital to make sure that there are systems within the network which encourage everybody to contribute and to feel that their contributions are valued. Successful networks have been able to acknowledge that leadership within the network may not necessarily come from the traditional places and have found systems that distribute leadership throughout. In this way they ensure that all adults within the network take responsibility for 'creating, validating and spreading knowledge about what works'. Those networks which report the greatest progress during their first year are generally the ones that have planned for distributed leadership from the earliest stage.

A group of primary schools linked through Excellence in Cities decided to look at structures to support art teaching for their pupils. One school was reluctant to take part as none of their teachers felt they had the expertise to be the art subject leader. The headteacher identified that one of her teaching assistants had a background in art and great enthusiasm for the subject and offered her a remunerated role taking part in the network on behalf of their school. The teaching assistant became an enthusiastic advocate with other teaching and non-teaching staff in the school on behalf of the network and its ways of working. Her commitment was identified by other network members as a significant factor in the success of the group in its work with external artists and improving the quality of assessment to support children's development of skills in art.

A structure for professional learning?

With all that we now know about the importance of school-to-school networks for professional development, the ways in which we can make network forms as successful as possible, and a policy context that incentivises and encourages collaborative working, we appear to have both the opportunity and the imperative to develop a structure which acknowledges networks as a mechanism for professional learning.

There are the benefits of creating local and national ways of transferring tried, tested and evidenced practice from one institution to another, and of creating a learning culture where one could use and adapt practices that have been developed collaboratively elsewhere. This is an increase in efficiency because we are not constantly reinventing that wheel. Networks within and between schools will help the teaching profession create and develop its own knowledge base, acknowledge the commonalities within the profession, supporting teaching as an intellectual activity and offering opportunities for distributed leadership and for teachers to both consume and generate knowledge (Lieberman, 1999).

It's a seductive idea, but it's not a simple one. Networks are a complex and organic form. Any system would need to acknowledge the multilayered and connected nature of networked learning as well as the tremendous variety of networks. We would also need to ensure that the work that has happened already is valued and promoted, that it was there for future networks to learn from. Networks can connect structures that currently exist or that may exist in the future. They are a framework where the knowledge base can be accessed and added to.

And this is no longer an unachievable aim. The internet provides us with models of constantly evolving, user-developed knowledge bases. Take Wikipedia for example: a free encyclopedia in ten languages with over 900,000 entries on the English language site, a knowledge base entirely created by those who use it. Anybody can add an entry on a subject in which they have an interest or some specialist knowledge and entries are amended or edited by other users. The knowledge base is always developing, evolving and becoming richer. Imagine an education knowledge base created, accessed and reviewed in a similar way by those working in education networks.

Of course, any structure for professional learning that was network-based would also need to acknowledge that any teacher may be a member of a number of professional learning communities. Their current needs may be met by networks that are multi-professional, multi-purpose, local or national, face-to-face or online, large or small. It would need to be appropriate for teachers at all stages of their careers and to help them to access the kind of learning that was most useful for them.

Many of these kinds of networks already exist and, as we have said, effective professionals in schools have been using and accessing networks to improve their practice for many years. So a structure for professional learning that was truly network-based would be less about creating new, organised networks and more about fostering collaboration and formally acknowledging the importance of looking beyond one classroom and beyond one school for professional development. The power of teacher-to-teacher learning is now widely recognised; school-to-school learning is becoming so. Our next challenge will be to develop effective network-to-network learning.

If we believe that every child has the potential to be a powerful learner, then they also surely have the right to access the best teaching, the best resources, the best methods and the best practice for their learning. By taking collective responsibility for the professional learning of all educators and ensuring that our individual knowledge is developed and shared, we are taking a collective responsibility for the educational development of all our nation's children.

References

CUREE (2003) *The impact of collaborative Continuing Professional Development (CPD) on classroom teaching and learning.* Centre for the Use of Research and Evidence in Education, June. EPPI review. Available at www.curee-paccts.com (see Publications).

DfES (Department for Education and Skills) (2005) *Higher standards, better schools for all.* Schools White Paper.

GTCE (2005) Further details of organisations and initiatives which support networks in education can be found at: www.gtce.org.uk/networksforteacherlearning

Hargreaves, D.H. (2003) *Education Epidemic: Transforming secondary schools through innovation networks.* London: Demos. www.demos.co.uk

HMSO (2004) *Children Act 2004.* London: HMSO.

Leadbetter, C. (2005) *The Shape of Things to Come: Personalised learning through collaboration.* London: DfES (ref. 1574). www.standards.dfes.gov.uk/innovation-unit

Lieberman, A. (1999) 'Networks'. *Journal of Staff Development*, 20, 3. www.ncsl.org.uk/networked/networked-introduction.cfm

MORI (2004) Teachers' Omnibus 2004 (Wave 2). Research Study conducted for the DfES. Available at: www.nerf-uk.org/software/ MORIsurveyteachers.doc?version=1

NCSL (2005a) *Learning about Learning Networks.* www.ncsl.org.uk (see Publications)

NCSL (2005b) *What Makes a Network a Learning Network?* – key messages for network leaders from phase two of the external evaluation of NCSL's

Networked Learning Communities programme. Available at www.ncsl.org.uk/nlc

NCSL (2005c) *What Are We Learning about Establishing a Network of Schools?* edited by Louise Johns-Shepherd and Darren Holmes. Available at www.ncsl.org.uk/networked/networked-wawla.cfm

NCSL (2005d) *Learning from Learning Networks* www.ncsl.org.uk/nlc (a short leaflet drawn from a longer paper entitled 'Learning themes from the Networked Learning Communities programme', which was presented at the International Congress for School Effectiveness and Improvement, Barcelona, January).

NCSL and CUREE (2006) *Systematic Research Review: the impact of learning networks on pupils, practitioners and organisations.* Available at www.ncsl.org.uk/networked/networked-research.cfm

NCSL and DfES (2005) *A Review of Networked-based Innovations in Education in the UK.* Available at www.ncsl.org.uk/networked/networked-research.cfm

Stoll, L., McMahon, A., Bolam, R., Thomas, S., Wallace, M. and Hawkey, K. (2006) *Professional Learning Communities: Source materials for school leaders and other leaders of professional learning.* London: Innovation Unit, DfES, NCSL and GTCE. Available at www.ncsl.org.uk/networked/networked-research.cfm

Warren Little, Judith (1982) 'Norms of collegiality and experimentation: workplace conditions of school success'. *American Educational Research Journal*, 19.

www.ebay.co.uk

www.wikepedia.com

5 New teachers and educational research

Anne Turvey, Institute of Education, University of London, and Hilary Kemeny, National Institute of Education, Singapore

As an English teacher, I get so many instructions about how to teach writing and what to teach and the assumption seems to be that this will make pupils better writers. But I'm not sure about this. And it really matters because the Literacy Framework that's behind a lot of it is like gospel in my school. I want to question it and I want some evidence to support my thinking and my experiences. Maybe that's what research is – weapons! I'm not really sure what my evidence might be or how I'm going to collect it. What do you guys think?

This chapter is about the work of students who are in their second year of the Master of Teaching (MTeach) course at the Institute of Education. It focuses on their development as 'researchers', and how this is shaped and supported by one particular module in the course: 'Research and Professional Practice' (RPP). The above quotation is taken from one of the online discussions that are central to the module: What is the value of educational research to the practitioner? The student's posting encapsulates a number of important features of the module that are, we will argue, characteristic of the students' engagement with the world of research in the early years of their teaching careers. These are:

- a commitment to improving one's own teaching through practice-based enquiry;

- understanding how such an improvement in practice must be based on an understanding of children's learning;

- a willingness to consider alternatives to current practice, at both an individual and an institutional level; and

- the importance of a framework for researching practice and guiding reflection.

This is a familiar rationale for an *action-based* approach to research and, in line with this, the module must help the students to understand the language, potential and limitations of different types of research. The 'criticality' thread running through this student's posting – 'I want to question it and I want some evidence to support my thinking and my experiences' – is also central to the module and in this chapter we will see how important this questioning of the status quo becomes to the students. What is missing from the above outline is what we consider to be distinctive about the RPP module: it takes an *inductive approach* to knowledge construction and the research is carried out within a *community* of shared values, practice-based exchanges, mutual support and critical questioning. Participants work together to construct their understanding of research in education, a process that begins with an examination of what it means for teachers to be research literate. At the end of the module, participants then reflect on how far their views on research literacy and research in education have changed. This is in contrast to many research modules in more traditional Master's courses, in which participants start with accepted definitions, before moving on to research approaches and methods.

For the students in this study, the module is the continuation of a process begun in the PGCE training year and extended into the first year of the MTeach course: reading educational research and critically evaluating it in the light of their experiences in schools. They are quite used to questions that bring together issues of practice and theoretical understanding. The students represented in this chapter have also worked together as an online community during the first year of the MTeach, reading together and discussing perspectives on pedagogy and children's learning. So, the students are not novices in undertaking both critical reading and small-scale research projects; what is distinctive in the RPP module is the requirement that as well as undertaking research of their own, participants consider critically the role of research itself, its principles and practices.

The module is taught in a mixed-mode style. There is an initial face-to-face (f2f) meeting at the beginning of the academic year where we launch the debate about research and education. This debate moves to the online discussion questions:

- What is the value of educational research to the practitioner?

- What is good educational research?

There are two further f2f sessions during the year, one held between the two online discussions. Assessed outcomes take the form of (1) a critique of a piece of published research and (2) a research proposal for the subsequent 'Practice-based Enquiry' module. Throughout the year, students communicate individually with their tutors and with each other; but it is the active collaboration, the shared process dynamic of the RPP module, that this chapter focuses on. The 'research community' is just one of a number of communities into which our new teachers are inducted in these early years and research does not always sit easily with them; but we think that the progress our students make from 'legitimate peripheral participation' (Lave and Wenger, 1991) to full, active participation in the wider community of research, as seen through their involvement in the RPP module, bodes well for the profession as a whole.

The process of the online discussions

Both online discussions begin with 'briefing papers' that outline important questions in the debate and set required reading dealing with aspects of educational research. For the first discussion, the one about 'the value of educational research to the practitioner', students read a paper by Strauss (1995) on the dilemmas and challenges of teacher research. In addition, the briefing paper grasps the nettle of David Hargreaves's well-rehearsed argument that teaching is not a research-based profession and that much of what is seen as 'research' in education is 'second rate'. Such research has had little impact, he maintains, on the improvement of practice and, unlike medical research, it doesn't produce enough 'practically relevant knowledge' (Hargreaves, 1996). Some of the contributions to this first discussion give a flavour of the students' collaborative and critical engagement with these complex issues.

- I'm not sure Hargreaves's medical model works for teachers and teaching. And anyway, all medical research is not good research. The doctors I know argue about research reports just like we do.

- I would question Hargreaves's assertion that there are few areas (of educational research) which have 'yielded a corpus of research evidence regarded as scientifically sound'. Perhaps we need to broaden our understanding of types of research that can be considered 'educational'.

- I was intrigued by how positive K was about the Strauss article and revisited it with much excitement and hence disappointment. I am struggling mainly with the personal point of view.

- I wanted to pick up on your reference to the difficulty of knowing whether or not to trust certain types of research.

- I'm not sure about L's idea – or was it in the article?! – of a central body managing research. I agree with you, X, that we need to see teacher research as part of a bigger picture, but ... I

don't want anyone to take overall responsibility for
administering research, even deciding what gets researched!

Aspects of 'criticality' and 'community' referred to earlier
characterise these contributions to the first discussion and to the later
one. The students are partly 'teaching themselves' how to assess the
research literature and quite early on in the year they are confident
enough to disagree with each other. They are working things
through in an atmosphere that encourages co-operation and
openness to critique. L, challenged here about her support for a
central body overseeing research, returns fire at once: 'I'm not sure if
M will see this, but I think she misunderstood my posting completely.'

In the course of the second discussion – 'What is good educational
research?' – there is a marked development in what we will call
'knowledge construction' about research itself, particularly in
relation to what is meant by 'methodology':

- What is a rigorous methodological approach? How will I know
  I'm doing it?

- I share your concerns about framing a question and establishing
  a sample group to target. What is more useful: mass, large-scale
  research with statistics and a wide sample base, or very specific
  small-scale research conducted in individual classrooms?

- My instinctive feeling is that it doesn't matter how big or small
  your analysis, providing your conclusions are tenable.

- I interpreted one of [Hargreaves's] points slightly differently to
  you, the criticism of teacher-research projects being 'too small to
  draw significant conclusions'. I think his argument is about
  inappropriate conclusions rather than scale per se.

- The 'relevance' and 'generalisability' issues worry me. I always
  appreciate how L doesn't expect her experiences on Jersey to be
  necessarily applicable in the London context and how she
  contextualises details of her experiences with comments about

the 'advantage of being a small island' where it's easier 'to share findings across the island's schools' … But does too much context mean your research is too narrow and not 'useful' beyond a narrow circle?

- How do you generalise from a case study? And someone explain to me in words of one syllable Bassey's fuzzy generalisations!! [Bassey, 1998]

Two case studies

James

James's involvement in the online discussions about research gives some indication of the value to him of a supportive community. It is *intellectual work* that the students are engaged in, an important characteristic of this group's interactions and partly a feature of it being the second year of the course: they have been communicating online for a full academic year. James is able to try out ideas and at the same time must respond to the ideas of others and, crucially, consider challenges to his own position. There is an interesting example of this in the first discussion: What is the value of educational research to the practitioner? In his initial posting, James tries a neat summing up: he refers to 'two general maxims which summarise my motives for reading any educational research', namely 'to gain tools which I myself can try out and use in my own classrooms' and 'to be given well-reasoned arguments, founded on sound evidence, which prove hypotheses about teaching and learning, thus providing me with the latest theory to apply best practice'. This provokes a number of responses from others in the group, responses that, broadly speaking, question what one calls 'your cut-and-dried view of research' and the difficulty of knowing what 'sound evidence' and 'best practice' are. 'You need to know the origins and agenda of the research and that's sometimes kept hidden', is one acute reply. 'I haven't worked out in my own mind what I think James would call the usefulness of research, the connection between what I read and what I do in my classrooms.' The fact that James opens himself up to this kind response is of course a feature of his personality; but what is significant here is the degree to which this is a representative way of working for this group and how it supports development and change.

Soon after this exchange, the students are involved in the second discussion about research: What is good educational research? James refers explicitly to 'my hazy understanding of effectiveness in relation to research' and the difficulty in 'proving that a particular strategy in my school or my classroom has relevance to others'. There is a less certain tone here and a subsequent recognition among the group that he is voicing a common concern, one that is recognised by all researchers: the tension between 'putting yourself in the picture', thus situating your own observations within a specific context, and notions of the 'validity' and the 'wider implications' of your findings. One catalyst for moving James and others beyond a general anxiety about the value of what they might be able to do in their own school or classroom is a discussion he has with a member of the group, K, about three things: 'a research focus', 'sample size' and 'evidence'. K is grappling with 'the need for a clear question' for some research in her primary classroom, since, she argues, 'in my experience the question you start with never fails to open up more questions than it answers. Do you think it matters if our projects evolve in the same way?' In an earlier posting, she addressed a problem that the group returns to many times: 'moving our work beyond the staffroom chat level to something that is going to have an impact beyond our own classroom/school/borough' and she wonders how a research project that focuses on just her own class, let alone a 'case study approach', can count as valid evidence: 'Would a class of 30 children be considered a big enough sample to draw generalisations from? Would a focus group of 6 children be considered a significant sample size?' James's response is worth quoting at some length:

I share your concerns about framing a question and establishing a sample group to target. My instinctive feeling is that it doesn't matter how big or small you base your analysis, providing your conclusions are tenable. For example, from your class of 30 (with context fully described) you might be able to suggest that some practice, say initiating successful group work using problem-based learning in a competitive setting, produced particularly successful results (which you might back up using some empirical data); but you wouldn't therefore conclude that you had proved this technique as 'effective'. This is my rather hazy understanding and suggestion. The challenge is to draw any sort of conclusion which you can actually infer from your research and which isn't self-evident from the outset.

Despite the rather confident tone, James is still feeling his way. He offers 'advice' to K partly as a response to her bid – 'Maybe others in the group can help with [my questions]' – and also as a way to elicit the views of others. He is testing the waters for his own research focus and his methodology and chooses this particular moment to outline his plans to the whole group, confident that he is speaking to a supportive but 'productively critical community' (his phrase from a later interview):

In my own research, I have been observing the lessons of a variety of teachers across a range of subjects and ages. I will also be observed and want to interview a cross-section of Caribbean-extraction boys who have been comparatively 'successful' in school. What I am looking at particularly at the moment, are the interactions that occur during lessons and what I want to try and investigate is what 'works' well for this group, which in our school, and most others, consistently underperforms. Any suggestions on this research and a good methodology to adopt would be much appreciated. Thanks to everyone for lots of ideas!

There follows an exchange on the 'problems of interviews' and how to analyse and interpret these. 'Will you try to code these in some "scientific way"?' James is asked. His phrase to K – 'context fully described' – is also taken up and the challenging question posed: 'If the context is too specific, how will you argue a general case?' These issues – handling interview data and generalising from specific examples – are clearly central to many research methodologies and our students have to familiarise themselves with the critical literature. But what is striking at this stage are the ways in which they are *working out together* what they see as the salient issues, as these emerge from discussion and from their own experiences in schools. Nothing is settled at this stage, as James's comments to a different member of the group on the same day demonstrate:

> The challenge for practice-based research, in what essentially must be a confined context, is to able to draw any significant conclusion – fuzzy or otherwise. I think it's important not to commit oneself to proving anything at the outset and to constantly situate your own observations within the context that they took place. That way we are allowing readers of our research to understand our findings and perhaps draw conclusions which are relevant to their own contexts … Is this too 'open' maybe, not proper research?!

We've given details of these exchanges as they demonstrate the way the discussion operates for James – and for others in the group. It is more than a forum for sharing ideas about 'good practice in the classroom', although it is often that as well; it is fundamentally about the culture of a learning community and depends on what Quicke calls: 'the generation of knowledge constructed through dialogue between all parties in a particular context rather than through the "top-down" application of a universal, "objective" professional expertise' (Quicke, 2000: 304). This construction of knowledge is characterised by a high degree of collaboration and communication and it involves critique and disagreement. James is able to think through issues around research in a context he regards as both safe and, at the same time, challenging. There are times when he and others appear to be 'taking a stand' on a particular issue or in response to the reading of a critical text, as a way to provoke discussion and question taken-for-granted assumptions.

This is a group dynamic that develops over time and it would not have been possible to this extent in the first year of the course. It is interesting that Quicke's comment about the culture of a learning community refers to a school or an actual physical space; but it is clear that such a community is being developed through these online discussions that are central to the MTeach course.

One of the assessed coursework assignments for the module is a critique of a piece of research literature. Students use an analytical framework based on the work of Brooker and MacPherson (1999) and Scott (2000). Writing this critique while at the same time organising your own research proposal furthers the process of the online discussions and effectively integrates the roles of research producer and research consumer. James chooses for critical review a book that he thinks will help him to understand more about the attitudes and academic achievements of Black Caribbean boys in schools: Tony Sewell's seminal work, *Black Masculinities and Schooling: How Black boys survive modern schooling* (Sewell, 1997). This is an interesting 'academic' question for him; but it also relates directly to that group of pupils he 'has difficulty getting through to' and with whom he feels his relationship is too often 'combative'. Thus he is sensitive to his own 'personal position' as a reader, particularly the fact that he is looking for 'if not answers from Sewell, then ways of understanding my situation and perhaps strategies for the classroom'.

James is drawn to Sewell's use of interviews in the research and sees that it might be an advantage to be interviewing boys he knows well. At the same time, he is also sensitive to his own position *as a researcher* and he argues cogently in his initial research proposal for the need to 'identify myself in the research', and to explain his motives to colleagues and to pupils, partly so that other people, particularly the pupils themselves, are not reduced to 'subjects of my investigation'. He regards interviews as 'a potentially empowering form', despite the problems, and when he observes that 'what people say cannot be taken at face value', it's clear that he has understood something of the 'deceptive complexity of interviews' (Freebody, 2003). He is uneasy about the conclusions Sewell draws from the interviews, alert to the dangers of 'a highly authoritative tone' in interpreting the responses of interviewees: 'Of course, this is a criticism that could be levelled at almost all interview-based research but the depth of the generalisations that Sewell draws, against the amount of evidence he cites, makes his validity questionable.'

Like many researchers before him, James doesn't resolve this tension around the interpretation of qualitative data; but it is significant that he is aware of the debates and that when he quotes from Blaxter in relation to Sewell's methodology – 'Generalisations from case studies must be handled with care' (Blaxter *et al.*, 2001: 187) – he understands the very real danger implied here. Of course, spotting the flaws in someone else's research does not guarantee that you will avoid similar pitfalls; but with James there is a productive link between the critique and the speculative way he handles his own interview data, aware of commonalities and variations, but still trying to learn from what the boys themselves say about 'effective teaching'.

As an English teacher, James is interested in the broader debates around gender and schooling, particularly in relation to boys' reading and writing and what he and many have seen as 'resistance to certain forms of literacy'. But he wants to move beyond his own subject area to consider 'patterns in teaching and learning in my school' that could help to explain his own difficulties – 'the disproportionately large amount of time in the classroom spent managing behaviour' – and, crucially, what he calls 'the potential for change'. He knows it is not possible to 'move beyond the socio-cultural debate' and that schooling is only part of the issue for these boys and for all children; but still, he wants to use the research project as an opportunity to 'examine my own practice and the practice of others, especially those teachers the boys themselves rate as "good", in order to help our boys fulfil their potential'. One of his sub-questions gives a sense of what interests him and shapes the research: 'What teaching strategies can be identified that might be of benefit to me and other teachers, which are transferable to our individual classrooms?'

Deciding on a research method – and explaining why a particular method is appropriate for what you want to do – is a challenge for all the MTeach students. As recently qualified, classroom teachers, they are drawn to 'action research', with its emphasis on problem-defining and problem-solving. James speaks for most of the students when he argues for what he sees as the value of 'research directly linked to practice', with a purpose that is 'always and explicitly to improve practice'. The group spends some time on issues of 'methodology' and the challenges presented in various definitions of 'action research' (Kemmis, 1993; Denscombe, 1998; Blaxter *et al.*, 2001), particularly: selecting the focus of the enquiry and studying the available literature; data collection and analysis; interpreting findings and using these to improve curriculum, teaching and learning. Each of these areas is fraught with difficulties and the students experience what one teacher calls 'false starts, brick walls and the sheer unpredictability of schools'. Clearly, James is motivated by professional self-improvement, but he also sees himself as part of a whole-school community, teaching with and learning from others, and this shapes his research methods. For example, he is keen to talk to colleagues about his research and this leads him into dangerous waters: sharing concerns about 'underachievement' and 'teachers' responsibilities in helping pupils to fulfil their potential'. Carrying out such interviews and analysing the results requires a great deal of sensitivity and skill, particularly in recognising and being explicit about the limitations of your methods. James grapples with one of the dangers picked up from his critical reading that has particular relevance for him: 'the criticism that the findings (in action research) relate to one instance and should not be generalised beyond this specific case' (Denscombe, 1998: 64). Here is his defence:

> I attempted to address this issue by making the scope of my research broad within my context, looking at classrooms and pupils outside my normal working scope. I engaged in what Denscombe describes as 'emancipatory' action research, research that attempts to make technical and practical improvements which in turn may improve systems. My research employed systematic self-reflection, as advocated by Denscombe, in order to deal with an issue that I feel strongly about in order to in some small way improve a situation through improving my own practice and the practice of others.

Of course this rationale raises as many questions as it attempts to answer: what, for example, is this 'self-reflection' James used and how did this help him to guard against the dangers of localisation or subjectivity; how did he disseminate the findings of the research to 'improve the practice of others' and what, if anything, has been put in place to monitor and evaluate the 'success' of any change in practice? The students on our course at the Institute of Education must address these and other problems with action research and it is often frustrating and difficult for them; but it is also the case that we encourage them to undertake research strategies – interviews, classroom observations, critical analysis of statistical information, questionnaires – within a community of active researchers that extends beyond their own situation and whose advice and critical perspectives they have already learned to value.

Shortly before submitting his dissertation, James was interviewed by one of the course tutors about the process of research: what had its value been to him; had his views about research in general as well as about his area of interest changed in the course of the module; what were his school's views about his work?

> I think the most significant thing is I had this expectation of finding answers, that not necessarily big questions but some definite questions would be getting answered. And ... it's not that I'm not getting answers for myself, but I'm certainly moving away from finding any sort of resolution, because the more you think about things the more complex it becomes. It's much less linear than I think I first expected, so you think you're going down one alley and you

suddenly find yourself splitting off down these three or four junctions and going off in lots of directions at the same time.

Yeah, I've moved on ... I've gone very broad-based and I'm trying to bring things together now and ... well, there's the whole issue of how boys respond to you in that situation ... having established some kind of rapport makes a huge difference – when you do the interviews ... But again, your evidence is highly subjective which is ironic since I said that about Sewell! But as a teacher you have a relationship with them already, and that's really interesting but I haven't worked it out yet, as a problem in research, I mean. Interpreting ... I think I've become particularly aware of the difficulty in interpreting evidence and having to look to other research, I s'pose I'm increasingly aware about having some integrity and honesty in the research ... and also making it meaningful.

Deborah

The case of Deborah highlights the relationship of the researcher to the communities to which she belongs. In common with James, Deborah values the MTeach community, particularly for the way it supports her as she examines the status quo in her school. Her experiences also show how tensions emerge in the course of identifying an area of research and carrying it out. In her contribution to the first online discussion, Deborah is positive about the way the course has supported her in her teaching and helped her to see herself as 'a researcher':

Action research was of great value to me when I did it last year for the first year of my MTeach. It helped me to identify a problem, decide on a strategy I wanted to test, and then test how successful my strategy was. Had I not been engaged in a research process, I probably would not have thought particularly hard about how to solve my problem, would only have adopted strategies from the repertoire I already possessed, and would not have critically reflected on the success of the strategies ... There's so much at first that's about just surviving or getting on top of classroom management that takes all your time and energy in the first year – but the MTeach made us think about our teaching as it affected the pupils' learning

146

and I think that automatically turns you into a 'researcher' from the
beginning.

The research she considers comes out of a problem in the school
that reflects a national trend – the declining number of students
who choose to study geography. Deborah shares the concern of the
senior management in the school where she has become head of
department, but it becomes clear that her interest in researching
this goes beyond questions of student numbers or the threat to
staffing: it is related to what she sees as the role of geography in
encouraging children to take a critical look at the world and their
place in it. She is interested in how children actually develop ideas in
geography, the concept of 'place', for example. How are their ideas
shaped by both the geography curriculum in school and by the
media? Might 14-year-olds begin to investigate for themselves what
she sees as a key principle in her undergraduate studies and in her
initial teacher training – the principle of 'contestedness' in relation
to how we see the world? Could they come to understand
something that follows from this: that what we refer to as 'place' is
not in fact fixed, but socially and culturally constructed? These are
some of the questions she poses in her research proposal and
understandably she struggles to find a tight focus for the research
project. 'If,' she asks in one of the online discussions, 'pupils could
choose the topic and maybe even the learning style, would this
affect motivation? Can I research the whole idea of student-led
enquiry or improving motivation?' She is critical of the current
emphasis on a 'personalised learning agenda' for what she sees as
largely a spin on target-setting wrapped up in a discourse of child-
centredness. She is aware of certain tensions between the way she is
situated as a head of department within an institution, and her own
interests in children's learning. In a contribution to that online
discussion about 'good educational research' she pinpoints what
becomes increasingly the issue for her: investigating 'a real-world
problem in geography in my school' and, at the same time, working

out how this relates to 'my own practice, my identity, values and beliefs about learning'. She attempts to reconcile these potential tensions through a series of pointed questions about her research:

- What do my colleagues see as an area that needs potential improvement?
- What do students see as an area that needs improvement?
- What are the priorities of senior management for my department?
- What is the current policy shift in terms of geography education?

Deborah's experiences highlight a significant factor in the way our students engage with research in the early years of their careers – namely the capacity of schools to be 'professional learning communities and manage time for professional development effectively' envisaged by the DfEE in Learning and Teaching (DfEE, 2001). If teachers such as Deborah are to have an input into curriculum development and pupil learning in their own classrooms, then they will need supportive contexts for practitioner research as well as the skills to engage in such research. As outlined at the beginning of the chapter, we attempt throughout the module to give our students what Stevenson refers to as 'a framework and a language for expressing assumptions, beliefs, ideas and value commitments, and an analytical framework for guiding reflection, critique and the search for alternative possibilities for practice' (Stevenson, 1995: 202). In addition to this framework and language for analysis at both the individual and the institutional level, the kind of 'reflexivity' advocated by Stevenson requires a school context that encourages practitioner enquiry from its newcomers as well as from experienced staff, a school that sees itself as a learning community, open to change and reflective about how it manages the professional development of staff. The kinds of induction our students experience in their schools in these early years do not traditionally deal with these questions of research. Moreover, what counts as research can raise questions and create tensions in our students' minds – as happens with Deborah and with others.

In an interview with her tutor towards the end of the academic year, at the time she is trying to set up an investigation that will involve a degree of pupil autonomy in the choice of topic and ways of working that are seen by some of her colleagues as 'experimental and high risk', Deborah refers to this tension.

> There is a problem with my research. And I think I would have more support in terms of time, perhaps, or just in terms of general interest if it was felt that what I was doing was meeting the school's objective ... one of the frustrations, I think is that [in my former school], there were a lot of people there who were doing Master's and it was a really vital kind of community that was going on. And in a way, the problems there were so massive that they could go, 'Right, let's go right back to the foundation, what is valid learning for these students? A lot are not gonna come out with particularly amazing results so what do we want them to be able to do as citizens?' Whereas at my school now I feel that they are just agreeing with the agenda of the Government and saying 'Yes, it is right that we should drive children through them, we should get them doing GNVQs which get them four extra GCSEs, because that's what gets it ... it looks better.' The school is doing very well within the Government's agenda. So, say 'personalised learning', something I'm interested in, but not just as another way of shaping the debate about raising standards, it's not really about personalised learning at all, because ... something's being done to you ... it's not about you as an individual being inspired to do something, and that's what I want to do, that's what I'm really interested in. Does this make sense at all?

We would argue that not only does this make sense, it pinpoints a particular aspect of our MTeach course that is central to its 'criticality'. Deborah is clearly developing that 'language of critique' referred to by Stevenson, in relation to such complex ideas as 'achievement', 'success', 'standards' and, of course, 'learning' in general. And without a language for examining educational claims and an ability to articulate alternatives, the result can be a willingness to accept the status quo, an acceptance one can hear her resist in this interview. And it is similar for many of our students as they pursue the questions that are important to them in understanding how their teaching relates to children's learning. We would like to conclude with a number of these responses, from both online postings and from interviews with tutors, that draw attention to the complex and problematic nature of educational research, and to its value in the professional development of a new generation of teachers.

- The research I'm doing has helped me to argue my corner about grouping by ability.

- I am very conscious of the growing body of research into formative assessment, which suggests that grading students' work can be counterproductive and unhelpful to the learning process. My main priority is the students' learning, but the agenda of the school managers is also important, so I suppose I have been, as Strauss describes in the article we read, 'pulled in different and sometimes opposite directions' by systems and orthodoxies on the one hand and ideas and visions on the other. I have had to negotiate this carefully in order to continue to work in the way that I believe is best while still being seen to conform to the expectations of the senior management.

- One thing I've done is make explicit the extent to which my practice is based on research. I was recently observed by a deputy headteacher, and decided to focus on the issue of assessment in order to avoid any conflict about my approach.

- I'm learning to see my observations as 'data', as part of 'proper research'. I'm thinking of what I did when I observed a class of boys in an English lesson and as far as I could see they didn't conform to some of the stereotypes that I think are becoming set in stone. This is important because policy decisions are based on this – like all-boy classes in my school or different books for boys to read.

- Rebecca says she is striving to do the best for the children in her class, yet feeling restricted by the tasks she is required to undertake and hindered by the time she has to give to these tasks. I know how you feel, and also I am amazed that it has taken us all so long to talk about this tension in our jobs. As NQTs last year, perhaps it has taken this long to even separate our own thoughts from what we have been absorbing as the status quo. There has been so much to learn about 'the way things are' that it is only now we are saying 'should this be the way things are?'

References

Bassey, M. (1998) 'Fuzzy generalisations and professional discourse'. *Research Intelligence*, 63, 20–4.

Blaxter, L., Hughes, C. and Tight, M. (2001) *How to Research.* Buckingham: Open University Press.

Brooker, R. and MacPherson, I. (1999) 'Communicating the processes and outcomes of practitioner research: an opportunity for self-indulgence or a serious professional responsibility?' *Educational Action Research*, 7, 2, 203–19.

Denscombe, M. (1998, 2003) *The Good Research Guide.* Maidenhead, PA: Open University Press.

Department for Education and Employment (DfEE) (2001) *Learning and Teaching. A strategy for professional development.* London: TSO.

Freebody, P. (2003) *Qualitative Research in Education: Interaction and practice.* London: Sage.

Hargreaves, D.H. (1996) 'Teaching as a research-based profession: possibilities and prospects'. Teacher Training Agency Annual Lecture. London: Teacher Training Agency.

Kemmis, S. (1993) 'Action research and social movement: a challenge for policy research'. *Educational Policy Analysis Archives*, 1, 1–4.

Lave, J. and Wenger, E. (1991) *Situated Learning: Legitimate peripheral participation.* Cambridge: Cambridge University Press.

Quicke, J. (2000) 'A new professionalism for a collaborative culture of organisational learning in contemporary society'. *Educational Management and Administration*, 28, 3, 299–315; in F. Banks and A.

Shelton Mayes (eds) (2001) *Early Professional Development for Teachers.* London: David Fulton.

Scott, D. (2000) *Reading Research in Education and Policy.* London: RoutledgeFalmer.

Sewell, T. (1997) *Black Masculinities and Schooling: How Black boys survive modern schooling.* Stoke on Trent: Trentham Books.

Stevenson, R.B. (1995) 'Action research and supportive school contexts: exploring the possibilities for transformation'. In S.E. Noffke and R.B. Stevenson (eds), *Educational Action Research: Becoming practically critical.* New York: Teachers' College Press.

Strauss, P. (1995) 'No easy answers: the dilemmas and challenges of teacher research'. *Educational Action Research*, 3, 1, 29–39.

6 The respect she thinks she deserves

John Hardcastle
Institute of Education, University of London

Teachers make sense of classrooms by drawing on their 'life experiences' as well as their professional knowledge. The relationship between these two ways of knowing is complicated and not well understood. This chapter looks at the way, and the benefits of so doing, that practitioners use various kinds of knowledge to present and interpret 'incidents' from urban classrooms, where multi-ethnicity, multilingualism, poverty and powerlessness are the defining features. Additionally, it considers how a combination of face-to-face contact and electronic communication has fostered collaborative ways of working as well as creating new opportunities for teachers to share and develop their professional knowledge.

'Teaching and Learning in Urban Settings' (TALUS) is a Master's-level module, a core module on the Master of Teaching (MTeach) course at the Institute of Education, designed for teachers working in cities. It is intended chiefly for practitioners in the early or middle stages of their careers. Teachers' practical knowledge and expertise provide the starting point for addressing the themes and topics covered by the course. Above all, TALUS aims to develop teachers' understanding of the impact of cities on schooling. The course themes are meant to provide a context for teachers' enquiries: linguistic and cultural complexity; multiple disadvantage; the educational potentials of high-density cultural resources; extremes of poverty and wealth; pupil mobility and rapid demographic change; and the impact of patterns of local decline and renewal on schooling.

TALUS's central concerns correspond closely to those of the UK Government's initiative, 'The London Challenge', which aims to support the development of London as a world-class city for education. Additionally, TALUS is meant to interest and support teachers seeking Chartered London Teacher Status (CLT). Indeed, both the module's content and the ways of working it has evolved correspond to the substance of the CLT scheme. However, the module starts from the position that teachers are the key agents of change rather than merely responding to external initiatives. TALUS assumes that how practitioners make meaning in relation to their work hinges on their implicit understandings of how children learn. Teachers need opportunities to make their understandings of learning explicit so that they can reflect critically on their practice in order to develop it. This may entail giving up old certainties, but it doesn't mean replacing old ideas with new ones in a programmatic fashion. Typically, it will involve a complicated process of intellectual repositioning – and risk-taking. And teachers will need support in this. For example, they will need to develop their picture of learning systematically in direct contact with, rather than at a distance from, the children they teach. Not surprising then that the design of the module is different from conventional top-down models of professional development, in which someone else's practice is regarded as exemplary. TALUS concentrates on developing teachers' professional understanding by their observing and recording practice in their own as well as in others' schools. The module's collaborative methods of study are intended to support reflective teachers working in especially challenging circumstances. And the mixed mode of learning – a balance of face-to-face contact and electronic correspondence – fits in well with teachers' day-to-day work. Online exchanges and discussions have been devised to encourage conversations among peers. Such exchanges aim to provide both practical and scholarly support for practising teachers, encouraging them to reflect on, and to deepen, their understandings of their own practice.

MTeach course participants are required to contribute substantially to three online postings. These postings involve responding to various online briefing papers (accessed through web pages), completing a series of tasks and discussing one another's ideas. By concentrating on systematic observations, recording and analysis of what goes on in classrooms, the tasks and discussions help teachers appreciate the complicated nature of barriers to educational achievement in cities, in order to understand and overcome them.

TALUS operates with a strong assumption that teachers, in partnership with various educational agencies, can contribute powerfully to finding new ways to break the link between poverty and educational underachievement. A further assumption is that research in education that draws upon teachers' first-hand experiences as well as their particular sense of local environments for learning might provide a more powerful instrument for urban school improvement than generalised guidance.

Teachers are potentially well placed to see what needs to be changed and developed in order to enhance the quality of what goes on in schools. Making sense of classrooms is a central part of their day-to-day work. And yet it can be hard for teachers to make explicit – and therefore make professionally available – the wealth of insights and understandings that shape their practice. Thus we have a paradoxical situation. On the one hand, practitioners who are immersed in the ongoing life of schools may miss the significance of things simply because they are taken for granted, unremarkable and part and parcel of their busy comings and goings. On the other hand, researchers, with limited knowledge of evolved ways of working, find 'ordinary' events hard to interpret. As yet, the practice of producing systematic descriptions and analyses, and sharing them with peers, remains underdeveloped. Of course, such descriptions and analyses, if they are to offer a depth of insight, will need to go beyond what is merely taken for granted to get at the underlying 'realities'.

Research training is not the main objective of the TALUS module (there are opportunities elsewhere on the course for this), but it informs the way that teachers use various kinds of knowledge to present and interpret incidents and episodes from their own and other people's schools. Researchers will be familiar with the distinction between *quantitative* and *qualitative* traditions in research. Much valuable work has focused on matters of *quantification,* where researchers have wanted to measure empirical data. Studies of classroom interaction, for example, have called attention to significant differences – systematic, asymmetrical relationships between teachers' and pupils' speech, the number of open-ended questions, changes of topic, and so on. Such questions will affect the focus of enquiry. Is it primarily on the teachers or on the pupils? If the aim is to study 'effective' teaching and learning, then will it be important to look at what teachers say and do as well as how pupils respond? Should the researcher record all that is said or 'select' interesting examples? One relatively 'objective' way of 'capturing' classroom interaction is to record what is said at three-second intervals, thus, ostensibly, avoiding problems of selection. However, such sampling methods may be wholly 'external to the life of the classroom' and disappointingly 'thin' on meaning. Ethnographically 'thick' descriptions of classroom life, by contrast, place great emphasis on giving rich interpretations of social environments. Teachers, given the right opportunities, frequently interpret classrooms in ways that are especially rich in interpretative insight.

In the context of teachers' professional development we need a holistic picture of the interpreter's task which takes into account the way practitioners 'read' classrooms by drawing on their interests and their life experiences as well as their professional knowledge. They bring to ordinary situations many different kinds of understanding. The relationships between teachers' various ways of knowing is both complicated and not well understood. A central objective of this chapter is to look at the way that teachers use various kinds of knowledge to interpret events in urban classrooms. Such classrooms are especially complicated social environments, where multi-ethnicity, multilingualism, poverty and struggles over status are constant features.

The dense web of implicit knowledge and professional knowledge that constitutes teachers' pre-understandings – that which enables them to make sense of what goes on – cannot be prefigured in advance in the way that top-down models of professional development frequently assume. To be able to reflect critically on their own practices in order to change them, teachers need to operate reflexively on their own multilayered understandings from changing critical perspectives. And they need support in this. Therefore TALUS allows practitioners to follow their individual developmental trajectories in the context of the course, guided and supported by their tutor and peers, none of whom have an 'official' agenda.

One way of trying to capture something of the human density of the life of classrooms is to describe *'events'* in fine detail. The aim of the tasks is to select from the life of classrooms critical *'incidents'* – *'moments'* or *'episodes'* – that contain features and structures that typically configure teaching and learning environments. Unavoidably, of course, in selecting an event or an incident the observer has already begun to shape the data. Essentially, in describing a moment in a particular lesson (an event that can never be repeated) the researcher constructs a narrative representation – a 'story' about what went on. Indeed, the place of narratives in *qualitative* research has attracted much attention in recent years (see Chapters 1 and 2). Such stories are shot through with the narrator's interests, assumptions and prejudgements. In giving a rich (but selective) account of events – by delving beneath the surface to reveal complicated meaning and significance – the observer's 'scientific objectivity' is inevitably compromised. It follows from this that giving rich description and explanation involves making inferences and attributing motives to the participants on the basis of what the observer brings to the 'evidence'. Ideally, another researcher using the same methods would produce identical findings. TALUS assumes that practitioners will bring out the particular meaning and significance of what goes on in their classrooms. That is what makes their readings of lessons rich – and especially so when their insights figure in conjunction with other kinds of knowledge. As enquirers, they are constrained to tell a plausible story that matches the evidence, but no two ways of interpreting the same event will be identical because people with different life histories will bring different pre-understandings to the task. Models of professional development need to be clear about what using various kinds of knowledge to make human sense of classroom events entails, because the process carries huge implications for learning to make professional judgements.

TALUS students were introduced to some of the issues involved in carrying out small-scale investigations by means of a starter task. The task involved looking closely at a given classroom incident and interpreting what went on. The incident was taken from an English lesson in an all-girls comprehensive school in West London. It was short – ten minutes in all – but it contains many typical features of urban classrooms.

It's the first lesson of the day and the class is working on their 'Island' project. Three Black 13-year-old girls are grouped around a table. They have drawn an outline of their island and they are colouring in features of the landscape. Later, they will provide a key. Their overall objective is to display the completed map on the wall by the end of the lesson. The observer was new to the school. The incident was not recorded. Rather, it was reconstructed from field notes. What the reconstruction signally fails to show is the atmosphere of the interaction, which at times is both tense and painfully slow. I have altered the original presentation slightly and included the beginnings of a reading of the incident.

9.10 a.m. Three girls on task (Louise, Nadine and Sabine) – they share crayons, glue stick, etc.

Nadine: Did you see the programme about sharks last night? It ate a man. *(Pause)* And a woman. It ate her ... *(indignantly)* WHAT ARE YOU DOIN' MAN?

Nadine breaks off the social conversation to criticise Sabine's drawing. She raises her voice and switches to London Jamaican Creole. Sabine has been colouring a river in brown crayon. She stops drawing.

Nadine: Sabine, de river blue! *(Pause)* Is not brown!

Nadine continues to speak London Jamaican Creole. *(Long pause – 30 seconds)* There is a palpable tension around the table.

Observer: Some rivers are brown. *(Pause)*

Observer: The Mississippi is brown.

(Pause – after a further 30/40 seconds, Sabine resumes colouring in)

Sabine: Dis Demerara.

Observer: In the United States?

Sabine: No.

Observer: Where then?

Sabine: It go t'[h]rough Mackenzie ... *(pause)* an' it finish up Georgetown.

Sabine speaks 'rural' (basilectal) Guyanese Creole.

Nadine: Where's that? In America?

Sabine: Guyana.

Observer: Are you from Guyana?

Nadine: She's been here two months, Miss. (*The observer leaves*)

The aims of the starter task were: to introduce the main themes of the module; to begin to tease out some of the issues involved in observing classrooms; and to consider the value of classroom observation for both teachers and researchers. The module participants were invited to look carefully at the account (given above) of the incident, and to comment briefly on what they made of it. The face-to-face discussion that followed the starter task was predictably wide ranging, but most participants commented on the fluid social relationships among the girls.

Eleven students were participating in the TALUS module. The majority of them taught in reception and primary classes in one of London's poorest boroughs. All the participants were educated overseas. They came from the United States, Canada, Australia, New Zealand, India, Hong Kong and the Caribbean. They were amused by Nadine's attempt to start a conversation about the TV programme, taking the view that this was 'social talk' accompanying the task. Most participants also expressed concern over Sabine's situation as a recent arrival. There was much speculation about why she had chosen to colour the river brown instead of blue. (Some suggested that Sabine might have been unfamiliar with mapping conventions, possibly because she had been educated in rural Guyana; others suggested that she was trying to represent the world as she remembered it.) Overall, the participants showed subtle insights into the way that Nadine's criticism of Sabine's work had served to establish differences in status between the girls. Nadine seemed to imply several things at once: 'you have made a foolish mistake', 'you are spoiling our display' and, perhaps, to a relative newcomer, 'we do things differently (properly) here'. Most, if not quite all, of the participants commented on the ambiguous shifts in language, the code switching, that went on. Nadine deepens her London Jamaican Creole whereas Sabine sticks to (and possibly deepens) her Guyanese Creole. There was little explicit attention paid to descriptive terms or the forms and structures of the language. Yet the shifts were noticed and linked tentatively to issues of identity, status and power. Crucially, these discussions revealed common implicit awareness of the impact of many of the features of urban classrooms: linguistic and cultural complexity; the complex nature of multiple educational disadvantage; pupil mobility and rapid demographic change.

Following on from the starter task, the module participants were set an online task to select a brief 'event', 'moment' or critical 'incident' that contained characteristic features of teaching and learning in urban settings. They could report on one of their own lessons or observe a lesson taught by one of their peers. They were advised to decide at the planning stage what the focus of their observation would be and to formulate a research question. Additionally, they had to make careful decisions about the kinds of data they intended to present and analyse. They were given a structure:

- a series of headings to help them organise their observations and record them systematically;

- a context – the lesson plan, materials and the syllabus;

- class notes – a brief characterisation of the pupils, the languages spoken, the ethnic composition, their histories as learners, the length of time they've been together and so on;

- field notes – the observer's record of what happened, including notes made at the time, but also subsequent recollections and reconstructions; and

- extracts from transcripts of audio or video recordings.

The materials were meant to provide substance for online discussion – they were posted in a designated online chat room – as well as for the second face-to-face conference.

I have elected to focus on one participant, to give depth to a picture of the way these small-scale enquiries developed. Nina was a Black primary school teacher in Hackney. She was educated in Canada, although her family came originally from Jamaica. For her first observation, she chose to look at an incident from her own class. During the 'numeracy hour' students in Year 5 were asked to work with partners in their ability groups to answer a series of questions on the topic of ratios. There were 29 children between the ages of 9 and 10 – 19 girls and 10 boys. The majority of the class had been together since nursery school. Three children had joined from neighbouring primary schools and one child had arrived recently from Lithuania. Ethnic and linguistic diversity was a marked feature of the group. There were children from Turkish, Caribbean, Nigerian, Vietnamese, Central European and indigenous British family backgrounds. Seven children were at various stages of learning English as a further language. Two children had severe special educational needs. Four children were identified as needing additional learning support (they were frequently withdrawn from regular classes). Nina describes 'social class background of the class as working class/underclass' and in support of this description she mentions that 17 out of the 29 children in the class receive free school meals.

Nina chose to record a middle-level (ability) maths group. The children were working independently when, after five minutes, they drifted off task. Michael, who was not a member of the group, joined them. He wanted to find out about a film crew that had been filming local flats. Nina chose this incident because Michael, a Black child who has special educational needs, significantly changed his usual pattern of behaviour. Michael had a speech impediment and was usually slow with his responses. He also had problems with short-term memory. On this occasion, he remembered specific details about the filming. In Nina's words, 'he is talking fine and quickly'. She wrote about the incident:

> [Michael] is making choices that are significantly different from his normal behaviour. His change in behaviour suggests that he is probably a lot more capable than what his teachers have assumed about him. What are the possible motives for his behaviour? Is he acting the role of the special needs child when he is in school?

In her analysis, Nina raises intriguing questions about Michael's behaviour. She was particularly interested in the social dimensions of the interaction, especially Michael's 'low status' and the 'role of the special needs child' that school afforded him. At this juncture she focused on the significance of maturity. Later, she would concentrate on the role of 'social talk'. In sum, Nina discovered that Michael could be both articulate and capable of concentration when the conditions were right – in conversation with his peers about something that interested him. This suggested to Nina that his teachers needed to revise their picture of his abilities.

Nina's second observation was in a primary school in the same inner-London borough. A significant difference between the two schools was that the second school had a large number of children from Muslim families. In the Year 6 class that she observed there were children from Somalian, Middle Eastern, Caribbean, Cypriot, Turkish and Bangladeshi backgrounds. The balance between the boys and girls was even. Some of the children were learning English as a further language and there were several children with serious learning difficulties. The majority of the children received free school meals. Once more, Nina chose to look at a primary maths class – the children were reading line graphs in independent learning groups. Again, she chose to focus on a Caribbean student, Margaret. Here is a key moment from her chat-room posting:

> The children were looking at how to read line graphs, and converting between miles and km. During the independent work,

> children worked with partners using the graph to convert miles to km.

> Margaret and Kate start to work as teacher is now at their table. Teacher explains the work to them. Sam who has been getting on gets praised for his efforts. Margaret responds.

> *Margaret*: He's smart that's why – I went and helped there and there, once we worked it out.

With her first observation, Nina had noticed that the picture she had of one of her student's abilities didn't match her data. She was therefore prompted to ask 'why she had underestimated Michael's ability.' The initial locus of her reflection was her own classroom. Now, when she looks at someone else's class, she discovers a similar instance of misrecognition. She asks, 'How is Margaret's performance affected by the (lack of) recognition afforded her [by the teacher]?' In essence, what drives Nina's enquiry is her sense that Black students don't get the recognition they deserve.

Moreover, Nina has realised that she was already well placed to begin to answer the questions she posed. Her realisation deepened in dialogue with her peers and with her tutor. Crucially, a picture of CPD that underestimates teachers' agency in directing their own practice-related enquiries is a fundamentally impoverished one. Such pictures fail to take account of practitioners' needs in controlling the pace and intensity of their development.

What follows are short extracts from informal postings. In the first instance they are addressed to the module participants. The later ones are directed towards the tutor. Crucially, these are ongoing, open-ended communications, which are not in any sense intended as finished pieces. Nina writes:

> [O]bserving in someone else's class is a difficult experience, because classrooms are very complex. Teacher and students who work together generally have a shared history ... that one does not scrutinize until you observe it in another classroom. (12.01.05)

Nina's point about teachers and students having a shared history is an important one which connects with practitioners' and researchers' readings of classrooms. While she is immersed in the ongoing life of her classroom she risks missing the significance of what she takes for granted. In a certain sense, then, Nina occupies the grey space between practitioner and full-time researcher. However, by observing her own as well as someone else's classroom, she extricates herself from the realms of the taken-for-granted. This is evident (in a small way) from what she says about implications for her own practice: 'I think that observing in this way, also made me more aware of my teaching practice ... and also, I saw children's behaviour from their point of view ... it is difficult to sit in any class, and listen for a period of time.' What has this to do with the knowledge and interests Nina brings to her analysis? She has this to say about the second incident:

> How does Margaret feel about her academic abilities? Margaret's comment to Sam reveals how she feels about her academic abilities. Her comment 'I helped too' ['He's smart that's why – I went and helped there and there, once we worked it out'] and the way it was said implies that Margaret might believe that although she is not as bright as Sam, she still wants acknowledgement and praise from her teacher for her contribution. (29.01.05)

Nina focused on Margaret's need for recognition. Nina's insights open windows onto the microprocesses of power in classrooms as well as raising questions about what the Canadian philosopher Charles Taylor (1994) calls 'the politics of recognition'. Nina is sensitive to the capillary workings of power. She understands the way that local hegemonies function in culturally diverse settings. Shortly afterwards, she introduces large-scale historical considerations, notably the 'African diaspora', that frame the incident differently:

> There is an interesting dynamic happening between the two girls. They are working jointly to be disruptive to the other children at the

table. I assume[d] that they are friends, but in fact they are rivals. Margaret, who is from the Caribbean, is a popular and well-liked girl at the school. Kate, who is Somalian, is more of a tom boy and does not have a large circle of friends. These two would not communicate with each other in any other circumstances, except in the classes in which they are required to work together. I wondered what the possible reasons are for this. I am aware of the cultural issues between Caribbean and African communities, because of the stereotypes that these two groups have about each other, and because of the history of how racism in the past has worked to divide black communities in industrial countries. Is this being played out between these two girls? And if so, how do they manage to overcome this to band together in the classroom? (29.01.05)

On the reading that is emerging, the key to Nina's understanding how the girls 'band together' in the classroom lies in grasping the function of the girls' 'social talk'. She formulates the problem as a question: 'What is the role of social talk versus productive [work-related interaction] in the classroom?' This question emerges from her insight that the girls' 'social talk' is not at all trivial, and that it has an important function.

There follows a sequence of postings – I shall concentrate on extracts from the ensuing dialogue between Nina and me. I responded:

What exactly are these children doing in their social talk and why is it so persistent? Surely they are trying to interest each other, establish their social identities and so on? So [is] it different in urban settings? ... Well, possibly so. To get any 'work' done they have to distribute their energies between socialising and 'working'. Their success may depend as much on their social intentions as on raw 'ability'. [H]ow do teachers negotiate these social intentions – do they stifle them to get stuff done? Where children's backgrounds are diverse, their social intentions will be various. Your other question – the one about how Margaret feels – her need for recognition – may be embedded in the social relations rather than in the individual psychology ... in which case teachers need to think hard about the functions of social talk and task-focused talk as part of a piece. (02.02.05: 9.27 p.m.)

166

There is a degree of informality about this exchange, but the relationship remains that of tutor and student. But keep in mind that this is not a personal correspondence. Other participants in the TALUS module were following the exchange and this was a consideration that speakers had to attend to. Moreover, this was not a conversation between friends or peers. Rather, it was an exchange between a White, middle-aged, male lecturer from the North of England and a Black Canadian, young female teacher, working in a London primary school. Missed meanings and misunderstandings were inevitable in an extended dialogue in which the participants were finding their way. A huge amount turns on making implicit prejudgements about one another's values and commitments. This 'conversation' is not like a face-to-face exchange, where the opportunities for reviewing and revising are limited by the need to keep going the to-and-fro of utterance and response. With email, utterances can be reviewed, revised, qualified and retracted. And yet, Nina's posting is not the same as written correspondence where letters are crafted, drafted and checked for accuracy. The conventions of emailing have not yet been settled – they remain fluid. Expectations about standards of accuracy vary. Crucially, the correspondents control the pace of the exchanges and consequently the rhythm of the correspondence is uneven. That said, in the context of the course, the onus of responding does not fall equally between the correspondents. The gaps between postings – there is no regular pattern – accommodate strategic thinking time. Nina writes:

> Hi John, I had a long day trying to come up with a response to your last email … here are my thoughts. What are they doing in their social talk[?]. I think it might be banding together against the two children who are working, as well as banding against the work, as if they are [in] rebellion. It seems to me, that if the two girls are not friends, then it is possibly this is a kind of showing off, but not against each other, but against the other children and possibly school. Yes, there is a hierarchy between the two girls but that is not immediately obvious particularly in their speech to each other. There

167

is a camarade[rie] ... Which implies a kind of respect, at least that she is prepared to get into trouble with her, if it came to that. As for whether it is different in an urban situation, I don't know. In Urban schools, you have to be a bit tougher on the outside in order to be accepted, and it might be difficult for a Somalian child who is relatively new to the country to understand this. Having said that, I feel that Kate is holding her own... Nina. (05.02.05: 9.10 p.m.)

This response came after an interval of three days. The mode of address is informal – 'Hi John' – and the 'voice' is personal – 'I had a long day trying to come up with a response'. Notice that there is a relatively high incidence of expressions indicating the tentative nature of Nina's reading of the incident: 'I think'; 'It seems to me'; 'possibly'; 'as for ... I don't know'; 'I feel that ...'. Notice, too, that parallels are beginning to emerge with interpretations of the starter task incident. Nina concentrates on the relationship between the two Black girls, Margaret and Kate (the recently arrived Somalian child). She reflects:

From the children's point of view being popular and well liked is much more important than being the smartest. The person who values the smartest child the most is the teacher, because in a lot of ways it defines our position and positively supports our roles. I think that for kids who don't feel they are up to scratch in that area, they opt out of that kind of rating system, and tend to instead go for other socially defined roles that allow them to maintain a positive status for them. They may not be as concerned with their ability to the same extent as their teachers, or schooling system, because for many urban kids being academically smart does not pay off in the end for them. (05.02.05: 9.10 p.m.)

Then, in a passage that makes explicit reference to her own experience, Nina suggests why Margaret is becoming disaffected with school:

Where I grew up, Black kids did not try to live up to these expectations because we knew, that the teachers had already wrote us off, and that Canadian multicultural idea only included our presence in a limited manner. I think that is still true for many black children in London. I suspect a lot of my black students ... by year five realize that, they are affected by what other people think about them and their race. So maybe Margaret is aware of those limitations that are placed on her from above. Just some thought in response to your last email. I could be wrong, as I have not had to think about this kind of stuff in a long time. (05.02.05: 9.10 p.m.)

I was intrigued by what Nina meant by, 'In Urban schools, you have to be a bit tougher on the outside in order to be accepted', so I responded:

'In urban schools you have to be a bit tougher on the outside in order to be accepted.' I agree, but I can't point to any 'evidence' that would settle the matter. And this is just what we want to explore. Maybe 'toughness' is related to urban ways of living where people from lower socio-economic groups are constantly trying to establish themselves as newcomers, as 'minorities' as people who have to establish their status in con[t]exts where status – and respect – is not automatically afforded. [T]heir lives are tough. Children – sometimes as a matter of sheer survival – have to establish their place in the local hierarchy i.e. in the school, the classroom – in relation to values that circulate among peers and communities ... Your personal experience drives your point home – it's not 'merely anecdotal'. [I]t's moving – and convincing. Your closing comments about Margaret's identity could be developed – and you could shed light on it from the knowledge you have got of what goes on. Perhaps, [too] you need to ask what [more] do I need to know – what could I read about – to add another dimension to my understanding? (07.02.05: 10.58 p.m.)

I had wanted to encourage Nina to use her life experience and also to read in an appropriate literature. With hindsight, of course, I might have phrased this differently. A week elapsed before Nina replied:

Hi john, [I] have had some time to think and get back to this paper – here are my thoughts, and can I say i need to make them my final thoughts ... I am almost afraid to respond, as i am sure you are going

to suggest that i read [?] text to support my thinking!! [A]nyways
here goes ... (16.02.05: 9.27 p.m.)

Nina seeks closure. She appreciates the scale of the implications of
her enquiry. Recall the way she closed an earlier posting: 'Just
some thought in response to your last email. I could be wrong, as I
have not had to think about this kind of stuff in a long time.'
What is beginning to emerge (this was confirmed subsequently in
face-to-face meetings) is that she has an academic background in
sociology as well as in Black Studies. She knows that she is re-
entering a huge field. She knows that her recent enquiries bridge
across to previous ones. To continue will involve revisiting
complicated – and possibly painful – issues. However, it would not
be right to discuss Nina's reasons for pulling back here. The point I
am making is that she needs to control the pace, the direction and
the intensity of her studies at a moment when she is fully
engaged. She continues:

> I don't know much about Margaret but this is the impression that
> she left on me. She is tough! She is the kind of girl when i was 10 i
> would have been afraid of, she speaks hard ... street vibe ... e.g.
> 'Ain't it though'. She is cool, popular and [h]as that confidence to
> pull it off. The other children in the class, seem to respect or at least
> like her as i did ... I think what you were saying about how they are
> in the world is a good point. I don't know about Margaret
> specifically, but from what i suspect and my experiences ... they
> [urban kids] are tough in order to survive, tough because it is how
> you get respect here, and tough because they do fight against the
> world ... I think that all urban kids are tough. They know more about
> the 'street life' and things that [are] way beyond them in years.
> (16.02.05: 9.27 p.m.)

Nina continues to make explicit reference to her life history: 'She is
the kind of girl when i was 10 i would have been afraid of'. She
empathises with the children in the classroom, as her remarks about
'toughness' show. The medium (email) allows her a measure of
control over what she withholds and what she discloses. It also

afforded a way of setting thoughts down, which proved relatively difficult when Nina came to write her assignment, as she notes:

> First, i want to apologize for my email on Thursday, because i realized that my last email may have been taken in the wrong way ... i have included the ideas that came out of online discussion. I did find an article on black underachievement that help me to find a way to explain Margaret's behaviour and now wish i could have chosen this for my as a focus for my dissertation ...

> I found it hard to find the words i wanted to say that would succinctly included all that we discussed in a few paragraph but that got harder and just did not make any sense. I have taken out some bits out of my original analysis ... (19.02.05: 4.24 p.m.)

Email postings have an electronic afterlife. They are reconsidered – and sometimes 'regretted' – much as spoken utterances are reconsidered and regretted after face-to-face conversations. We recall conversations to evaluate them. In some ways, of course, online postings are close to conversational speech. But, as with written language, they have a certain 'materiality' that doesn't go away. Nina wrote anxiously about the demands that academic writing were making on her resources, finding it hard to condense her thoughts. She also continued with her scholarly enquiries between postings. In particular, she read independently in an appropriate literature outside the course. Moreover, she was becoming conscious that the issues she was dealing with – the marginalisation of Black students and the workings of local hegemonies in urban schools – could have had a central place in her dissertation. Crucially, Nina drew on her life experiences – growing up Black, female and working class in Toronto – to shed a powerful light on London classrooms.

Nina wrote about Margaret in her final assignment:

> Margaret may already be becoming aware that because of her [...] situation (she lives in an estate in [name of an inner-city borough], a poor urban community) where Black people don't appear (to her) to

171

be achieving economic success, she may be coming to a realization
that her financial security is not dependent on how well you do in
school, it's about how resourceful you are ...

Up to this point in the course, the concentration had been on
observing, recording and analysing classroom interaction. But Nina
went on to cite relevant literature on the workings of institutional
racism and to criticise the limitations of 'multiculturalism' in
Canadian schools. Making sense of Margaret's situation involved
revisiting – and reappraising – her own educational experiences. In
her concluding remarks, she made positive suggestions about ways
that schools might 'encourage discussions about their social worlds,
and help them to understand how their social worlds impact on
them'. Thus, she addressed many of the core themes of the TALUS
module. In sum, she took the opportunities that the course afforded
to make her understanding of classrooms explicit and to reflect
critically on her own and other teachers' practice in order to develop
it. Crucially, this did not entail exchanging 'old' ideas for new ones
or learning about 'best practice'. Rather, it involved a complicated
process of reflection and intellectual repositioning – and risk-taking
– in dialogue with her tutor and her peers.

At the start of this piece, I claimed that teachers make sense of
classrooms by drawing on their life experiences as well as their
professional knowledge. Nina's story is intended as a case in point.
Additionally, I suggested that relationships between various ways of
knowing are complicated and not well understood. Teachers'
professional development is rarely linear and new teaching skills
and professional understandings are not simply added on to existing
ones building-block fashion. Rather, teachers make progress
unevenly in relation to their evolving understandings about what
their work entails. The nature of such work is continually shifting,
shaped by changing priorities and new responsibilities in schools. To
see teachers' development properly, we have to consider the whole
picture. The processes of reflecting and repositioning that are at the

core of teachers' development require adequate support and guidance. In this instance, the support and guidance came via semi-formal electronic correspondence and face-to-face meetings. No single set of determinations shape individual developmental trajectories. Teachers necessarily make sense of their responsibilities and the demands that schools make on them in the light of a multiplicity of prior experiences, understandings, commitments and interests. In Nina's case, the striking relevance of her life history to the task of understanding children's behaviour might easily distract us from appreciating the intellectual nature of her journey. What emerged powerfully over several weeks was her *theoretical, scholarly* interest in the fate of 'underperforming' Black students in urban schools.

Reference

Taylor, C. (1994) *Philosophy in an Age of Pluralism: The philosophy of Charles Taylor in question.* Cambridge: Cambridge University Press.

7 Online task design on the Master of Teaching

Adam Unwin
Institute of Education, University of London

Introduction

Technologies in education have often been seen as providing the answers to expanding demands for continuing professional development (CPD), and information and communication technologies (ICTs) are often promoted by politicians (and sold by retailers and software manufacturers) as the solution to effective learning. The rhetoric, however, often neglects the serious point that it is not the availability of the technology that is important, but how it is used. The most ambitious CPD for UK teachers utilising ICTs to date is the New Opportunities Funds (NOF) training which started in 1999. The aim of this programme was to train and develop all teachers' ICT skills and understanding, with particular emphasis on development of classroom practice. This programme is now considered to be at least partially successful, but this was after a lot of problems in the early stages. In fact, it was the highlighting of such problems that prompted interim evaluations and redesign of NOF training. Design as well as planning and delivery weaknesses were identified with this form of CPD. These design weaknesses included the lack of long-term strategies to encourage practice-based research, creativity, ownership of learning and communities of practice. This chapter focuses on the role of e-learning on a course aiming to provide meaningful CPD for newly qualified teachers (NQTs). In this case, ICTs play a crucial part in encouraging a form of CPD that is collaborative and allows the development of practice-based research, creativity, ownership of learning and communities of practice (in some way the antithesis of NOF). It investigates the design of the online tasks and activities that students participate in on the Master of Teaching (MTeach) course at the Institute of Education, University of London. Tutors have needed to develop their own pedagogical expertise in the light of using new technologies. This is based on a belief that professional learning can exist for teachers in a non-hierarchical way via sharing practice, and that this online collaborative work, which is classroom-focused, cross-phase, cross-subject and cross-experience, allows a non-skills-based approach to CPD. In this chapter, to analyse and explore these important processes, a framework is used (and critiqued) that highlights the relationship between technology, pedagogy and content.

The chapter starts with a review of some of the main research and pedagogical issues that exist with learning technologies in contemporary higher education (HE) and CPD settings. It then introduces a framework which has potential in this and other cases for analysing and designing courses where learning technologies are an integral feature. The main part of the chapter focuses on specific pedagogical design issues on the MTeach course. With online courses there are many technological design decisions that need to be made, such as the website layout, the conferencing software and other questions about user interface and access. These are important issues but not the focus of this work, which concentrates on the nature and structure of the online tasks (with what and how we expect participants to engage in these tasks). This central part of the chapter reports on how the course team has developed the online tasks and also uses some small-scale research with a group of MTeach students to examine their experiences of participating in these tasks. Where relevant, both the process and outcome of task design is critiqued using the analytical framework. The conclusion pulls together key issues and identifies implications for designers of CPD courses.

Learning technologies in HE

In the increasingly market-driven climate of HE in the UK there is often pressure to increase the use of ICTs, especially in creating and developing more online courses. Contemporary HE has responded to technological change (particularly the internet) with an expansion of modes and methods of course delivery. However, with these changes it is important to consider the design and pedagogies involved with such course developments. ICTs in education (especially the use of online environments) are relatively new and tend to change quickly, but practitioners' understanding of how to use them for effective teaching often lags behind. Laurillard, in her writing on the effective use of learning technologies in HE, sets the scene: 'Learning technologies are unfamiliar and complex. Few of the current generations of academics have ever learned through technology, so practice develops slowly and theory hardly at all' (Laurillard, 2002: preface). Seale (2003) and colleagues investigate learning technologies in post-compulsory education. In this overview, Oliver, like Laurillard before, argues that continual change does not provide stability for research of practice, which has consequently tended to be limited: 'Learning technology often seems an amnesiac field, reluctant to cite anything "out of date"' (Oliver, 2003: 3). Although there is a concern over the lack of theoretical frameworks on which to develop HE courses for CPD, Oliver suggests there is a consensus view, but this has not yet developed into a theoretical position.

> Generally, learning technologists just do not believe the 'default', transmissive model of education ... They believe that learning arises from thoughtful experimentation (experimental learning), from

176

> questioning (critical thinking), from the intertwining of practice and reification, debated with peers (communities of practice). By deeming transmissive e-learning to be 'of questionable value', we have taken a theoretical stand – but are we, individually and collectively, aware of what stand we have taken?
>
> (Oliver, 2003: 154)

There is also within the debate in this book recognition of the potential tension between technology and pedagogy. Most software used is designed for commercial rather than educational use. Even software aimed at the education marketplace is often designed using a self-teach model. The danger is that technology drives the pedagogy and that it encourages a 'transmission' approach whether this is via a presentation package or within a virtual learning environment (VLE). Wilson refers to 'pedagogic poor' applications of technology: 'I groan at the thought of students faced with death by PowerPoint both in the lecture theatre and now in the VLE' (Wilson, 2003: 14).

These concerns over pedagogy amongst the learning technology community resonate with our concerns as educators. As teacher educators working on a Master's-level course providing CPD for new teachers, which includes substantial online components, we are clear that the course is not about downloadable presentations and readings or pre-packaged 'manuals' on responding to the latest government initiative. What we feel is crucial is that those teachers have the opportunity to discuss with each other and make sense of theoretical concepts, and to question policy and practice, within the context of their professional lives. As NQTs their professional lives are very busy and very focused on their classrooms and their day-to-day teaching. There are thus clear design implications for tutors, especially for the online elements where teachers are not physically together. A subsequent section of this chapter explains in some detail how the course team has responded to these challenges by reporting on practice and research on a core module named 'Understanding Teaching' (UT) specifically designed for NQTs.

A framework for design?

The growth of e-learning has typically led to numerous sources of advice to course designers. Some models have been very influential, such as the 'Five Stage' model (Salmon, 2000). Our experience over the early stages of developing the MTeach is that this model raises some useful and valid issues about design and implementation, for instance the need to build in (technical) support and social/group cohesion icebreaker activities in the first stages of online programme development. However, it is rather simplistic and mechanistic in parts and does not address the complexities of teachers' learning that need to be investigated and 'un-picked' further to provide a better understanding of the wide range of factors at play in online learning environments.

A conceptual framework that addresses more of the complexities that are involved is that of Mishra and Koehler from Michigan State University, USA. In a similar vein to the views of the UK academics cited above, they acknowledge the lack of theoretical grounding of research in the area of educational technology. They emphasise three issues which have restricted the development of more unified theoretical and conceptual frameworks, one being the (over) focus on the technology: 'Part of the problem, we argue, has been a tendency to only look at the technology and not how it is used. Merely introducing technology to the educational process is not enough' (Mishra and Koehler, 2006: 3). The second is the large number of case study approaches to reporting developments and practice which, they argue, only provide the first step in building understanding. The third is the rapid change in the technologies that are available.

Mishra and Koehler propose a conceptual framework to address some of the shortfalls in analysing the role of ICTs in education, which they have named Technological Pedagogical Content Knowledge (TPCK). They have developed Shulman's (1986: 9) idea of Pedagogic Content Knowledge (PCK). The argument is that, to be

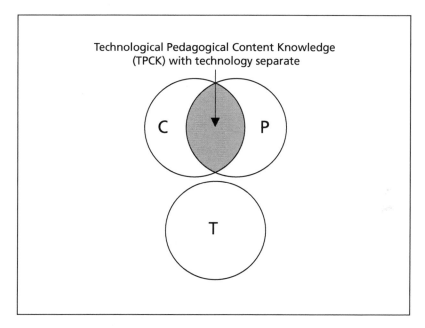

Figure 7.1 Pedagogy (P), Content (C) and Technology (T) Knowledge, with Technology separate

Source: Mishra and Koehler (2006: figure 3)

effective, teachers – in our case, university tutors – not only need to know about the subject matter and about how to teach, but they also need to understand appropriate pedagogies for that particular subject, topic or concept. PCK has been very influential in teacher education and has been adopted widely (but not unquestioningly) both for initial teacher education and for teachers' CPD. Mishra and Koehler have introduced Technology Knowledge (TK), which is knowledge about the technology and how to use it. Their diagram is shown in Figure 7.1 (Mishra and Koehler, 2006: figure 3).

Mishra and Koehler propose that this diagram represents what generally happens in both educational practice and debate about the use of technologies – that technologies are seen and treated as separate from content and pedagogy. They argue that this is not a

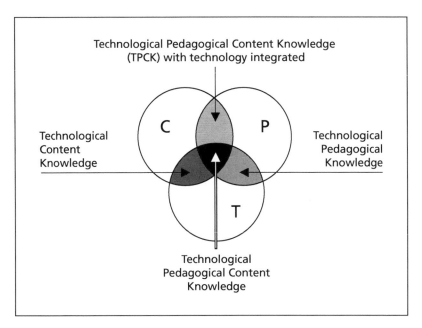

Technological Pedagogical Content Knowledge
(TPCK) with technology integrated

Technological
Content
Knowledge

C   P

Technological
Pedagogical
Knowledge

T

Technological
Pedagogical Content
Knowledge

Figure 7.2 Technological Pedagogical Content Knowledge (TPCK) with Technology integrated

Source: Mishra and Koehler (2006: figure 4).

useful way of treating learning technologies; the relationships are 'complex and nuanced' and technologies may actually constrain content. They suggest that TK needs to overlap as shown in Figure 7.2 (Mishra and Koehler, 2006: figure 4).

Mishra and Koehler argue that this framework allows a potential model for analysing as well as designing resources, methods, structures and desired outcomes, especially where ICTs are an integral or growing part of a course. They identify a change which many of us in education can relate to, namely that in the past there was a tendency for content to be a driver of course development, and pedagogy (and technology) followed. Whereas now, they claim, the pervasiveness of technologies has forced educators to rethink pedagogical issues. They do not, however, raise the possibility that technology now drives pedagogy, something which is highlighted as a concern earlier in this chapter.

TPCK and the MTeach

The TPCK model provides a helpful analytical framework for evaluating course and task design, which has become relevant to teacher educators because of its PCK foundation. This section explains the make-up, context and process of the development of the MTeach course team and attempts to assess the relevance of applying a TPCK framework to the way they worked on the design of the modules and tasks. This is followed by a focus on a particular module to try to evaluate the development of TPCK achieved by tutors within the design of the online tasks.

The academic course team is currently made up of ten staff who, all but one, are PGCE tutors from six secondary subject areas and primary education. Generally, work on this course forms a minority part of their contract. The conditions for a high level of PCK exist; all staff are experienced teacher educators with a willingness to share critical reflections on their own pedagogies, including varied experiences of using technology. It has been a challenge for the course team to design and develop this course over the last five years. Team meetings are well attended, open and developmental, allowing genuine debate and criticality. Staff who previously had not worked together seemed to gain confidence and value the cross-subject, cross-phase learning that takes place. Because this course was new and was planned with technologies as an integral part from the outset, the team needed to design the tasks and sessions carefully in an integrated way, taking into account pedagogies, content and technologies. The key to this design process, although not overtly stated but apparent from experience and observation, is to encourage within the tasks a pedagogy of social constructivism, so that students (the new teachers) make sense of their school experiences and reading via interaction with professional colleagues. This allows them to develop their understanding and construct knowledge within a 'situated' learning community.

The team came with varied TK as well as their subject specialisms and ideas about pedagogy. The design of a new course allowed staff to work to their strengths and the sharing of knowledge and techniques about ICT or content or pedagogy was reciprocal. Aspects of the TPCK model resonate with the way the course team worked. For example, some of the team are perhaps what we could call 'ICT enthusiasts', arguably with high TK, and their understanding of the potential of particular ICTs enabled the course design to have a richer TPCK than if there were no enthusiasts. Once the course was up and running and staff experienced using the new technologies (initially mediated by the enthusiasts), it could be argued there was a move to higher levels of TPCK generally. An indicator of this is a special interest group (SIG) on ICT and Pedagogy, which grew out of this team in the first year of the course and is now an established group open to all University staff.

There are important ways, however, in which the team designed the course and tasks that do not fit so well with the TPCK framework. The main weakness in the model is the lack of presence of the learner. This is similar to criticisms of Shulman made by Banks *et al.* (2005) where a main concern is that, in essence, the PCK model is teacher-centred. This can be taken a stage further, in that the TPCK model also fails to highlight the importance of other 'knowledges' that Shulman later introduced, such as knowledge of learners and knowledge of educational contexts. The MTeach team, for instance, took great store in considering these two 'knowledges' in the design of the course. This is first exemplified by the fact that the course has three routes specifically designed for teachers at different stages of an early teaching career: the 'P' route (post-

PGCE) for NQTs, the 'I' route following an induction year, and the 'E' route for more experienced teachers (three years plus).

By looking further at the 'P' route, we can illustrate how knowledge of learners and their educational contexts is at the forefront of the online course design. The course team knows the NQT year is probably one of the busiest and potentially most stressful in a teaching career. To avoid overload for these new teachers, the two modules they undertake are run over the whole of an academic year rather than being completed in one term. The integration and balance of both face-to-face (f2f) and online elements are designed very much with the learners' needs in mind. This allows flexibility via the online tasks as to when they undertake study periods. The timings and subject focus of these tasks are carefully planned to fit in with the typical issues and pressures of an NQT year. The tasks require participants to use (reflect and analyse on) their day-to-day experiences as new teachers. The idea is that the sharing of experiences, the grappling with classroom issues, and the use of readings and theoretical frameworks encourage students to build on previous knowledge and understanding and make sense of the educational contexts in which they are situated. The online environment provides a crucial, supportive and challenging space in which to do this with peers. What is clear here to us as teacher educators designing and running a CPD programme is that the TPCK model misses out crucial factors especially to do with the role of the learner in this process. The TPCK model alludes to complexities and nuances that can come from using learning technologies, but fails to address the importance of considering educational contexts, the role of learners and their previous knowledge, all of which are core factors affecting the learning of NQTs. In contrast, for us these issues are the starting points of course and task design decisions.

To reflect, experiment and discuss how a specific part of the course has developed against the TPCK model, there follows a closer examination of the 'Understanding Teaching' (UT) module based on a small-scale piece of research which was carried out with students taking this module. It is the longest-running 'core' module for NQTs, and for most of the teaching team it was the first module they worked on with new technologies. Table 7.1 illustrates the interplay of f2f and online tasks in the UT module.

Table 7.1 Structure of module

Timing	Tasks	'Understanding Teaching' (UT) module activity	Mode
September		Inaugural evening	f2f
October	1	Starter task (classroom management focus)	online
November		Saturday conference	f2f
Nov./Dec.	2	Classroom interactions	online
Jan./Feb.	3	Learning, progression and achievement	online
February		Twilight/Saturday tutor group meeting	f2f
March	4	Evaluating teaching	online
April/May	5	Developing pedagogy	online
June		Coursework in progress conference	f2f
July/August		Coursework write-up	online/f2f

As discussed above, the content, focus and timing of these tasks were carefully designed by the course team to be relevant and pertinent to the issues NQTs encounter in their schools and classrooms. Each of these tasks, accessible via the MTeach website, follows a pattern which has been designed and developed by the team: an opening page/section delineates briefly the aims, purpose and context of the discussion. From this, participants can move either to the task itself or to a background paper written specifically by course tutors drawing on key literature in the field and listing carefully selected, recommended background reading. The task usually offers a choice of questions as well as links to two or three digitised core readings. Participants are encouraged to read the background paper before they choose the task and to engage with the digitised readings before composing their response to the task (usually 300–500 words) by a specific date. This is posted into a password-protected online tutor group conference area. In a further step, they are required to submit by a specified date at least one additional posting per online discussion in response to the contributions made by their peers.

The research

A small-scale practitioner enquiry was designed to investigate students' experiences and perceptions of participating in the UT online tasks. The idea behind this was to move them from reporting on how they approached the tasks to commenting on what aspects of the tasks worked well (or not) and why they felt this was the case. A questionnaire was sent to 14 students (see Appendix 7.1) who were full-time teachers across a range of subjects and phases in both primary and secondary schools. The questions (5, 6 and 7) that were concerned with the design aspects of tasks were deliberately open-ended without a prescriptive list of choices or a Likert scale. The rationale for this was to try and see the students' overall opinions, experiences and perceptions rather than them commenting on specific design elements of the tasks referred to earlier (e.g. introduction, background paper, tasks, digitised readings, postings, responses, and so on). This enquiry is exploratory and small scale in nature, but will act as a pilot for further research in this area which can include more students and modules and wider data-collection methods such as interviews.

Findings

Some key issues emerge from this enquiry which are useful for CPD course designers to take on board when using online discussion groups. It was clearly the case that students valued the situated nature of the tasks, in that they were asked to reflect on and explain their own teaching experiences and that this was an interactive and shared process. Also significant is that students tended to see tasks as holistic and not as a series of interconnected parts; however, they did identify the second stage of the online discussions as less useful than the first stage, something discussed in more detail below.

There were several design aspects of the tasks that were identified as important and positive by the students, namely that:

- they were focused around their classroom experiences;

- they enabled the making of meaningful connections between theory and practice;

- they encouraged being reflective in the light of wider research;

- they helped them think about and develop wider teaching strategies;

- they facilitated interaction and sharing of ideas with colleagues;

- there was easy access to the tasks/readings (downloadable);

- the timing (within the school year) and the flexibility of the tasks (personal control over when to work on them) was well thought out.

There were fewer responses about negative experiences with the tasks, but it was clear that responding to other students' postings was seen as less useful than other parts of the tasks.

To experiment with the TPCK model in the context of this research, this section includes a simplified outline of the UT module in terms of technology, pedagogy and content which is followed by a discussion about the implications for course design. It is useful to remind ourselves that it is the level of TPCK in the course team and the online tasks, not the students' TPCK, that we are considering in this case.

Technology

This is the password-protected website of resources including digitised readings, digitised exemplars, shared files and e-journal access. The website hosts the online tasks and acts as a portal to the online tutor group where participants engage in asynchronous postings required by the online tasks and facilitated by a tutor.

Pedagogy

An underlying pedagogic ethos of the course/module is that of social constructivism. That students (the new teachers) make sense of their school experiences and reading via interaction with professional colleagues. This allows them to develop their understanding and construct knowledge within a 'situated' learning community.

Content

The UT module aims to develop students' understanding of the following via (digitised and other) readings and reflections on their teaching:

- classroom interactions;
- learning, progression and achievement;
- evaluating teaching; and
- developing pedagogy.

The main findings illustrate a high degree of TPCK in the task design up to initial posting and reading of each others' postings. Students said they found these parts worked and were useful, and they felt they were developing and progressing. Interestingly, this was less the case at the stage where they were required to respond to each others' postings. One then needs to ask why this was? One could argue it was not the technology that was the barrier (this had worked fine in the earlier stages of online task engagement), but rather the design of this stage/aspect of the task. This aspect of the task is more open-ended and the learner would benefit from more directed structure, purpose, exemplification and, perhaps, a more creative approach to the design. In other words, there needs to be more thought about both the pedagogy and content aspects of this stage of the task. This is a positive example of using the TPCK framework, as it reminds us to consider all factors when approaching design, even at individual stages of a task.

Although the course team did not use the TPCK framework when designing the online tasks, it is apparent that tutor TPCK was (even if unconsciously) at work. The team adopted an integrated approach to the design of tasks where the available technology was used to create an environment that allowed constructivist ideas about pedagogy and learning, and where content emanated from classroom experiences and carefully selected readings.

The clearest findings of this research were about issues that are not made explicit by the TPCK model. What was important for students was the fact that the tasks were focused around their classroom experiences, there was interaction with colleagues, and the timing and flexibility of the tasks worked well. These are issues about educational contexts, the role and previous knowledge of learners and, as explained earlier, were the starting points to the way we designed the course. The TPCK model, by not including specific reference to the learners, creates a potential analytical gap which can miss out on the importance of considering these particular factors in any course or task design. Thus one should be cautious about adopting the TPCK framework in a simplistic and unquestioning way. Without due consideration of the learners and their contexts, course and task design is less likely to be effective.

Conclusions and ways forward

Design of courses that use learning technologies (especially the internet) is important as the plethora of options available increases. However, it is important not to accept 'the latest' learning technologies without question. Consequently, theoretical models and frameworks that allow critiques of design can be very useful. TPCK seems to include strengths and weaknesses. The strengths are that it can provide a tool for thinking about the design of courses. In particular, it flags up the important issues of pedagogy, content and technology. It also emphasises, or reminds us of the need to consider, the interrelationships between these factors, particularly as learning technologies continue to grow at a rapid pace. Criticisms of the TPCK model concur with other writers' concerns with Shulman's early formulation of PCK which seem to have been at least partially transferred to this new model, such as the lack of discussion about a learner's (previous) knowledge and the process of learning.

The key design features that emerge from reviewing both student and course team experience with the online tasks is that the tasks require students to relate theory and concepts to their current teaching and then explain this to others. Interaction with peers is seen as important. These aspects of design correlate with the findings of Daly and Pachler (see Chapter 2) and Pachler and Pickering (2003), who have analysed the online discussions and established the formation of 'communities of (professional) practice' (Wenger, 1998) where theory–practice issues are discussed critically and situated learning develops.

What is clear is that the MTeach participants value the collaborative nature of this online work where they are making meaningful theory–practice linkages and connections based on their own and others' day-to-day teaching experiences. The design of the course and the tasks has been crucial in facilitating this non-hierarchical, non-transmission mode of professional development and learning.

References

Banks, F., Leach, J. and Moon, B. (2005) 'Extract from new understandings of teachers' pedagogic knowledge'. *Curriculum Journal,* 16, 3, 331–40.

Laurillard, D. (2002) *Rethinking University Teaching: A conversational framework for the effective use of learning technologies.* London: Routledge Falmer.

Mishra, P. and Koehler, M. (2006) 'Technological Pedagogical Content Knowledge: a new framework for teacher knowledge'. *Teachers College Record,* 108, 6, 1017–54.

Oliver, M. (2003) 'Looking backwards, looking forwards: an overview, some conclusions and an agenda'. In J. Seale (ed.), *Learning Technology in Transition, from individual enthusiast to institutional implementation.* Lisse, Netherlands: Swets and Zeitlinger.

Pachler, N. and Pickering, J. (2003) '"Talking teaching" – the Master of Teaching'. *Change,* 6, 2, 38–45.

Salmon, G. (2000) *E-moderating: The key to teaching and learning online.* London: Kogan Page.

Seale, J. (ed.). (2003) *Learning Technology in Transition, from individual enthusiast to institutional implementation.* Lisse, Netherlands: Swets and Zeitlinger.

Shulman, L.S. (1986) 'Those who understand: knowledge growth in teaching'. *Educational Researcher,* 15, 2, 4–14.

Wenger, E. (1998) *Communities of Practice: Learning, meaning and identity.* Cambridge: Cambridge University Press.

Wilson, R. (2003) 'Embedding learning technologies into institutional practices: a further education perspective'. In J. Seale (ed.), *Learning Technology in Transition, from individual enthusiast to institutional implementation.* Lisse, Netherlands: Swets and Zeitlinger.

Appendix 7.1

Questionnaire

Background

The focus of this research is to find out about your experiences of participating in the online tutor group. More specifically I would like to find out how this was facilitated by the design of the tasks. At this stage I am trying to keep most of the questions open-ended and do not want to restrict or direct your answers. Do use continuation sheets if necessary.

It may be useful to read all the questions before answering.

1. Name: 2. Age:
3. Do you have a computer with on line access at home?
4. Describe briefly any previous experience (before the MTeach) of online tutor group work/study you have been involved in:

The MTeach course

5. Describe briefly how you worked on the UT online tasks
6. What aspects/parts of the tasks worked well for you?
   Why do you think this was?
7. What aspects/parts of the tasks did you find less useful?
   Why do you think this was?
8. Please feel free to add any other views or comments you have about the design and structure of the tasks.
9. Are there any other questions you think I should have asked about online task design?

Thank you very much for completing this questionnaire. It can be returned either by the postage paid envelope or via email to a.unwin@ioe.ac.uk . If possible please return this by Friday 15 July.

8 Teachers' professional development
Not whether or what, but how
Jon Pickering
Institute of Education, University of London

Introduction

This chapter draws on my research into teachers' experiences of professional learning. The teachers are recent graduates from the Master of Teaching (MTeach) course at the Institute of Education, University of London, a mixed-mode Master's course for teachers working in educational settings in London and the south of England. The research findings are based on interviews with a group of 20 MTeach graduates[1] from the course between December 2004 and December 2005. The study's findings are set against the current model in England of continuing professional development (CPD). This is a model that is predominantly concerned with measuring the impact of CPD in terms of student achievement through the implementation of policy initiatives. This model can be seen to have narrowed the purposes, content and modes of in-service teacher education, by creating a reductivist discourse of effective teaching and learning (Wrigley, 2004). Based on evidence from the teachers in this study it is suggested that there should be a new model of CPD. This will have as its focus the process of development, namely the 'how' of teachers' learning, which needs to be as central as the 'what', its content. This process should be located as much as possible in a cross-curricular, cross-phase, cross-experience approach to learning, which acknowledges and celebrates *all* teachers' experiences, expertise and insights, rather than privileging the voices of those who have their professional status through their appointed position. The CPD process would then be truly collaborative, active and engaging.

The English CPD landscape: best practice or collaborative learning networks

Best practice

Key to this research is an examination of the blurring by the Department for Education and Skills (DfES) in England and its associated agencies of professional development and professional learning. This examination is carried out by contrasting the views of 20 teachers about their diet of CPD with the Government's CPD strategy document (DfEE, 2001) and the recent guidance, *Leading and Coordinating CPD in Secondary Schools* (DfES, 2005). These documents focus mainly on professional development, which is defined as being about 'increasing teachers' skills, knowledge and understanding' (DfEE, 2001, see www.teachernet.org.uk). This highly technicist view of teacher development suggests that an increase is best achieved by a standardised approach to CPD, in which knowledge, skills and understanding are 'delivered' to teachers, and thereby transferred, by a combination of top-down experts and examples of best practice. This is certainly the view of the MTeach graduates in the research.

The best practice model of CPD has been challenged also by Fielding *et al.* (2005), in a research report for DfES, in which the teachers they interviewed advocated a 'joint practice development' model rather than the Government's preference for transfer of best practice. In the research for this chapter, 20 teachers of varying experience, phase, subject specialism and school type were interviewed. Their views echoed those of Fielding's sample, in as much as the teachers most valued professional learning that was a genuine shared dialogue over time, in which teachers reflected and acted upon individual and collective experiences of teaching.

In summary, the teachers were saying that what was missing from their professional learning was:

- engagement with their *learning at a meta-level*;

- real *collaboration* that led to change in practice; and

- any sense of *their responsibility* for their CPD,

and that what they wanted was:

- to be engaged actively in their CPD, not to be passive recipients of other people's (often poorly delivered) sessions.

CPD programmes and opportunities

The experiences of participants on the Institute of Education's MTeach course are in stark contrast to many of the main professional development courses for teachers in England and much of the school-based and external training/INSET that they encounter. These professional development courses range from FastTrack for teachers in the beginning stages of their careers, Leading from the Middle (LftM) for subject leaders and middle managers, the National Professional Qualification for Headship (NPQH) for aspiring headteachers, and the Leadership Programme for Serving Headteachers (LPSH) for experienced headteachers. Although there has been a shift towards learning as opposed to training on these courses, they remain largely technicist, positioned as they are in DfES's CPD strategy (DfES, 2001). This one-size-fits-all approach is often characterised by 'delivery' that is timed, prescribed and read out from a script, leading to it being anecdotally referred to as 'CPD by folder'! The strategy overtly links CPD to performance management and school improvement and is focused on the passing on of national strategies to large groups of teachers en masse, not on individual or small group needs.

The process of many of the current CPD courses, no matter how interactive or evidence-based they are – and these are rare according to the 20 teachers in the study – is essentially a deductive, directive one. Knowledge of teacher development resides in the programme or course facilitators and is passed on to participating teachers, and is only then mediated by the teachers' experience. It is a 'received wisdom' or 'grand narrative' approach to knowledge construction, leading to professional development. CPD has become a large and growing part of the education 'market' in England in the last 20 years, fuelled mainly by national strategies (curriculum initiatives in the case of the Literacy, Numeracy and Key Stage 3 strategies), as well as school leadership programmes such as LftM, NPQH and LPSH. Within CPD provision Master's courses are seen to play a part, albeit a minor one. The recently inaugurated Postgraduate Professional Development Programme, funded by the Training and Development Agency (TDA) for schools (formerly the TTA), may be an exception to this rule. However, it still appears to be linked to government initiative-related CPD. Master's courses are still regarded as relating more to personal choice of an intellectual, non-professional nature by individual teachers, rather than being 'of use' in impacting on classroom practice or whole-school development. Indeed, funding from government agencies for the MTeach at the Institute has not been forthcoming because the course was not regarded, in the view of the TDA, as impacting directly on the classroom.

What teachers in England are currently faced with through the Government's website (www.teachernet.gov.uk/ professionaldevelopment/) is not just a rationale for the need for and value of CPD, but also a vast array of CPD guidance, pathways and professional networks. If teachers also wish to access the website of the General Teaching Council for England (GTCE) (www.gtce.org.uk/cpd_home/) or that of the National College for

School Leadership (NCSL) (www.ncsl.org.uk/programmes/), they will find a rich choice of CPD opportunities. Much of the CPD that comes from the GTCE and NCSL appears to try to move away from the delivery, top-down model of the national strategies, and locates CPD in local teacher networks. There are, for example, currently three GTCE learning networks: Achieve (for education professionals promoting racial equality and diversity in schools), Connect (for those who lead in CPD in schools) and Engage (for teachers starting their careers). These can be accessed at www.gtce.org.uk/networks. These networks are open to members of the GTCE, as is the Teacher Learning Academy (www.gtce.org.uk/), which, as the website claims, 'seeks to support learning communities within and beyond schools that enrich teaching practice and support innovation'. As to the NCSL, the development of its online community learning environment, talk2learn, is, according to its website, 'open to an increasingly wide range of school leaders – including headteachers, deputy heads, middle leaders and bursars'. This online community provides access to a wide network of colleagues, experts and policy-makers with whom school leaders can 'debate, discuss and share ideas'. talk2learn is a crucial part of NCSL's Learning Gateway. The Learning Gateway is a managed learning environment, which supports the NCSL core business of delivering CPD to school leaders. In addition to these CPD opportunities, there is also a large and growing volume of research available, through the National Foundation for Educational Research (NFER), at www.nfer.ac.uk and the Evidence for Policy and Practice Information and Co-ordinating Centre (see EPPI-Centre, 2003, 2005 and www.eppi.ioe.ac.uk).

Professional development or learning?

In the Government's CPD documents mentioned earlier, there are references to professional learning, but the fine distinction between development and learning is not teased out or problematised. Learning is not articulated as the more personal, holistic process of professional development (Bolam, 1993; Day, 1999; Craft, 2000; Earley, 2005). Rather, in the DfES discourse, as was noted in the Introduction, learning is seen as the acquisition of knowledge, skills and understanding. This is a limited view of learning about teaching, which pays little regard to recent work about the effective learning of children and adults (see Watkins, 2005, for a more detailed analysis).

Improved teaching (and, by implication, pupils' learning) is best achieved by a standardised approach to CPD, in which knowledge, skills and understanding are 'delivered' to teachers by a combination of top-down expert witnesses and the transfer of good practice from teacher to teacher and school to school. In their study for the DfES, Fielding *et al.* (2005) challenged the view that transfer of good practice was the most effective form of professional development. In the study, teachers talk about the need for the mutuality of the CPD process and the need to see CPD as a learning partnership, not as the 'giving and receiving' relationship of transfer, but as what the research team came to call 'joint practice development'. Although not defined, joint practice development is seen as a validation of 'the existing practice of teachers who are trying to learn new ways of working and acknowledges the effort of those who are trying to support them' (Fielding *et al.*, 2005: 3). This emerges from 'their having developed creative ways of working and the complex task of opening up and sharing practice with others' (ibid.).

The GTCE and NCSL networks notwithstanding, the unswerving central emphasis on CPD as the means of improving standards (i.e. pupil performance) inevitably means that episodes of professional learning tend to be gauged by their potential for impact on pupil achievement. In practice, achievement refers to pupil performance in national tests and, therefore, the emphasis is ever more limited. There is an inevitability that this will create a reductionist view of the provision of CPD, whereby most courses and training are designed almost specifically with impact on pupil performance in mind. This leads to a highly instrumentalist view of CPD. It exists fundamentally to improve the performance of pupils, and, in so doing, underplays the value of professional learning as an end as well as a means. In this way, the tendency of writers like Guskey (2000) to suggest evaluating CPD through a hierarchical typology is unsurprisingly welcomed by the dominant, impact-based CPD discourse. Guskey's five measurable features of CPD are ordered as follows:

- participants' reactions;
- participants' learning;
- organisational support and change;
- participants' use of new knowledge and skills; and
- pupil learning outcomes.

What the teachers in this study say runs counter to this hierarchy, foregrounding instead the need for the content and mode of delivery to engage them *first,* if CPD is to then benefit the pupils. Teachers' learning and, therefore, the rate and nature of their professional development are dependent on a combination of highly complex and human factors that do not fit neatly into a simple hierarchical and linear typology, which positions teachers' learning relatively low down the hierarchy.

What is good professional learning for teachers?

The research

In the research for this chapter, 20 MTeach graduates, teachers of varying experience, phase, subject specialism and school type were involved in the exit and follow-up interviews. Ten of the teachers had between two and five years' teaching experience, six had between five and ten, and the remaining four had between ten and twenty years' experience. Twelve were secondary school teachers, two came from the post-compulsory sector, five were primary school teachers (including one from a special school) and one worked in an Early Years setting. Fifteen of the teachers were female; five were male. This sample is similar to the overall gender balance of the MTeach course. Although most of the teachers came from schools in London, several came from schools on the London fringe and two worked in schools over 50 miles from the Institute.

It is important to acknowledge the self-selecting nature of those who undertake the MTeach course and of those who took part in the interviews. Teachers in England who enrol for Master's-level courses represent a small minority of the profession, compared with those who are involved in accredited professional courses and training and with those who do not take up any professional learning other than one-day INSET courses or school-based training. Moreover, the uniqueness of the MTeach course, particularly in its work with newly qualified teachers (NQTs) and teachers of only one or two years' experience, suggests that MTeach participants are a particular breed, characterised by strong personal and professional drive. As one of the stated underpinning principles of the MTeach course is to develop a questioning, critically informed disposition towards educational orthodoxies, it is to be expected that the participants have a tendency to also question the focus, value and efficacy of much of their CPD.

Nonetheless, these teachers have valid views to offer about the nature and content of CPD in England. The analysis of their responses provides the substance of this chapter. Data sources include individual and group interviews, and questionnaires. Analysis of these qualitative data is thematic and will be considered in the concluding section for its significance, in relation to the hierarchical typology of CPD impact by Guskey (2000), noted above. In addition, in November and December 2005, 11 of the MTeach graduates were asked to reflect on the best CPD they could recall.

This they subsequently posted in an online discussion group. Some of them had to go back a long way.

> It pains me, therefore, to have to write this, but the best inset I have attended was the first one, back in the September of 2001. I fear this may not meet the criterion of 'recent', but it was a model of how to run a staff training session and has simply not been beaten.
>
> (Andrew)

This example was chosen not just because it was simply the best experience, but it contrasted so markedly with the usual CPD diet, as Andrew himself noted: 'I have sat through so much bad INSET, that I actually find it difficult to differentiate the merely boring from the utterly intolerable.'

As noted earlier, four key themes emerged from the data. Careful scrutiny of the exit and follow-up interviews from December 2004 to December 2005 identified what the 20 teachers regarded as features of good and bad CPD, as listed in Table 8.1.

Table 8.1 Features of continuing professional development

Good CPD	Bad CPD
Learning	Teaching
Co-constructing	Judging
Learning	Entertaining
Learning	Performance
Internal	External
Interactive	Passive (esp. PowerPoint)
Challenging	Patronising
Optional	Forced
High level	Low level
Individual/group needs	Mass needs
Ongoing	One-off
Information (new knowledge)	Instruction (been there before)

In the subsequent online discussions, the four key themes of the study were developed and refined. It is the comments from the teachers that are the core of the thematic evidence that emerged from the year-long research study.

Learning and metalearning – theme 1

The first theme from the interviews was the need for these teachers to feel engagement with *learning* in general and their *learning at a meta-level* when involved in CPD. In good CPD the learning challenges them, taking them, as one of the teachers, Angela, remarked, slightly 'out of their comfort zone'. Although this was often done, and needs to be done, in subject or phase groups, the opportunity to come into contact with teachers cross-phase, cross-subject and cross-experience was highly stimulating. To some extent this is untypical even of the forward-thinking learning networks that have been set up by the GTCE and the NCSL. Here networks are either hierarchically constituted, as with aspiring or serving headteachers at the NCSL, or where they are experience and position related, as for CPD leaders in the Engage strand of the GTCE networks and for teachers starting their careers in the Connect strand.

These learning exchanges on the MTeach course could be at general level, as a primary school teacher, Millie, remarked: 'I enjoyed the academic stimulus and the contact with other teachers, whom I would otherwise not normally come into contact with.' However, it did also lead to practical benefits with regard to the sharing of practice, or Fielding *et al.*'s (2005) joint practice development, to improve learning. A secondary teacher, Leanne, noted how she adapted a suggestion from Millie, the Year 2 teacher above, to her own practice: 'Yes, and someone from your group, when we first started "Leading Learning", someone brought up "Bubble Time", I can't remember who it was. Was it M (primary)? Right, Years 7–13 now book a "bubble" with me every week.'

This learning is stimulated also when the course or training is an ongoing, not an isolated one-off, experience. As both Theresa and

John observed, this could also be an experience that was somewhat removed from the current favoured type of INSET or course.

> One good form of CPD I've been lucky to experience on an ongoing basis over the last year is the observation of NQTs. This wouldn't be regarded as a traditional form of CPD, but I feel more than anything over the past year, it's made me reflect upon and improve my own practice.
>
> (Theresa)

> Probably the best example I had last term was training on transition from Reception to Year 1. This has been part of an ongoing training program looking at how to plan and create high quality learning opportunities for young children that are not overly formal but challenge children to learn through play. Why was it good? Well, I think one of the key reasons was that it wasn't an isolated experience but one that was in a sequence of three. I strongly believe that isolated INSET experiences often have little sustainable and lasting impact as they get gradually subsumed back into the morass of day to day classroom life and other competing priorities.
>
> (John)

Engagement with learning works best when the CPD experience is refreshing, informative and stimulating. Bad CPD seems at times to distance itself from or ignore learning, as Craig describes: 'Another failing of INSET/CPD is that so much of it is not about learning, which is why we all work in schools in the first place.' However, more than this, a key ingredient is the amount of learning that teachers themselves do, both in its nature – the challenge referred to above by Angela – and the time to reflect on one's learning commented on by John. Craig sums this up when he describes:

> The best INSET I experienced was during my first year as a BT. This involved all the teachers spending a day experiencing what going to different classes was like. Each group went to three classes, my group went to Maths, RE and PE, we were taught by our colleagues for about 40 minutes and had time to ask questions, complete activities, etc. This INSET was excellent as it gave/reminded everyone of what it

felt like to have to move around the school and attend different classes as well as revisiting the atmosphere of sitting in class and sampling the different teaching styles of the subject teachers. Essentially it was about learning and whatever improves our understanding of learning is a valuable use of teacher time.

Collaboration – theme 2

The second key theme about good or bad CPD was the extent to which real *collaboration* took place. Collaboration was characterised by the sharing and enacting together of practice and learning in a non-hierarchical way, reflecting the benefits noted above of a non-hierarchical approach to CPD. Theresa noted the benefits of the non-judgemental nature of such an approach, when talking about her NQT observations mentioned earlier.

> The follow-up dialogue with the NQT is equally useful, providing a forum for discussion about approaches – not all one way. I think the two-way nature is really important, and I always hope the NQTs go away feeling inspired to look at things differently, rather than just feeling 'judged'.

Another secondary teacher, Laura, developed this thinking by noting the mutual benefits possible from collaborative CPD whilst commenting on the rarity of such opportunities.

> I totally agree that CPD should involve more observation of peers. We are always told that we should share good practice but this is rarely formalised. You seem to be enjoying this aspect of your role and it is great that it is has two-way benefits.

The teachers in this study also said that genuine opportunities for collaboration enabled them to develop, through their CPD, both the individual meaning-making and co-construction of knowledge that characterises successful learning communities (Watkins, 2005). In describing his best-ever CPD experience, back in 2001, Andrew remarked that:

> [The] training, a twilight session, was on assessment, and drew on the Inside the Black Box work from Kings. Summaries of the research were available, and a member of the Kings team gave a short and stimulating presentation on their findings. Crucially, the meeting broke down into subject teams to allow colleagues to discuss the relevance of the research to practice in the school, and to construct a shared understanding – a pedagogy – of assessment.

And Craig reinforces the benefits to all parties, not just the recipients, of the sharing and enacting of good practice:

> By referring to observing and follow-up discussions with NQTs you have identified the very practical learning and reflection which is a big part of our BT training. I also think that the learning conversations which we can have with NQTs, BTs, etc are an invaluable part of *our* [my emphasis] CPD.

Responsibility – theme 3

The third theme that featured strongly in the analysis was that these teachers felt that what was lacking in their CPD diet was an articulation of *their responsibility* for their CPD. This was not just in terms of what they needed personally but also what they had to contribute to the professional learning of others.

With regard to their own needs, the teachers had a general distrust of, and disregard for, mass INSET sessions, which were undifferentiated and simplistic.

> My school management assumes that a staff of 60+ can all usefully be given the same lectures. I remember one Tuesday afternoon when they thought they were doing something clever by bringing someone in to talk about learning styles or something equally vital to understanding education. Unfortunately, I learnt nothing.
>
> (Andrew)

The teachers were also surprised and frustrated that their needs were not identified, let alone met. Craig, responding to Laura's comments about a bad INSET session on display, commented:

> [It's] obvious from your posting that good INSET/CPD must have an identifiable, practical application. I think this is essential, as teachers do not have the luxury of spare time to idly consider the latest trend in CPD/INSET. Does your school canvass teachers for their training needs? It sounds like the Display session was not based on demand by teachers.

And, in responding to John, he repeated this view, using an interesting metaphor to illustrate the decontextualised and irrelevant nature of much bad INSET: 'Good INSET is surely about responding to identifiable teaching and learning needs whereas bad INSET is often parachuted into our diaries without real context.'

With regard to making contributions to their own and others' CPD, some had been able to contribute what they had learned on the MTeach course, especially the findings from their practice-based enquiry. For a primary school teacher, Jane, this had benefits for the school and for her own learning.

> I have used my Research to inform curriculum development across the school. I have since been involved in Leadership and Management Training and was able to come to this course with prior knowledge, which was useful. I am much more aware of my own learning and it has given me a more positive approach and attitude towards myself … I have moved much more towards being a 'reflective teacher' whose 'errors' are now seen as learning experiences.

For Claire too, in the post-compulsory sector, her research in particular and the course in general brought benefits to her college and herself.

> As a department we've set up a Good Practice Group, of which I'm a part. I also fed back my findings from my research project. I hope and feel it has made an impact on my teaching and made me realise the benefits of keeping my finger on the pulse of theory.

However, it has not all been plain sailing and the contributions that some of the teachers have wanted to make have not always been received with universal acclaim, as Debbie, a secondary school teacher, noted:

> [In] my school there was a sense of, 'we've got so much to do how can you possibly spend time doing this when you should be doing all the other stuff?' And, although I have shared with my department what I did, and I've implemented certain things in our workshops, it's very hard to share across school, because it's not really understood.

This resistance to others' contributions and their wish to contribute to CPD, particularly if they seemed *too* innovative, could be disheartening. Angela said in her secondary school it was a:

> ... bit demoralising [when some teachers don't engage with the thinking behind new ideas] because you know how much benefit it has. You want other people to see how much benefit it has. People don't necessarily see it ... You try to get others to look at new, different ways of doing certain things. I am getting some resistance from older members of staff.

In their research, Fielding *et al.* (2005) noted that teachers benefited most from professional development activities which engaged them in learning about their practice in an atmosphere of trust and mutuality. The distrust that teachers may have about CPD, that it is imposed on them regardless of need and experience, may explain some of the resistance noted above. For the teachers in my research, distrust often took the form of trusting more in practising teachers in general as CPD leaders, rather than in experts from outside. Also, they tended to trust and benefit more from teachers working in similar contexts. Talking about a generally bad whole-day INSET experience, Theresa said that '[the] part of the day that many people did find useful was a set of "spotlights" from staff on ways they're using ICT already. So why not spend the INSET teaching each other, rather than sitting in front of an "expert" all day?'

What also tied in to a feeling of professional contribution to their

CPD was the element of choice that they had, which per se often led to more enjoyable and fruitful CPD experiences. As Laura noted:

> On joining my new school in September I attended an internal course on using Interactive Whiteboards run by the school's ICT Manager. The format was a PowerPoint presentation combined with demonstrations over an hour. Questions were answered throughout. It was effective because it was a very practical session with demo. There was also a chance to try out some of the things he has taught us ... The training was also optional and I chose to go so that might be significant – it was not imposed blanket training that we get on INSET days!

Active engagement – theme 4

The fourth and final theme emphasised the need for CPD to be active and experiential. These teachers wanted to be *engaged actively* in their CPD. They did not want to be lectured to and at by external or internal experts, mainly because they did not learn much from the experience.

> One bad example of CPD came last term, when a guy ... came to do a whole school INSET. There were a number of things that made it ineffective: firstly, he spent a lot of time trying to entertain us with jokes, anecdotes and QuickTime videos of sheep saying their times tables. Vital in a long INSET, yes, but not at the expense of learning ... In short, the INSET had all the elements of a bad or average lesson – a focus on teaching and 'entertainment' over learning, and a lack of ways to ensure any learning there was had been sufficiently embedded by the learners.
>
> (Theresa)

They often resented this all the more because they knew that they would be heavily criticised as teachers if they taught in this lecture style, as Theresa and Craig, independent of one another, emphasised:

> It amazes me that approaches that would be criticised by Ofsted in a

lesson observation seem to be the preferred model (government or otherwise) for the 'teaching' of teachers.

(Theresa)

I have also thought many times how come we are expected, encouraged to teach in a certain way yet CPD/INSET is usually a lecture in a way that would create serious discipline problems within the classroom context. It really does lend a 'do as I say and not as I do' approach to much of our CPD.

(Craig)

Often the over-reliance on and inappropriate use of technology only compounded the problems of the lecture-style, 'stand-and-deliver' approach to delivering CPD.

I remember another interminable hour-long instruction on the use of data (when I'd just spent a year – again on the MTeach – processing enough data to break a mainframe); this last one rambled on in a vague manner, with the lecturer talking to number-packed 'PowerPoint' slides, captured from page after page of 'Excel'. Colleagues battled on, man- and woman-fully peering valiantly at the screen, cocking their heads on one side and trying to stop the numbers dancing in front of their eyes. Occasionally, the instructor would randomly throw-in some really impressive theoretical concept (which she had just learnt on her course at Kings) which regrettably had little connection with the ostensible purpose of her talk. On one of these occasions, I thought to myself 'do they run their classes like this? There'd be a bloody riot'.

(Andrew)

What then is active engagement in CPD for the teachers in this study? Nancy, a secondary school teacher, gave this recent example from her school.

Because we're going to have OFSTED soon, in the INSET we were going to be told about how OFSTED grade lessons. This school is really going for the upper end, we're looking for excellent for everything. We had the deputy head and head teacher leading the session. What happened was the deputy head had this totally interactive session, absolutely. First of all we had to stick post-it notes on each others' heads and try and describe the best cartoon we've seen. Then we were sticking post-it notes on our heads about what makes a good lesson. What do you think are the characteristics of a good lesson? We had to stick all of them on the wall. Then we had a different teacher read it out to the group. Then we watched videos and discussed them with the person next to us, what we thought the grade should have been for that. Then we looked at some feedback for a lesson observation. We were trying to, just by reading the text, decide what the level of the lesson would have been. So it was the most interactive thing I had and there was all this opportunity for learning more and discussing, which was really great. But meanwhile the head teacher was writing the observation sheets out for the whole thing. So she was observing the lead session. And at the end she went and gave us her feedback about what she thought was good about the session. She actually graded the deputy head in front of everybody and it was really good. It doesn't happen very often, but it was really practising what you preach.

John, from his primary school perspective, sums up Nancy's example when he reflects on the good features of his course on children's transition from Reception to Year 1.

The day itself was effective because there was a very high degree of interactivity between participants, coupled with a bond that we were pursuing the same goals of creating a more appropriate, play-based curriculum. ALL of the people delivering presentations etc. are current classroom practitioners which helps no bounds when it comes to question the do-ability of what is being advocated.

Overall: issues and impact

Returning to the earlier summary of the research findings, these 20 teachers have indicated that what they find most enhances their professional learning are:

- an engagement with *learning* – the pupils' and theirs;

- real *collaboration* with people they trust;

- a sense of *their responsibility* for their CPD; and

- *active engagement* in their CPD, not being passive recipients of expert advice.

However, how does this sit with Guskey's (2000) five-stage hierarchy of effective CPD, especially the ultimate need for it to impact on pupils' achievement? From the evidence presented it might seem that these teachers are only interested in CPD from the point of view of their reactions, their learning, organisational support and their use of new knowledge and skills and that they are not looking for, or concerned with, evidence of impact on pupils. Are they, indeed, seeing CPD from a somewhat professionally self-indulgent perspective as some teacher-researchers do (Brooker and MacPherson, 1999)? One of the teachers raises this as a possible issue, when giving an example of some INSET that he regarded as bad.

> I will pick a three-morning course on autism, mainly because I feel it was bad INSET yet also useful. The basic set up was detailing about the disorder, its many facets and suggestions for classroom practice. The three mornings were mind-bendingly boring, consisting of three people reading off PowerPoint presentations (the new OHTs!) and making only occasional links to classroom practice that seemed completely abstract. There were almost no opportunities for discussion and this seemed a major handicap to making the days a success, as we were unable to compare our experiences, admittedly with children of hugely different backgrounds. Yet, I did feel I took away quite a bit of factual knowledge that helped me have a better understanding of the autistic child in my class. So I suppose some bad INSET can have good impacts. I suppose this leaves the question: is INSET bad because it is badly done and delivered or bad because it doesn't result in any learning?
>
> (John)

This is a perfectly valid issue to raise. Perhaps badly done courses and INSET are less of a failure where they impact on pupil performance. However, it is also valid to raise again the issue that many of the teachers commented on in the section on learner engagement. This is that, if we accept that what is good pedagogy in the teacher–learner setting of a school or college leads to good learning and good performance, then surely this must apply in the teachers' CPD context. If, as school teachers, they are encouraged to use a form of Kolb's (1984) learning cycle (do–review–learn–apply) or Watkins *et al.*'s (2002) evidence that teaching-learning processes work best when there is:

- activity, with reflection and sense-making;
- collaboration for learning;
- learner responsibility for learning; and
- learning about learning,

then this will surely work also with regard to their own CPD. This approach resonates clearly with Bruner's (1996) four models of folk pedagogy, in which learning develops through:

- being shown;
- being told;
- constructing meaning; and
- joining a knowledge-generating community.

The teachers in this study said that most of their professional learning, external and internal, does not get much beyond Bruner's second stage. For them, for CPD to be successful, the complete focus does not need to be on pupil performance such that the means and the ends of the CPD are totally outcome-focused. For the teachers it is the purpose, content and pedagogy of the CPD that brings about effective teacher learning. It is this that will challenge, contextualise, resonate with and improve their practice. It will definitely not be:

> ... too many of us still sitting in bare halls, lured by free coffee and biscuits, to watch PowerPoint and doodle. Exactly what would students do in that situation? ... We had a guy in to talk about (and that's what he did) values education. He gave us his CV. It was impressive. He had a PowerPoint and a little piece of video. I think he was telling us to teach a value a month. None of us were really sure, and surely that's the point. As teachers we have a clear aim, and we assess how much closer the students are to reaching that aim. We use this knowledge to feed into their future learning, just as Andrew said, no recognition of prior knowledge, our current practice, or assessment for learning. I think the biggest lesson is the lack of focus – what are we learning?
>
> (Leanne)

Instead of this sterile atmosphere and non-learning outcomes, good CPD should be more learning-focused, engaging, collaborative and reflective, like Theresa's NQT observations.

> I often feel quite privileged to have a job that allows me to watch other staff teach. I always take something from the lessons – from good ones, it can be an actively good idea that I'd like to try. From others, it might be that, in sitting at the back watching the behaviour of disaffected students and the teacher's response to them, I reflect on whether I'd do anything better in their situation.

Concluding remarks

This research suggests that the professional development of teachers in England needs to adopt a different conceptual model, a new design, if it is to meet both the professional and personal learning needs of teachers and to then impact on pupil learning outcomes. In the new design, the focus on the process of development, namely the 'how' of learning, will be as important as its content, the 'what'. At the heart of this process should be a cross-curricular, cross-phase, cross-experience approach to teachers' learning, rather than a focus on skills-based, information-centred development. In this way there needs to be a distinction between development (growth and gradual professional unfolding) and learning (Abbott's (1994) 'reflective activity' which is both retrospective and forward-looking). This is so that development, the more professional aspect of teacher learning, is seen only as a part of the richer and more influential holistic learning that individual and collaborative reflection and activity bring.

The new CPD design is located in, and reflects, teachers' experiences, rather than privileging the voices of those who have gained professional status by virtue of their appointed status. Accordingly, teachers will then be better prepared, through a learning-centred model, for the challenges they are likely to meet throughout their careers. The current focus on performance management and school improvement is replaced by one in which, as Abbott suggests, teachers' CPD draws on 'previous experience to understand and evaluate the present, so as to shape future action and formulate new knowledge' (1994: 12).

The changing (inter)national and local context of teachers' CPD will influence, and be influenced by, four tensions, which are as yet unresolved, but highly stimulating, areas for dialogue about a new design for CPD. These are:

1 the needs of the system (top-down best practice) as opposed to local needs (bottom-up joint practice development);

2 the provision of central training (delivery) as opposed to locally clustered collaborative opportunities (discovery);

3 new technology being used to transmit knowledge the old way (presentation) as opposed to new technology used to enhance learning and metalearning (dialogue); and

4 teacher networks that reflect group interests/hierarchies

(exclusive) as opposed to networks that encourage mutuality based on an 'everyone can contribute' approach (inclusive).

At the heart of this chapter have been the voices of the MTeach graduates. It feels right then to end with a quotation from one of the teachers in the research study. As an illustration of these four issues, he suggests, as the others in the study did, that paradoxically we know what works to bring about effective teacher learning – discussion, not lecture – but seem happy to put on and 'endure' what we know does not work nearly as well.

> Bad CPD/INSET is similar to a manufactured boy/girl band. It might look nice, be catchy and fashionable but will you remember it by this time next year? Probably not, unless it is really awful. This brings me to INSET I endured on Emotional Intelligence or EI. INSET on ET would have been more useful or relevant! This seemed like a really desperate attempt to repackage and resell something that has been around for years. Most of my senior colleagues merely nodded their heads, recognising that this was merely rebranding, and possibly it would have been better to have an interesting 30-minute discussion rather than a three-hour lecture by PowerPoint.
>
> (Craig)

Note

1   One of the students was not an MTeach graduate but a student from another Institute course, who had written widely on CPD. To avoid constant reference to this, the research sample will simply be referred to as the MTeach graduates. All names have been anonymised.

References

Abbott, J. (1994) *Learning Makes Sense: Recreating education for a changing future.* Letchworth: Education 2000.

Bolam, R. (1993) 'Recent developments and emerging issues'. In General Teaching Council for England and Wales, *The Continuing Professional Development of Teachers*. London: GTC.

Brooker, R. and MacPherson, I. (1999) 'Communicating the processes and outcomes of practitioner research: an opportunity for self-indulgence or a serious professional responsibility?' *Educational Action Research*, 7, 2, 203–19.

Bruner, J. (1996) *The Culture of Education*. Cambridge, MA: Harvard University Press.

Craft, A. (2000) *Continuing Professional Development: A practical guide for teachers and schools*. London: RoutledgeFalmer.

Day, C. (1999) *Developing Teachers: The Challenge of Lifelong Learning*. London: Falmer.

Department for Education and Employment (DfEE) (2001) *Learning and Teaching. A strategy for professional development*. London: TSO. Available at: www.teachernet.gov.uk/professionaldevelopment/

Department for Education and Skills (DfES) (2005) *Leading and Coordinating CPD in Secondary Schools*. London: TSO.

Earley, P. (2005) 'Continuing Professional Development: the learning community'. In M. Coleman and P. Earley (eds), *Leadership and Management in Education: Cultures, change and context*. Oxford: Oxford University Press.

EPPI-Centre (2003) *The impact of collaborative CPD on classroom teaching and learning: how does collaborative CPD for the teachers aged 5–16 age range affect teaching and learning?* EPPI-Centre, Institute of Education, University of London.

EPPI-Centre (2005) *The impact of collaborative CPD on classroom teaching and learning: how do collaborative and sustained CPD and sustained but not collaborative CPD affect teaching and learning?* EPPI-Centre, Institute of Education, University of London.

Fielding, M., Bragg, S., Craig, J., Cunningham, I., Eraut, M., Gillinson, S., Horne, M., Robinson, C. and Thorp, J. (2005) *Factors Influencing the Transfer of Good Practice*. Research Brief RB615. London: DfES.

Guskey, T. (2000) *Evaluating Professional Development*. New York: Corwin Press.

Kolb, D. (1984) *Experiential Learning: Experience as the source of learning and development.* Englewood Cliffs, NJ: Prentice-Hall.

Watkins, C. (2005) *Classrooms as Learning Communities.* London: RoutledgeFalmer.

Watkins, C., Carnell, E., Lodge, C., Wagner, P. and Whalley, C. (2002) *Effective Learning,* Research Matters 17. London: Institute of Education, University of London, International School Improvement Network.

Wrigley, T. (2004) 'School effectiveness: the problem of reductionism'. *British Educational Research Journal,* 30, 2, 227–44.

Websites

Evidence for Policy and Practice Information and Co-ordinating Centre (EPPI-Centre) www.eppi.ioe.ac.uk

General Teaching Council for England (GTCE) www.gtce.org.uk

National College for School Leadership (NCSL) www.ncsl.org.uk

National Foundation for Educational Research (NFER) www.nfer.ac.uk

Teachernet www.teachernet.gov.uk

Part 3
Relation to national policy

9 Control or empowerment?

The professional learning of Scottish teachers in the post-McCrone era
Jim O'Brien
Centre for Educational Leadership,
University of Edinburgh

Introduction

> There is no such thing as a British educational system. Scotland, although a small country has been a constituent part of the United Kingdom since 1707 with its own distinctive and autonomous education system.
>
> (O'Brien, 1995: 9)

The post-devolution settlement in the UK has led to suggestions of increasing divergence, particularly in social policy and educational policy and practice, in the four 'home' countries since May 1999 when the Scottish Parliament was re-established with the Scottish Executive as the devolved 'government'. The Scottish Executive is fully accountable to Parliament, and has responsibility for educational policy at national level and for ensuring that education authorities and other institutions and bodies operate within that national policy framework (Pickard and Dobie, 2003). As Scotland is a small country, this has been progressed in a largely consensual way – epitomised perhaps by the acceptance of proportional representation in the Parliament and a coalition Executive (Scottish

Executive, 2003). While the educational problems and issues are recognisably similar, separate jurisdictions are adopting different policies and solutions, and are worthy of study and exploration (Raffe and Byrne, 2005), so it is interesting in this volume to see chapters from the constituent parts of the UK. Scotland, in particular, with greater devolved powers than Wales (O'Brien and Jones, 2005), while being 'similar to other national systems which have embarked upon the regulation and re-professionalisation of teacher education along "competence" lines' (Hartley, 2002: 251), appears determined to assert its educational distinctiveness and to pursue different approaches, policy initiatives and 'Scottish solutions for Scottish problems' in the face of issues and problems emerging globally. Or is it merely a mediation or Scottish interpretation of New Labour policies for consumption north of the border (Mooney and Poole, 2004)?

Certainly education can lay claim to enhanced policy distinctiveness. Since devolution, Scotland has engaged in a national debate (Munn *et al.*, 2004) about the purposes of education and schooling and has established by statute its national education priorities (www.nationalpriorities.org.uk). The importance of teaching and professionalism were reaffirmed as part of the 'McCrone Agreement' (Scottish Executive Education Department (SEED), 2001) between the Scottish Executive, the teacher unions and the teacher employers – education authorities (EAs) – as there are no 'opted-out' schools and less than 5 per cent of schools are independent and private. Teacher professional development and school re-culturing are at the heart of this agreement, but worrying signs are appearing that this is more difficult to realise than perhaps anticipated by politicians and civil servants (Audit Scotland, 2006).

This chapter offers an analysis of the emergence of policy and the Scottish Continuing Professional Development (CPD) Framework (Christie and O'Brien, 2005) based on a series of professionally endorsed standards, and locates the emergence of an expert teacher standard – Chartered Teacher (CT) – firmly within this framework. The development phases for CT are reviewed and assessed in terms of the degree to which these Scottish developments address or inform issues associated with teacher professional learning, e.g. important themes of partnership, the role of higher education (HE), professional accreditation and the role of the General Teaching Council for Scotland (GTCS), and the developing CPD profile associated with the principal teaching union, the Educational Institute of Scotland (EIS), will frame the discussion.

A framework for CPD: the policy dimension

Scotland for several decades has had a graduate teaching profession; the content and approach of HE initial preparation courses have been closely controlled by the Government and, until recently, Her Majesty's Inspectorate of Education (HMIE) – since 2001 repositioned outside government as an executive agency. In the 1990s, during the Thatcher Government, there were discernible attempts to 'reform' teacher education (note 'education' and not 'training') and competence was one lever used. Policy on the content, nature and duration of courses leading to teaching qualifications (TQs) was published by the Scottish Office Education Department (SOED, 1993) and revised by the Scottish Office Education and Industry Department (SOEID) (1998a). The competence-based guidelines, which despite the terminology were to all intents and purposes mandatory, generated debate and concern, but were relatively quickly implemented by the Scottish teacher education institutions (Stronach *et al.*, 1994; Christie, 2003).

How has CPD developed in Scotland and why is there now a standards-related framework? Marker (1999: 924) claims that historically in Scotland

> ... professional development has been one of the poor relations of the education service. Teachers have not been willing to campaign for it at

221

the expense of salaries or class size; the authorities have regularly had to sacrifice it to meet their statutory responsibilities; successive governments have advocated it without providing the necessary resources.

The context for the development of CPD in Scottish education is discussed by Ross (1996), who offers an overview of how staff development in secondary education developed through a series of phases between 1975 and 1990. From fairly informal approaches reflecting individual motivation and commitment, it moved to being centrally managed and controlled. Boyd (2005: 18–31) provides an interesting brief history of teacher-related CPD in Scotland. He tracks the changes in emphases and priorities (some aspects will be very familiar to readers from other parts of the UK), including the 'marketisation' of government funding of INSET and the emergence of a range of new 'providers'. In Scotland, as a result of the rejection of 'opting out' policies, this has led to enhanced roles for EAs initiated primarily by the former Strathclyde Region (at the time the largest education authority in western Europe) and to the growing gulf between the 'centre and periphery'. He then goes on to critique various associated 'delivery' models such as the highly centralist 'Postman Pat' model involving centralised decisions about what CPD was needed, especially in relation to the major curricular reforms of the 1980s and 1990s, and the development and 'delivery' of CPD activities where 'in-service training was done to people rather than being done with them' (Boyd, 2005: 33). This model reflected the over-centralised nature of Scottish educational policy-making of the time. The next phase involved a 'cascade' model of CPD whereby designers and 'experts' were often involved in creating robust so-called 'teacher-proof' activities and then training a range of people to deliver these materials at EA or, in some instances, school level, e.g. the staff development and appraisal 'training the trainers' initiative of the early 1990s. Boyd (2005: 45) reflects that this led to a 'mushroom effect' whereby classroom teachers, as recipients of the cascade effect, 'are the mushrooms in the dark room and it is not difficult to see why CPD is not always regarded as an enlightening experience'.

Sutherland's report (1997), as part of the Dearing Inquiry, highlighted the lack of structured teacher CPD involving HE. He argued that a framework for CPD would help to retain teachers in the profession, improve the quality of teaching and consequently benefit school students (Livingston and Robertson, 2001). This proved to be a powerful influence on policy development, as Sutherland's report was followed by SOEID's (1998b) consultation proposals to develop a framework of professional development for Scottish teachers which might contain 'guidance for teachers, schools, and education authorities on the competences, standards and qualifications required in the wide range of teaching and management roles that teachers undertake at different stages in their careers'. It was recognised that, while there was a clear statement of competences and a standard for initial teacher education (ITE), there were no related statements identifying further competences and no coherent framework of opportunities or qualifications available to the Scottish teaching profession to recognise enhanced professional skills, knowledge and attributes.

Much of the standards-based development was under way or was being planned prior to the teacher industrial unrest of the late 1990s, but the resolution to that unrest, the McCrone Agreement in 2001, followed a major review of teachers' pay and conditions, and resulted in a contractual obligation for all fully registered teachers to undertake an additional 35 hours of CPD annually. The Teacher's Agreement thus endorsed the significance of CPD for all teachers, and motivation and individual work satisfaction were declared as important goals for CPD. This is fundamentally different from the agendas focused on system and school change that had driven CPD developments previously. Some tension has been generated because the additional 35 hours is largely in addition to any CPD in relation to the CPD Framework undertaken by fully registered Scottish teachers.

Such activities are not recognised as contributing to the contractual obligations of teachers. Accessing the provision at Chartered Teacher or Standard for Headship is regarded as a voluntary not a contractual activity while the CPD arrangements during the induction year remain essential and integral to the process and are discussed below.

The CPD framework consists of four standards, in their original or revised versions, plus the CPD experiences and opportunities suggested for educational leaders. While the actual development of the framework was relatively unplanned and non-sequential (Table 9.1) and has been described as 'haphazard' (O'Brien and Draper, 2003), there are clear linkages between its elements, namely an Induction Standard (O'Brien and Christie, 2005; Draper *et al.*, 2006; Draper and O'Brien, 2006); an expert teacher standard – Chartered Teacher (Kirk *et al.*, 2003; O'Brien and Hunt, 2005); a revised Standard for Headship (O'Brien and Torrance, 2005); all apparently building on the existing Standard or Benchmarks for Initial Teacher Education (QAAHE, 2000). Unlike England, there are no standards planned, as yet, for particular school roles such as special educational needs co-ordinators (SENCOs). Such specific standards might have been predicted given the aims of the 1998 consultation quoted above.

There is no published rationale for Scottish policy-makers having chosen a standards-based CPD framework, but Purdon (2003, 2004) suggests that such a framework allows closer political control over teachers' professional lives. Critics of standards-based teacher education and CPD have emerged everywhere since such standards have appeared. Humes (2001: 15) posits an interesting perspective on teachers and standards:

> What is it that teachers profess? It is doubtful if most teachers would answer that question by saying they profess a set of competences or a list of benchmarks. A more likely response is that they would appeal to values and principles concerned with such things as the worthwhileness of learning, their commitment to helping youngsters to develop, their desire to help them achieve, their belief in education as a fundamental right, its importance for democracy and social justice.

Humes goes on to suggest that CPD provision should allow exploration of such fundamental aims and values.

The Scottish standards certainly contain many statements related to values and refrain from atomistic reduction of skills and competences by providing illustrations of possible actions and approaches which would evince the standard in action. However, the emergence of these standards has resulted in what Patrick *et al.* (2003) consider to be two sets of competing discourses in Scottish education: performativity versus autonomy *and* managerialism versus pedagogic excellence. They argue that the conceptualisation of teaching in simplistic terms as a set of measurable outcomes engendered by the CPD framework risks undermining the autonomy and professionalism that it claims to enhance. Menter *et al.* (2004: 102), however, indicate that: 'Scottish developments appear to be based on a continuation of a public service ethic, trust in teachers, and an absence of performativity.'

Table 9.1 The Scottish Teacher Standards Framework – development timeline

Date	Stage	Standard or official publication
1993	Initial Teacher Education	*Guidelines for Teacher Training Courses* (SOED, 1993*)*
1998	Initial Teacher Education	*Guidelines for Initial Teacher Education Courses in Scotland* (SOEID, 1998a)
1998	Headship	*Standard for Headship* (SOEID, 1998c)
2000	Initial Teacher Education	*The Standard for Initial Teacher Education in Scotland: Benchmark Information* (QAAHE, 2000)
2002	Teacher Induction	*The Standard for Full Registration* (GTCS, 2002)
2002	'Expert' or Chartered Teacher	*Standard for Chartered Teacher* (SEED, 2002b)

| 2003 School Leadership Framework | *Continuing Professional Development for Educational Leaders* (SEED, 2003) |
| 2005 Headship | *Ambitious Excellent Schools: The standard for headship* (SEED, 2005) |

The individual standards emerged through different processes involving varying degrees of professional consultation and reflecting the ongoing centralist tendencies evident in Scottish education policy-making. For example, the McCrone Report expressed major disquiet about the then probationary period and recommended a period of 'stable employment' for newly qualified teachers (NQTs), with guaranteed improved induction support (Draper *et al.*, 2006). The General Teaching Council for Scotland (GTCS) was responsible for the development of the Standard for Full Registration (SfR) which underpins the new induction arrangements. The SfR (GTCS, 2002) reflected the work of the national induction project and discussions within Council and consultation with HMIE and SEED officials. McNally (2003: 160), the national development officer, describes the nature of the process and the control of the outcome of the SfR, stating clearly that the SfR:

> ... itself was driven by an official imperative to build a near replica of the ITE benchmarking standard (Quality Assurance Agency for Higher Education, 2000) and brooked practically no alternative to a competence-based view of professional practice.

McNally's interpretation of events suggests strict central governmental control and yet the GTCS as the principal professional body of the Scottish teaching profession appears comfortable with this and has subsequently endorsed other standards in the framework. Teachers have accepted the SfR despite its complexities, because the general approach to standards in Scotland has been promoted as a 'commonsense' approach to codification of teacher skills and abilities, and an examination of any of the Scottish

226

standards will illustrate that they assiduously attempt to avoid the 'technicist' approach favoured by the Teacher Training Agency in England, for example. Additionally, resources were provided to EAs and schools to pay for teacher participation in the new Teacher Induction Scheme, about which there was very little consultation, which got under way in 2003. For an NQT, the Teacher Induction Scheme includes the guarantee of a year's placement in one or two schools, a reduced teaching load (70 per cent) and the support of a more senior member of staff. The remaining 30 per cent of the inductee's time is designated for development activities, again reflecting the central role played by CPD in the agreement that followed the McCrone Report. HE has no formal role in the induction scheme despite currently having a major role in the other standards within the framework, where partnership between the profession, the employers and HE institutions has been a condition of involvement and has been officially endorsed in assorted documents and statements by SEED and GTCS.

The EAs and schools have responded with varying degrees of success to the challenges that the new induction scheme provides, and GTCS has shared its evidence in a series of published reports based on surveys conducted. With regard to CPD, some of the issues raised by induction respondents are illuminating (Pearson and Robson, 2005: 2.4.4):

- Most local authority CPD was of variable quality.

- Much of the local authority CPD seemed to be a repeat of content previously covered in ITE, where the input had often been of a higher quality.

- The SfR was often used as the framework for local authority CPD but was not a tool recognised by most schools.

While the potential of this early CPD entitlement is perhaps not yet realised, a possible outcome may be the desire of those satisfying the

SfR to continue to seek out and engage with quality CPD activities as their needs change with experience. The Economic and Social Research Council (ESRC) project (McNally *et al.*, 2003) on early professional development, not due to report until 2008, may offer critical insights into how new professionals actually learn.

The induction scheme has been criticised for its hasty implementation and inadequate consultation (O'Brien and Christie, 2005; Purdon, 2003). Indeed, Draper *et al.* (2004) suggest there is evidence from the first year of the scheme in secondary schools that many supporter teachers had not even read the SfR and were blissfully unaware of the nature of the competences they were assessing, formally reporting on and using to discuss the inductee's developing CPD agenda. A major finding (O'Brien and Christie, 2005: 200) and of concern for the associated ongoing nature of teacher CPD in Scotland was the 'absence of *conceptualising* or *reflective practice* from teachers' vocabulary' and the

> ... evidence that most instructional support of probationers is at the level of practical craft knowledge which does not go beyond 'what works'. There is a danger that, as supporters develop probationers within a fairly narrow range of classroom practice and probationers, in turn, strive to please their supporter-assessor, current practice will stagnate.

Clearly there is scope for interpretation of purpose associated with the development of the Scottish Standards Framework, e.g. the Induction Standard and associated processes involve both support and formal summative assessment by the same person; it is about development, surely, but are there also elements which may be designed to secure conformity or maintain what exists rather than invite experimentation and encourage a degree of supported risk-taking? Do similar comments apply to the Chartered Teacher (CT) initiative? The overtly stated purpose of the CT grade is to 'provide the best, experienced teachers with opportunities to remain in teaching, to embrace new challenges, improve their skills and practice and to be rewarded accordingly' (GTCS, 2003: 5, quoted in Forde *et al.*, 2006: 138). 'Expert' or accomplished classroom teaching is thus recognised, valued and rewarded. The Standard for Chartered Teacher includes 'collaboration and influence' as one of its core professional values and personal commitments; the relevant statement reads:

> [T]he Chartered Teacher will be committed to influencing and having a leading impact in team and school development, and to contributing to the professional development of colleagues and *new entrants to the profession*.
>
> (SEED, 2002b: 6; emphasis added)

Clearly this suggests an expectation that CTs will be instrumental in change, renewal and the re-culturing of Scottish education, but is this clearly understood and supported by the profession, employers and policy-makers? Or has there been a classic fudge of the issues surrounding this important development?

An example of policy to practice: the Chartered Teacher Standard and programme

The Standard for Chartered Teacher again emerged from that possible watershed in Scottish education – the McCrone Agreement. There were important implications for Scottish teacher career structures, especially by the suggestion that there should be a national programme for CT status, which,

> ... should be open to all experienced classroom teachers ... It would constitute a personal achievement, rather than a post ... it would require completion of a challenging and structured programme of relevant and accredited CPD, over a period of four years, aimed at improving teaching and other professional skills.
>
> (SEED, 2002b: para. 4.12)

The development phase of the Chartered Teacher initiative is well documented (Kirk *et al.*, 2003; O'Brien and Hunt, 2005). Enhanced teacher capacity and accomplishment in the classroom are part of the quality 'Kitemark' of the new status and – importantly – grade of teacher, not a post with responsibilities. The initial intention, however, was to have an 'expert' teacher emulating the English 'advanced skills teacher' (Lee, 2004). The new standard was to have two pathways: one associated with *teaching and learning*, the other with *leadership and management*. The standard was to include a core of competences for all and a set of electives for specific responsibilities, e.g. special educational needs, but such a dual and specialist approach was abandoned post-McCrone in favour of a process that defined the generic competences for a CT, produced an exemplar programme of activities that would issue in the achievement of the standard and the development and evaluation of a 'pilot' programme. Part of the project brief was to consult widely with the teaching profession and to involve them in shaping the outcomes, including the associated arrangements for any validation and accreditation of formal programmes of CPD should they be endorsed. From this emerged the largest and most comprehensive consultation on educational matters conducted in Scotland, which involved a series of public meetings, surveys issued to all Scottish teachers, focus groups and discussions with all the major stakeholders.

The standard was developed through iterative consultation and testing with stakeholders, and was informed by consideration of the literature on teaching quality and the statements or policy documentation associated with the notion of 'expert' teacher found in other educational systems in North America (National Board of Professional Teaching Standards (NBPTS)), Australia (Australian College of Education (ACE)), England and Wales, and other European countries. Many Scottish 'accomplished' teachers were identified and interviewed. The evidence gathered in this way suggested that four dimensions should be central to the standard, namely:

- professional values and personal commitments;
- professional knowledge and understanding;
- professional and personal attributes; and
- professional action.

Partnership and the role for HE are essential elements of CT programmes. All consortia that seek to have accredited provider status granted by GTCS have to evidence partnership with an HE institution. Why is this deemed so important? The rhetoric of partnership has been around for decades, especially in relation to ITE, but the nature and experience of partnership varies between geographic areas of Scotland and specific HE institutions involved in teacher education. There has been reluctance in the past for Scottish teachers to take on new partnership roles in ITE, as evidenced by the abortive attempt to introduce school-based mentors for student teachers in the 1990s; this might partially be explained by the proposed resource model. Similar resistance by teachers has not been evident in the introduction of 'supporter' or mentor roles for the new induction arrangements, perhaps because resources were provided by SEED to EAs and schools to provide for individual teachers, but it is only now that there is some serious investment in the training of mentors in a range of SEED-supported 'pilots' across the country, as part of a raft of experimental work on coaching and mentoring associated with building capacity through CPD, especially in leadership.

Nevertheless, GTCS and SEED have been consistent in endorsing the concept without really determining what structures and processes should pertain. Partnership is claimed at various levels of educational policy-making, not least with the partnership of SEED, GTCS and the teacher unions in agreeing the post-McCrone settlement and overseeing its progress. As intimated above, that 'progress' is increasingly questioned and there are suggestions that the expected re-culturing will not occur because of continuing teacher resistance to change.

For the Chartered Teacher initiative, much had been learned from the development in 1998 of the original Standard for Headship and its associated programme, the Scottish Qualification for Headship (SQH) (Reeves *et al.*, 2002; O'Brien *et al.*, 2003), and the importance of *involved* partnership between HE and the teaching profession; the need for professional accreditation and recognition of prior learning; and the benefits of context and work-based learning to engage candidates in reflective activities with perceived focus and purpose and associated action aligned to their daily responsibilities. When consulting on the CT proposals, it was clear that those responding wanted a rigorous but grounded experience. Universities were deemed able to provide rigour through validated programmes but there were concerns about existing postgraduate degrees being too academic and theoretical, with little practical benefits for classroom teachers; this ignored the advances made in the development of such programmes and especially the increasingly dominant paradigm of work-based assignments designed to provide practical and professional insights and action in schools and classrooms. During the pilot phase various modules were designed and tested and evaluated. Kirk *et al.* (2003: 74) indicate that many

> ... evaluations specifically asked about the relevance of the module to the classroom. The replies from teachers suggested they were very relevant, gave insights into their own classrooms, and made them reflect on their own practice ... they had become more reflective, analytical and self-critical, that their professional confidence had increased and that it had changed the way they taught in the classroom.

The Chartered Teacher development programme that emerged from the consultation period was essentially qualification-based, involving the acquisition of a Master's degree offered by several consortia, all of which had to have as a lead partner a university that would validate the degree and thus provide quality assurance as to its rigour and intellectual content, and whose programmes or provision leading to CT status were then subjected to rigorous professional accreditation by GTCS, involving scrutiny of documentation and formal meetings wherein the consortia individually justified their proposals. The principle of partnership in consortia was designed to provide a 'checks and balances' arrangement whereby the programmes remained balanced with grounded experience and academic rigour.

In relation to the standard for Chartered Teacher, my own institution, building on existing partnerships, determined through dialogue various stages of partnership with prospective CT partners – several EAs, a national charity interested in education, and the Scottish Council of Independent Schools – which the consortia might agree. This resulted in partnership levels ranging from remaining informed about developments to joint design and development plus joint teaching of provision with teachers and employers. Our CT partnership group meets several times a year and 'approves' all proposals for the initial development of new programme modules, believing that it would be inappropriate merely to offer existing pre-CT postgraduate CPD modules as these might not necessarily reflect important attributes of CT provision, e.g. work-based learning elements. We have thus created a new postgraduate degree – MTeach – that on successful completion satisfies CT status and remuneration arrangements (O'Brien and Hunt, 2005). Other consortia have their own partnership arrangements, and several universities and their partners have moved successfully to have a range of pre-existing modules and postgraduate degrees accredited by GTCS.

Kirk *et al.* (2003: 79) posed the question 'Will the national machinery responsible for overseeing Accreditation of Prior Learning (APL) be robust enough to ensure that high uniform standards are upheld across the country?' A major concern was that the experience and accomplishments of existing teachers should be recognised and rewarded but that the process guarantee rigour. Universities had well-developed systems for the APL and of Prior Experiential Learning (APEL) and these play an important part in the CT 'Programme Route', with often expanded amounts of credit being approved compared with more traditional postgraduate degrees. Recognising that many teachers may already have the requisite skills and dispositions associated with the CT grade, an alternative route is provided by GTCS. This requires a candidate to complete the obligatory Module 1 and self-evaluation exercise with an accredited provider and then to complete a portfolio and commentary that is presented for assessment by GTCS. This involves members (including university personnel and field practitioners), approved by GTCS, of a National Assessment Panel established by Council; consideration of a claim by two independent assessors working independently of each other; and a visit to the claimant's school to discuss the claim. Some of the learning experiences claimed are described by one of the national assessors in the GTCS CT magazine (Spring 2005: 7; www.gtcs.org.uk/Publications/) in addition to the importance of providing appropriate evidence in support of a claim and critical analysis of their enhanced teaching and accomplishments. This 'professional' or 'Accreditation Route' does offer a genuine alternative means of securing the status of CT and offers a demanding and rigorous experience but without the associated degree, and, some would claim, with less of an immediate developmental experience (www.gtcs.org.uk/ ProfessionalDevelopment/).

One of the interesting developments associated with CT is the emergence of the EIS, by far the largest teacher union, as a partner in a consortium with the University of Paisley providing an online CT programme. This has proved popular with teachers across the country, not least because of the fee discount associated with union membership. The provision builds on earlier collaboration between the two institutions to develop an online course for EIS Union

Learning Representatives (Alexandrou, 2006). The EIS appears to be positioning itself as a potential major provider of CPD in Scotland, but has recognised the benefits of working with established institutions such as Learning Teaching Scotland (LTS) and the universities. There is potential at local level through EIS Learning Representatives for tension with the employing EAs and their systems of CPD provision and it will be interesting to see how the Learning Representative initiative matures. Using ICT to 'deliver' CPD is becoming commonplace, with systems and virtual learning environments (VLEs) such as 'WebCT' and 'Blackboard' dominant with respect to CT provision. Our own institutional experience in offering Module 1 in an online environment is that CT candidates prefer 'face-to-face' learning and the sense of community this involves. This is contrary to the EIS/University of Paisley experience and to the experience of GTCS itself, as the Accreditation Route is supported by a 'Blackboard' system that provides candidates with tasks and prompts in support of their reflection and construction of their portfolio of evidence. Online communities of professional practice and reflection appear to work in that many of the 200+ successful CTs have been involved in some measure with ICT support. Where continuing research is perhaps necessary is in relation to the content-driven provision through VLEs, which may emulate 'traditional' delivery methods and may not harness the potential, nor circumvent the limitations, of such systems.

Conclusion

To date, only a limited number of Scottish teachers have accessed CT provision, and some policy-makers are beginning to query the investment. My own view is that this is a 10 to 15-year project and that once those teachers who have entered the profession since 2003 get to the point of accessing CT provision (after five years of classroom experience) then there will be an increase in numbers coming forward. The reasons for teacher reluctance so far are complex but perhaps reflect the post-McCrone 'flattening' of school management and associated disappointment and resentment; the reality of many promoted teachers with conserved salaries; the personal expense incurred by accessing the CT programme, no matter which route is taken; the natural conservatism of an ageing professional group; or perhaps because of continuing uncertainty about the 'role' of the CT. As noted above, there are no formal responsibilities for a CT, it is a grade of teacher not a post, but there are clear expectations in the Standard for Chartered Teacher that a CT will 'bring to his or her work more sophisticated forms of self-scrutiny, demonstrate a higher capacity for self-evaluation and a marked disposition to be innovative and to improvise' (SEED 2002b). The Standard also confirms that the CT 'will be committed to influencing and having a leading impact in team and school development, and to contribute to the professional development of colleagues' (SEED 2002b). Leadership in learning would appear to be an important facet of any CT, and this will be a test of the processes leading to the award and how CTs subsequently maintain or further develop their enhanced expertise. There is an emerging awareness of the differences between being an expert teacher and being accomplished enough to influence and lead other professionals. For some, the concept of an expert teacher is associated with raising student achievement, and that is often a prevailing notion in developed educational systems, but there is as yet little definitive evidence that standards-based teacher reform actually results in sustained enhanced student achievement.

Hartley (2002: 253) forewarned in a discussion of central controlling pressures associated with standards that 'The "standards movement" in teacher education may beget a pedagogy which is didactic and traditional' and that 'standardisation of teacher education (and of teaching itself) may not produce motivated teachers'. As yet, it is too early to say if the outcomes of the post-McCrone settlement and the influence of the Standards Framework on teacher development and professional learning in Scotland will result in enhanced pedagogy or a reification of the dominant 'best practice' model not necessarily informed by research, debate and experimentation. What of control or empowerment? There is evidence of tension between both of these concepts in the Standard for CT and other standards and in their subsequent implementation and the official hopes for change. The question of post-McCrone re-culturing and teacher professional development remains a fertile area for research, not least because Audit Scotland (2006) has expressed doubts in its recent 'value for money' analysis of the outcomes so far of the teachers' agreement, and castigates the Scottish Executive for not establishing targets at the outset so that achievements could be measured. Who is to say if that were a deliberate strategy to dispense with targets and thus avoid a discredited approach to development, or a device to dissipate any failure to re-culture the teaching profession in Scotland?

Bibliography

Alexandrou, A. (2006) *EIS Learning Representatives: An evaluation of the Educational Institute of Scotland's first cohort of Learning Representatives.* Edinburgh: EIS.

Audit Scotland (2006) *A mid-term report: A first stage review of the cost and implementation of the teachers' agreement A Teaching Profession for the 21st Century.* (Prepared for the Auditor General for Scotland and the Accounts Commission.) Edinburgh: Audit Scotland.

Australian College of Educators (2000) *Standards of Professional Practice for Accomplished Teaching in Australian Classrooms.* Deakin, ACT: ACE.

Boyd, B. (2005) *CPD: Improving professional practice.* Paisley: Hodder Gibson.

Christie, D. (2003) 'Competences, benchmarks and standards in teaching'. In T. Bryce and W. Humes (eds), *Scottish Education,* second edition (post devolution), pp. 952–63. Edinburgh: Edinburgh University Press.

Christie, F. and O'Brien, J. (2005) 'A Continuing Professional Development Framework for Scottish Teachers: steps, stages, continuity or connections?' In A. Alexandrou, K. Field and H. Mitchell (eds), *The Continuing Professional Development of Educators: Emerging European issues*, pp. 93–110. Oxford: Symposium.

Draper, J., and O'Brien, J. (2006) *Induction: Fostering career development at all stages*. Edinburgh: Dunedin Academic Press.

Draper, J., O'Brien, J. and Christie, F. (2004) 'First impressions: the new teacher induction arrangements in Scotland'. *Journal of In-service Education*, 30, 2, 201–23.

Draper, J., Christie, F. and O'Brien, J. (2006) 'Meeting the Standard? The New Teacher Education Induction Scheme in Scotland'. In Townsend, T. and Bates, R. (eds), *Handbook of Teacher Education: Globalization, standards and professionalism in times of change*, pp. 391–406. Dordecht: Springer.

Forde, C., McMahon, M., McPhee, A.D. and Patrick, F. (2006) *Professional Development, Reflection and Enquiry*. London: Paul Chapman.

General Teaching Council for Scotland (2002) *The Standard for Full Registration*. Edinburgh: GTCS.

General Teaching Council for Scotland (2005) *Chartered Teachers Report from Questionnaire. Strategies for the future and general update*. Edinburgh: GTCS.

Hartley, D. (2002) 'Global influences on teacher education in Scotland'. *Journal of Education for Teaching*, 28, 3, 251–5.

Humes, W. (2001) 'Conditions for professional development'. *Scottish Educational Review*, 33, 1, 6–17.

Kennedy, A. (2005) 'Models of Continuing Professional Development: a framework for analysis'. *Journal of In-service Education*, 31, 2, 235–50.

Kirk, G., Beveridge, W. and Smith, I. (2003) *The Chartered Teacher*. Edinburgh: Dunedin Academic Press.

Lee, M. (2004) 'Advanced Skills Teacher'. In H. Green (ed.), *Professional Standards for Teachers and School Leaders: A key to school improvement*, pp.123–39. Abingdon: RoutledgeFalmer.

Livingston, K. and Robertson, J. (2001) 'The coherent system and the empowered individual: continuing professional development for teachers in Scotland'. *European Journal of Teacher Education*, 24, 2, 183–94.

McNally, J. (2003) 'Developments in Teacher Induction in Scotland and implications for the role of higher education'. *Journal of Education for Teaching,* 28, 2, 149–64.

McNally, J., Boreham, N. and Cope, P. (2003) 'Researching Early Professional Learning'. Paper given at the British Educational Research Association Annual Conference, Edinburgh, September 11–13.

Marker, W.B. (1999) 'The professional development of teachers'. In Bryce, T.G.K. and Humes, W. (eds), *Scottish Education.* Edinburgh: Edinburgh University Press.

Menter, I., Mahony, P. and Hextall, I. (2004) 'Ne'er the twain shall meet? Modernizing the Teaching Profession in Scotland and England'. *Journal of Education Policy,* 19, 2, 195–214.

Mooney, G. and Poole, L. (2004) '"A land of milk and honey"? Social policy in Scotland after devolution'. *Critical Social Policy,* 24, 4, 458–83.

Munn, P., Stead, J., McLeod, G., Brown, J., Cowie, M., McCluskey, G., Pirrie, A. and Scott, J. (2004) 'Schools for the 21st century: the national debate on education in Scotland'. *Research Papers in Education,* 19, 4, 433–52.

National Board of Professional Teaching Standards (2002) *The Five Propositions of Accomplished Teaching.* Available at: www.nbpts.org/about/coreprops.cfm (accessed 18 March 2006).

O'Brien, J. (1995) 'Some notes on the Scottish educational system'. In J. O'Brien (ed.), *Current Changes and Challenges in European Teacher Education,* pp. 9–14. Edinburgh: Moray House Institute of Education in association with COMPARE-TE.

O'Brien, J. and Draper, J. (2003) 'Frameworks for CPD: the Chartered Teacher Initiative in Scotland'. *Professional Development Today,* 6 (Winter), 69–75.

O'Brien, J. and Christie, F. (2005) 'Characteristics of support for beginning teachers: evidence from the new induction scheme in Scotland'. *Mentoring and Tutoring,* 13, 2, 191–205.

O'Brien, J. and Hunt, G. (2005) 'A new professionalism? Becoming a Chartered Teacher – part I'. *Teacher Development,* 9, 3, 447–65.

O'Brien, J. and Jones, K. (2005) 'Politics, professionalism and pragmatics: teacher professional development and learning – perspectives from Wales and Scotland'. [OBR05265] *Symposium: International Perspectives on Teachers' Professional Learning: The ways in which it is understood and provided for.* AARE Conference, Paramatta, New South Wales, November. Available at: www.aare.edu.au/05pap/alpha.htm#O (accessed 18 March 2006).

O'Brien, J. and Torrance, D. (2005) 'Professional learning for school principals: developments in Scotland'. *Education Research and Perspectives,* 32, 2, 165–81.

O'Brien, J., Murphy, D. and Draper, J. (2003) *School Leadership.* Edinburgh: Dunedin Academic Press.

Patrick, F., Forde, C. and McPhee, A. (2003) 'Challenging the "New Professionalism": from managerialism to pedagogy?' *Journal of In-service Education,* 29, 2, 237–54.

Pearson, M. and Robson, D. (2005) *Experiences of the Teacher Induction Scheme: Operation, support and CPD.* Edinburgh: GTCS.

Pickard, W. and Dobie, J. (2003) *The Political Context of Education after Devolution.* Edinburgh: Dunedin Academic Press.

Purdon, A. (2003) 'A national framework of CPD: continuing professional development or continuing policy dominance?' *Journal of Education Policy,* 18, 4, 423–37.

Purdon, A. (2004) 'Perceptions of the educational elite on the purpose of a National Framework of Continuing Professional Development (CPD) for teachers in Scotland'. *Journal of Education for Teaching,* 30, 2, 131–49.

Quality Assurance Agency for Higher Education (QAAHE) (2000) *The Standard for Initial Teacher Education in Scotland: Benchmark information.* Gloucester: QAAHE.

Raffe, D. and Byrne, D. (2005) 'Policy learning from "home international" comparisons'. *Briefing 34.* University of Edinburgh: Centre for Educational Sociology. Available at: www.ces.ed.ac.uk/ (accessed 18 March 2006).

Reeves, J., Forde, C., O'Brien, J., Smith, P. and Tomlinson, H. (2002) *Performance Management in Education: Improving practice.* Published in association with BELMAS. London: Paul Chapman.

Ross, H. (1996) 'The management of staff development in Scottish secondary education: 1975 to 1990'. *Scottish Educational Review.* 28, 1, 37–49.

Sachs, J. (2003) *The Activist Teaching Profession.* Buckingham: Open University Press.

Scottish Executive (2003) *A Partnership for a Better Scotland: Partnership agreement* (Scottish Labour Party and Scottish Liberal Democrats). May. Available at: www.scotland.gov.uk/library5/government/pfbs-00.asp (accessed 18 March 2006).

SEED (2000) *A Teaching Profession for the 21st Century* (The report of the Committee of Inquiry into the professional conditions of service of teachers. 'McCrone Report'). Edinburgh: SEED.

SEED (2001) *A Teaching Profession for the 21st Century* (the Agreement based on the McCrone Report) www.scotland.gov.uk/library3/education/tp21a-00.asp (accessed on 18 March 2006).

SEED (2002a) *Continuing Professional Development*. Edinburgh: SEED.

SEED (2002b) *Standard for Chartered Teacher*. Edinburgh: SEED.

SEED (2003) *Continuing Professional Development for Educational Leaders*. Edinburgh: SEED.

SEED (2005) *Ambitious Excellent Schools: The standard for headship*. Edinburgh: SEED.

SOED (1993) *Guidelines for Teacher Training Courses*. Edinburgh: SOED.

SOEID (1998a) *Guidelines for Initial Teacher Education Courses in Scotland*. Edinburgh: SOEID.

SOEID (1998b) *Proposals for Developing a Framework for Continuing Professional Development for the Teaching Profession in Scotland*, Consultation Document. Edinburgh: SOEID.

SOEID (1998c) *Standard for Headship*. Edinburgh: SOEID.

Stronach, I., Cope, P., Inglis, B. and McNally, J. (1994) 'The SOED "Competence" Guidelines for Initial Teacher Training: issues of control, performance and relevance'. *Scottish Educational Review*, 26, 2, 118–33.

Sutherland, S. (1997) 'Report 10: teacher education and training: a study'. In National Committee of Inquiry into Higher Education, *Higher Education in the Learning Society* (The Sutherland Report) Norwich: HMSO.

10 Teacher development

A question(ing) of professionalism
Norbert Pachler
Institute of Education, University of London

Educational policy, teacher professionalism and teachers' professional development

The discussion in this chapter starts from the premise that we live in an era that is characterised by rapid societal and technological change and that, as a central feature of society, schooling and education are invariably affected by what appears at times to be acute pressure for change. With Hoban (2002), it is argued here that professional teacher learning, together with other factors such as school structures, approaches to leadership, political considerations and socio-cultural contexts, etc, is of central importance to educational change.

In the UK, current educational change is, among other things, driven by the Children's Act and the publication by the Department for Education and Skills of the *Five-year strategy for children and learners* (DfES, 2004). The document sets out the following five strategies for systemic transformation of children's services, education and training:

- Greater personalisation and choice, with the wishes and needs of children's services, parents and learners centre-stage;

- Opening up services to new and different providers and ways of delivering services;

- Freedom and independence for front-line headteachers, governors and managers, with clear simple accountabilities and more secure streamlined funding arrangements;

- A major commitment to staff development, with high-quality support and training to improve assessment, care and teaching;

- Partnerships with parents, employers, volunteers and voluntary organisations to maximise the life chances of children, young people and adults.

In view of proposals for such fundamental educational change (cf. the Every Child Matters and Workforce Remodelling agendas), it comes as little surprise that Bentley (2003: 11) argues for different organisations with different functions. He also notes that there is a need for these organisations to work together systematically and across boundaries between health, housing and learning.

> It also requires resilient institutions to interact far more creatively with the resources – social, economic, cultural and knowledge-based – that surround them in local communities. It is the combination of individual behaviour, social context and formal organisational process that produces a radically improved outcome.

This fundamental change, it is argued here, also raises significant questions for teacher professionalism.

In his paper on teacher professionalism (2002: 11), Whitty asks what type of teacher professionalism is appropriate for 'new times'. Through his sociological perspective on teacher professionalism (2002: 7), he reminds us of Hoyle's (1974) distinction between 'professionalism', 'those strategies and rhetorics employed by members of an occupation in seeking to improve status, salary and conditions' and 'professionality' – the 'knowledge, skills and procedures employed by teachers in the process of teaching'. Furthermore, he notes Hoyle's distinction between 'restricted' and 'extended' notions of teacher professionality. A look at recent literature on teacher development suggests that Hoyle's terminology still enjoys popularity (see e.g. Evans, 2002).

Later work with John (Hoyle and John, 1995) suggests that debates around teacher professionalism invariably focus around knowledge, autonomy and responsibility. Furlong *et al.* (2000: 4–6) discuss Hoyle and John's perceptions of teacher professionalism and stress the importance of possession of technical or specialist knowledge 'that is beyond the reach of lay people'. They also foreground the need and ability to exercise professional judgement in complex and unpredictable situations in relation to their own and their clients' interests. According to Hargreaves (1994: 9), traditional notions of professionalism – characterised by esoteric knowledge, specialist expertise and public status – are being superseded by an emphasis on 'discretionary judgement within conditions of unavoidable and perpetual uncertainty'.

Neo-liberalism, neo-conservatism and managerialism are arguably the order of the day; trust in the professions is seemingly on the decrease. And there is a trend towards 'commercialised' modes of professionalism (Hanlon, 1998) and a 'marketised culture of schooling' (Whitty, 2002).

> The new forms of accountability impose forms of *central control* – quite often indeed a *range of different and mutually inconsistent* forms of central control. Some of the new modes of public accountability are in fact internally incoherent. Some of them set targets that cannot be combined without fudging: for example, universities are soon to be told to admit 50% of the age group, but also to maintain current standard. Others are incoherent because they require that targets be achieved by following processes that do not dovetail with targets and can't be made to dovetail with those targets. Again, universities are to treat each applicant fairly on the basis of ability and promise: but they are supposed also to admit a socially more representative intake. There's no guarantee that the process meets the target ... Schools are to prevent classroom disruption: but they are not to exclude disruptive pupils ... Incompatible or barely compatible requirements *invite* compromises

and evasions; they undermine both professional judgement and institutional autonomy.

(O'Neill, 2002: 4)

Consequently, at the beginning of the twenty-first century, government-sponsored notions of extended professionalism focus on managerialism rather than social welfare models, and teachers find themselves caught up between the aspirations of the state and traditional notions of professionality.

The question arises how these tensions impact on teachers' professional development. Patrick *et al.* (2003: 237), in their examination of 'new professionalism', argue that teacher development 'must move from technicist emphases to a model that integrates the social processes of change within society and schools with the individual development and empowerment of teachers'. They posit that this development must start at the stage of initial teacher education (ITE), which is currently characterised by a tension between 'education' and 'training'. They, rightly, go on to ask whether continuing professional development (CPD) should be predicated on a functionalist training model or on a model based on the facilitation of critical reflection and enquiry as a basis for pedagogical excellence. According to them, concomitant tensions exist around accountability and performativity versus professional autonomy and CPD that is undertaken willingly or compelled (p. 238). In their view (p. 240), ITE in the UK – including the period of probation which is called 'induction' – currently stresses:

a specific and simplistic conception of professionalism: firstly, that the professional is one who is competent and develops excellence only in respect of measurable pre-defined standards; and secondly, that professional skills can be described readily, defined meaningfully and delivered through simple transfer (with values, attitudes, knowledge and understanding being classed as subsets of general teaching skills).

And they express the fear that CPD is following this tendency.

To a considerable extent CPD in the UK has in recent years been linked to the so-called Standards Framework (currently under review),[1] which is located within a competence-based approach to teaching along managerialist interpretations of leadership and school effectiveness, setting out detailed characteristics and descriptions of the skills and behaviours required in order to perform teaching roles at different stages of development.

> Continuous professional development has all too often been little more than an eclectic and unrelated assortment of in-service training events, narrowly focused on frequently changing policy initiatives and externally imposed agendas, pieced together reactively by individual teachers in response to extrinsic priorities rather than sought out proactively according to intrinsic training needs. In other words, the notion of *training* has prevailed which tended to be informed by the need to seek information about how to comply with changes in legislation or demands made by school development plans rather than gain a deeper understanding of issues concerning subject pedagogy or pupil learning. Significant and frequent changes to the educational landscape have meant that there has been little time for teacher professional learning about embedding new approaches, techniques, skills, knowledge, understanding and/or insights into personal practice.
>
> (Pachler *et al.*, 2003: 9)

In addition, this piecemeal or 'injection' approach to CPD can be seen to countervail attempts to redefine teacher professionalism in so far at least as it tends to be based on and constructed to operationalise prescriptions made by others as well as on performativity, for example the current preoccupation with impact measures and managed delivery of national strategies and frameworks. Also, it leaves little scope for theory-informed approaches which articulate with specific conceptualisations of teacher learning and personalised development agendas and for approaches that are characterised by an emphasis on values, attitudes, a social agenda and personal change. In other words, it is not conducive to the three main types of teacher development delineated by Bell and Gilbert (1994), namely personal, professional and social.

Teachers' professional development can be seen to be key in achieving extended professionalism but, as Evans rightly notes (2002: 124), the process of transformation from a 'restricted' to an 'extended' professional is less than clear. One aim of this chapter is to explore aspects of this transition and how it can be brought about. In order to achieve this, and in an attempt to secure conceptual clarity, it seems necessary to explore definitional bases here. Evans (p. 130), for example, defines professionality as 'an ideologically-, attitudinally-, intellectually- and epistemologically-based stance on the part of an individual, in relation to the practice of the profession to which s/he belongs, and which influences his/her professional practice'. She goes on to define teacher development as 'the process whereby teachers' professionality and/or professionalism may be considered to be enhanced' (p. 131) and she distinguishes attitudinal and functional development. Here the question arises whether attitudinal and functional, i.e. performance-related, development follows the same processes. Furthermore, Evans deems development to incorporate change 'that would generally be categorised as learning' (p. 132).

Professional development: some issues and initiatives

When the Labour Government came to power in 1997, its central policies revolved around 'education, education, education'. Education was hailed as *the* single most important factor for the nation's growth and development. What has followed is a period of intense change for the teaching profession.

For present purposes, one significant development was the publication in 2001 of a strategy for CPD aimed at 'giving teachers increased opportunities for relevant, focused, effective professional development, and to place professional development at the heart of school improvement' (Department for Education and Employment, 2001: 3), predominantly by developing school-based approaches. This has been followed by the development of online support in the form of the TeacherNet website.[2] Relevant information can also be found on the TDA website.[3] In addition to detailed information about the so-called Standards Framework, which maps out the various different standards that apply at the different stages of a teacher's career from ITE, through Induction to Threshold, Advanced Skills Teacher and Headteacher, it also includes resources which aim to guide visitors to the website through possible professional development routes. In their totality the standards comprise a worrying array of behavioural descriptors and competencies, closely linked to statutory and non-statutory government requirements and frameworks. In the proposed revised standards there will also be descriptors for so-called Excellent Teachers. In small print they fill a poster-size document and set out what is expected of teachers across the following elements:

- knowledge and understanding
- planning and setting expectations
- teaching and managing pupil learning
- assessment and evaluation
- pupil achievement
- relations with parents and the wider community
- managing own performance and development
- managing and developing staff and other adults
- managing resources; and
- strategic leadership.

In 2004, the Secretary of State for Education handed an extended remit to the Teacher Training Agency, now the Training and Development Agency for Schools, to bring 'improved national coherence' (Clarke, 2004) to CPD.

Overall, the standards can *inter alia* be seen to be prescriptive and seeking to impose a particular normative view of core professional values, knowledge and skills, and to be too prolific in scope in order to be covered satisfactorily in the time available (see also Lambert and Pachler, 2002: 228). They are predicated on a view of teachers as technicians and curriculum 'deliverers' 'whose task is to inculcate a narrow core of knowledge, the attainment of which, it is assumed, will result in quality of education' (Reid and O'Donoghue, 2004: 562). Among other things, such an approach not only takes little to no account of the provisional nature of knowledge – other than by way of regular revision – and it sits ill at ease with the diverse range of capabilities needed to navigate our globalising, 'post-modern' world characterised to a large extent by uncertainty and rapid change. In particular, they take little account of the inter-agency dimension of teachers' work, i.e. the need increasingly not only to work across subject discipline boundaries but also across traditional boundaries of education and care professions. Reid and O'Donoghue (2004: 563) point out that lists of standards tend to remain fixed and 'ossify' rather than being dynamic and open to change, which is at odds with the requirements of a knowledge society. In addition, but unsurprisingly, the standards agenda tends not to be driven by specific theoretical or conceptual insights but by political and/or ideological/anti-intellectual considerations in so far at least as ITE and teachers' CPD are important mechanisms through which policy agendas can be realised (see also Reid and O'Donoghue, 2004: 559).

In 2003, the Organisation for Economic Co-operation and Development (OECD), together with the Centre for Educational Research and Innovation (CERI), inaugurated a forum on 'Schooling for Tomorrow' (see www.oecd.org) holding periodic conferences for international exchange on matters of educational policy-making and practice in the context of the growing complexity of societies. Among other things, the work of the forum has led to the development of future schooling scenarios. Three main scenarios have been developed, each comprising two sub-scenarios:

1 Attempting to maintain the status quo – school systems seek to resist pressures to change
   a Bureaucratic school system continues
   b Teacher exodus – the 'meltdown scenario'

2 Re-schooling – major reform and renewal of schools
   a Schools as core social centres
   b Schools as focused learning organisations

3 De-schooling – widespread disestablishment of school systems
   a Learning networks and the network society
   b Extending the market model.

Irrespective of whether any of these specific scenarios will become a reality or whether they come into being in the way envisioned by the OECD and CERI, there are clear implications for teacher education and teachers' professional development from this work. Even if the current status quo is maintained, rapid changes in society will increase the tension between current conceptualisations of education and schooling and what is required in order to meet the needs of young people of the future. It is argued here that schools will sooner rather than later have to face up to the challenges of the so-called knowledge economy and society. Information and communications technologies (ICTs) have a significant role to play in meeting these challenges; but a detailed discussion of this role would go well beyond the scope of this chapter. Suffice it to note here that they have at least two leverage points, namely that of provider of information as well as of an infrastructure for collaboration (see e.g. Goldman, 2001).

Hargreaves reminds us (2003: 21) of Revans's Law which states that 'for an organisation to prosper, its rate of learning must be at least equal to the rate of change in the external environment'. Scardamalia and Bereiter (1999) make the point that although schools are learning organisations in the sense that they promote learning, few would meet the definition of learning organisations to be found in organisational theory: 'Indeed, from an organizational standpoint schools are often seen as bureaucratic institutions particularly resistant to the kind of purposeful change from within that characterizes learning organisations' (p. 274).

Scardamalia and Bereiter envisage two ways in which schools could develop into learning organisations in the sense envisaged by organisational theory: an overhaul in management and the organisation of work in order to perform traditional functions better, or a more radical transformation in which the functions of the school are changed. Option one, for them, would involve a reduction in the layers of management, with teachers being given greater responsibilities and being more involved in corporate decision-making. The second option is to reconfigure what is taught and learnt in schools and how it is taught and learnt in line with the requirements of life in a knowledge society through experience. In order to achieve this, they posit, the role of students has to change fundamentally from that of clients to members and workers. In other words, Scardamalia and Bereiter propose a change in the function of schools 'from that of service provider to that of a productive enterprise to which the students are contributors' (p. 275). To achieve this, they argue, a collaborative knowledge-building approach is required where 'the basic job to be done shifts from learning to the construction of collective knowledge' (pp. 275–6).

Scardamalia and Bereiter are quick to point out that problem- and project-based learning are insufficiently 'radical' in nature to achieve this transformation; problem-based learning, because it tends to consist of work on set and fictitious rather than real knowledge problems, and project-based learning because it tends to focus on the production of tangible products rather than on knowledge itself (p. 278). In terms of teacher education and teacher professional development, key implications arise in relation to shifting educators' conception of knowledge as 'stuff in the mind' to 'knowledge as resource or knowledge as product, as something that can be created and improved, bought or sold, discarded as obsolete or found to have new uses' (p. 276).

Hargreaves argues that what is needed is a move away from the traditional input-process-output model of effective schools, which emphasises schools' agency in making a difference despite social and economic conditions. He (2003: 24–6) holds that what is needed is a deeper understanding of the cultural and structural underpinnings and he puts forward a conceptual framework which explains the quality of a school in terms of its intellectual, social and organisational capital. Innovation in education, in his view (p. 27), comes through the creation of new professional knowledge and means that education professionals 'learn to do things differently in order to do them better'. Professional development can be seen to have a key role to play in this process.

One teacher development initiative responding to these challenges has been implemented in recent years by the National College for School Leadership (NCSL) in the form of networked learning communities (NLCs). There is not the space here to engage in detail with the conceptual and theoretical discussion underpinning the notion of networks or learning communities. Suffice it to note that the approach sponsored by the NCSL can be seen to only do partial justice to it at least in terms of the model of learning upon which it is predicated. Butler *et al.* (2004: 436), for example, argue for an analytical theory of learning 'that encompasses the social and the individual without oversimplifying the contribution of either, and that explains individual and collective development in the context of learning communities'. The documentation about the NLCs currently available lacks a detailed engagement with attendant conceptual and theoretical work in the field of learning communities beyond brief references. Importantly also, the NCSL does not set out a detailed conceptual and theoretical framework for the learning processes underpinning its NLCs beyond a vague notion of the main knowledge bases and so-called levels of learning involved. Indeed, the implementation of NLCs is accompanied by a research programme which intends to determine how individual networks develop and what networked learning (activities) might look like.

The NLCs of the NCSL aim to establish mutual support among clusters of schools (six plus, average of ten), local authorities (LAs) and universities through collaborative enquiry. The NLCs programme, match-funded to the tune of £50,000 per network per year over four years, 'aims to transform schools into learning organisations, capable not just of doing what they currently do better or responding more effectively to current demands and environment, but of generating a capacity for continuous innovation, adaptation, problem generation and recreation' (NCSL, no date).

According to McGregor *et al.* (2004), NLCs are characterised by four non-negotiable design principles:

- moral purpose;
- shared leadership;
- enquiry-based practice; and
- systematic engagements with three fields of knowledge: what we know (the knowledge of those involved); what is known (the knowledge from theory, research and best practice); and new knowledge (the new knowledge to be created together).

They note that networked learning operates mostly through particular activities such as:

- collective planning;

- joint work groups;

- joint problem-solving;

- shared CPD; and

- collaborative enquiry groups.

Apart from the seemingly high level of prescription imposed by the NCSL, another concern about the programme is the fact, as the promotional literature makes clear, that one important level of learning within NLCs is the notion of leadership for learning and leadership development. In other words, the programme 'seeks to invest in the capacity of headteachers, network leaders and other leaders within schools to create the enabling and facilitating conditions for networked learning' (NCSL, no date). This sounds barely distinguishable to us from the managerialist discourse of recent years.

The missing links

The approach to CPD for teachers, as conceived by the UK Government, is not without tensions and, at least to some extent, at odds with extended notions of teacher professionality, be they defined more traditionally in relation to depth of subject knowledge and specialist pedagogical expertise or less traditionally with reference to teachers' ability to cope with uncertainty and change. On the basis of the evidence examined here, Whitty's assertion (2002: 18) that 'teacher education on the ground remains something of a compromise between the aspirations of the state and those of the profession' is very true.

In view of the various initiatives and developments sketched out above, government policy in relation to CPD aims to have a profound effect upon teachers' identities and work practices, in particular in terms of their 'effectiveness' and in terms of the impact on their work, whatever that may mean and however it may be defined. In Whitty's terms (2002: 11), the state can be seen to be preparing key professionals for leadership in the new marketised culture of schooling and to be trying to prevent others 'from perpetuating an outmoded social service version of professionalism even if they cannot be won to the new agenda'. There can be seen to exist a particular tension between teachers as autonomous professionals and teachers as delivery agents of central government initiatives such as, for example, the Key Stage 3 framework. Nevertheless, the NLCs initiative seems to us to point in the right direction.

The UK Government's CPD strategy (DfEE, 2001: 12) identifies the maxim 'learning from each other ... learning from what works' as summarising the type of approach it wants to encourage. Whilst the Government's commitment to a CPD strategy and the collaborative orientation of what is aimed for are commendable, the 'what works' and 'good practice' agendas that they are predicated on are hugely problematical. With Edge and Richards (1998: 569) we hold that the notion of 'best practice' is 'an illegitimate importation from an inappropriate paradigm and that its use threatens to undermine the very values that its proponents espouse'. The 'good practice' or 'best practice' discourse is underpinned by an assumption that what works well for one teacher with a particular educational biography, values, methodological position, particular characteristics, working in one specific socio-political context at a particular point in time will necessarily work equally well for another teacher with different characteristics working in a different context, etc. Moreover, the discourse implies that there exists a best way of achieving specific goals and that this best way can be made generally available. This, Edge and Richards argue, is delusional on at least three counts:

1   Characterising individual accounts of practice as best undermines the status of particular understanding by holding out the prospect of general application.

2   By emphasising the status of particular practices, best practice downplays the importance of the individuals concerned ... Furthermore, only the successful voices ... are heard, and their presence in this form can serve as much to undermine the confidence of teachers as to encourage them.

3   (Like) ritual magic, it is not open to challenge: best practice is by definition best, so any failure to achieve it arises not as a result of flaws in its own constitutions but because the correct procedures are not being followed or the teacher has the wrong attitude.... Unchecked, it leads to the de-skilling of teachers, who are seen as technicians responsible for learning-delivery systems.... It leads to the establishment of orthodoxies suitable to education's political masters.

(Edge and Richards 1998: 570–1)

Yet, in view of the impossibility and impracticability of all schools and all teachers innovating on all fronts, not only is there a need for prioritisation in order to avoid innovation overload, but there is also a need for innovation transfer: '... every school re-inventing the wheel would be a prodigious waste of time and energy' (Hargreaves, 2003: 38). Hargreaves distinguishes two kinds of innovation, front-line innovation and levelling-up (p. 39). By front-line innovation he means primary involvement in the generation of new ideas and knowledge creation processes and testing them out; by levelling-up he means learning from others and adoption of second-hand practices. What is needed, he argues, is a system that is conducive to what he calls 'transferred innovation', i.e. a system in which schools transfer so-called good practices that possess high leverage, are credible and have a low level of 'stickiness' (p. 50). Hargreaves views practitioner-champions as particularly important in the transfer process. We consider collaborative, enquiry-based approaches to teacher education and professional development to play a central role in this respect.

There is a need for a professional development framework that takes account of the above and is based on notions of teacher agency and a re-professionalisation of teaching based around a focus on learning, participation, collaboration, co-operation and activism (Sachs, 2003: 30–5). First, Sachs's position foregrounds the importance of learning. With reference to Wenger (1998: 2) she stresses the transformational potential of learning who we are and what we can do. As such, learning affects teachers' identity and goes well beyond the accumulation of skills and information. Implicit in effective learning is active participation by teachers in attendant processes through collaboration, co-operation and collegiality. By activism Sachs refers to teachers' moral purpose of teaching and education which requires of them intellectual and political engagement as well as risk-taking.

Some of the Master's level provision at the Institute of Education, University of London, notably the Master of Teaching, is promoting these fundamentals in the context of a reciprocal, symbiotic relationship between practice and intellectual reflection referenced to relevant conceptual and theoretical frameworks and supported by electronic forums (see e.g. Lambert and Pachler, 2002; Pachler *et al.* 2003; Daly *et al.*, 2004). Also, the Institute is currently in the process of re-modelling its ITE programme and aims to strengthen collaborative, enquiry-based processes. Reid and O'Donoghue (2004: 565–6) identify two major obstacles to enquiry-based approaches to ITE: a considerable weight of institutional inertia in schools and an imbalance of authority between students and their mentors as well as rhetoric often not being matched by reality. They conclude that the answer lies in the establishment of communities of enquiry.

In view of this and with reference to Whitty's notion of a need for collectivist forms of association 'as a counter-balance not only to the prerogative of the state, but also to the prerogative of the market' (2002: 24–5), we want to discuss briefly the merits of three particular approaches to the professional development of teachers, namely the notions of 'productive pedagogy' (Gore *et al.*, 2004), 'case-based learning' (Shulman, 1996) as well as 'inquiry as a stance' (Cochran-Smith, 2003; Cochran-Smith and Lytle, 2001). These three approaches, and their theoretical underpinnings, can be seen to have the potential to show the way in the transformation from restricted to extended notions of professionalism; to respond to the challenge of relating professional development to experience and professional practice whilst at the same time providing strong links to conceptual and theoretical integrity; and to address the challenges facing the education system in times of unprecedented change.

The notion of productive pedagogy, which was developed by the Queensland School Reform Longitudinal Study research team (QSRLS, 2001), appeals particularly with a view to injecting much-needed intellectual rigour into ITE. It provides an analytical framework and consists of 20 items across four dimensions as well as key associated questions (see Table 10.1).

Table 10.1 Productive Pedagogy

Intellectual quality

Higher order thinking	Are higher order thinking and critical analysis occurring?
Deep knowledge	Does the lesson cover operational fields in any depth, detail or level of specificity?
Deep understanding	Do the work and response of the students provide evidence of understanding of concepts or ideas?
Substantive conversation	Does classroom talk break out of the initiate/respond/evaluate pattern and lead to sustained dialogue between students, and between teachers and students?
Knowledge problematic	Are students critiquing and second-guessing texts, ideas and knowledge?
Metalanguage	Are aspects of language, grammar and technical vocabulary being foregrounded?

Relevance

Knowledge integration	Does the lesson range across diverse fields, disciplines and paradigms?
Background knowledge	Is there an attempt to connect with students' background knowledge?
Connectedness to the world	Do lessons and the assigned work have any resemblance or connection to real-life contexts?
Problem-based curriculum	Is there a focus on identifying and solving intellectual and/or real-world problems?

Supportive classroom environment

Student control	Do students have any say in the pace, direction or outcome of the lesson?
Social support	Is the classroom a socially supportive, positive environment?
Engagement	Are students engaged and on-task?
Explicit criteria	Are criteria for student performance made explicit?
Self-regulation	Is the direction of student behaviour implicit and self-regulatory, or explicit?

Recognition of difference

Cultural knowledges	Are diverse cultural knowledges brought into play?
Inclusivity	Are deliberate attempts made to increase the participation of all students of different backgrounds?
Narrative	Is the teaching principally narrative, or is it expository?
Group identity	Does teaching build a sense of community and identity?
Citizenship	Are attempts made to foster active citizenship?

Source: QSRLS, 2001

The four principles can be seen to align broadly with academic, personal, social efficiency and social reconstructionist agendas and require a deep understanding on the part of the beginning teacher 'of important concepts through meaningful learning experiences that occur in an environment that supports learning and values diversity' (Gore *et al.*, 2004: 376). Among other things, such an approach makes increased intellectual demands on teachers and their pupils. It requires a focus on processes as well as content, and an engagement with foundation disciplines as well as a re-evaluation of the purpose and structure of practical teaching experience. And, of course, it has considerable implications in relation to teacher development.

Case-based learning, which has been promoted for ITE in the USA since the 1990s by Shulman (1996) and which to some extent is used on the Master of Teaching, also has a lot to offer, particularly a revised version of his organisational principles (1996: 202–3) which incorporates the use of new, digital video technologies and uses multimodal accounts and instantiations of particular situations and issues. Shulman (1996: 199) argues that cases, which make use of the power of narrative – following Bruner (1986) he considers narration an account of the vicissitudes of human intention – are by definition situated in place, time and subject matter rather than generic. Cases 'serve as the building blocks for professional reasoning, professional discourse, and professional memory'. In other words, they can stimulate broader conversations within learning communities. And cases are ways of 'parsing' and 'chunking' experience so that practitioners can examine and learn from it and use such units for critical reflection. This emphasis on the practical dimensions of teaching, whilst possessing a clear theoretical underpinning, offers a useful complement to school-based experience which is not always as carefully structured and scaffolded as it needs to be in order to lead to meaningful learning experiences. Shulman's (1996: 208) maxim that 'we don't learn from experience; we learn by thinking about our experience' suggests that multimodal cases, authored by (beginning) teachers offer fruitful triggers for professional thinking.

In relation to what Lieberman and Miller (1994) have called 'culture-building', rather than skills training, Cochran-Smith and Lytle (Cochran Smith, 2003; Cochran-Smith and Lytle, 2001) propose the development of an enquiry stance on teaching which is transformative and critical and which is linked not only to standards but also to social conscience and professional growth. This approach also holds significant promise for ITE and professional development in order to facilitate the transition from restricted to extended professionalism. Cochran-Smith and Lytle see the concept of 'inquiry as stance' located in a 'knowledge-of-practice' paradigm – as opposed to one of 'knowledge-for-practice' and 'knowledge-in-practice'. They see knowledge-making as a pedagogic act and they deem the enquiry approach to allow teachers, by working in collaboration with peers, to make their own knowledge and practice and that of peers problematic. Cochran-Smith and Lytle (2001: 48) start from the premise that:

> the knowledge teachers need to teach well is generated when teachers treat their own classrooms and schools as sites for intentional investigation at the same time as they treat the knowledge and theory produced by others as generative material for interrogation and interpretation.

Networks, in which teachers combine their efforts to construct knowledge, are viewed as the main structural vehicle for teacher development. Cochran-Smith and Lytle (2001: 49) interpret stance as a disposition which makes different perspectives visible and problematic. Through these perspectives research questions are framed, as are the positions teachers take towards knowledge and how knowledge relates to practice, as well as towards the purposes of schooling. They distinguish 'inquiry as a stance' from more 'traditional' notions of enquiry, which in their estimation mostly take the form of 'time-bounded projects'. Enquiry as a stance, on the other hand, is a social and political act of 'working together within communities to generate local knowledge, envision and theorise their practice, and interpret and interrogate the theory and research of others' (p. 51). Central to the difference between 'traditional' and 'alternative' approaches for Cochran-Smith and Lytle (p. 53) is the perspective on knowledge. Enquiry as a stance is predicated on a conception of teacher knowledge which does not imply certainty, expertise and 'state-of-the-art' or 'best' practice. It avoids expert–novice distinctions as they can be seen to perpetuate an 'in-the-head' model of professional development which focuses on individuals and their differences instead of common intellectual projects. The searching for significant questions becomes as important as problem-solving. Key questions include (p. 52):

- Who am I as a teacher?

- What am I assuming about this child, this group, this community?

- What sense are my students making of what's going on in the classroom?

- How do the frameworks and research of others inform my own understandings?

- What are the underlying assumptions of these materials, texts, tests, curriculum frameworks, and school reporting documents?

- What am I trying to make happen here, and why?

- How do my efforts as an individual teacher connect to the efforts of the community and to larger agendas for schools and social change?

Key processes involved in the transformation from restricted to extended professionalism, therefore, appear to be engagement in teacher development which is characterised by: non self-referential reflection, i.e. reflection which goes beyond what one might call navel-gazing by making explicit reference to relevant conceptual and theoretical background reading and/or the experiential bases of peers; hypotheses formulation, testing and refining; and participation in (online) learning communities and practice-based enquiry.

Conclusion

This chapter has argued that the 'new times' we live in require new notions of teacher professionalism and new forms of professional education and development. The future can be seen to lie in democratic and discursive, i.e. collaborative, notions of professionalism (Whitty, 2002: 23–5). In a recent paper emanating from the medical world, the model of professionalism envisaged here is aptly described as 'involved professionalism' (Boyasak *et al.*, 2004). Table 10.2 compares the model of involved professionalism with the traditional and market models and stresses the importance of the 'sociality' of decision-making, knowledge and learning. It is this notion of 'involvedness' in professional teams and activities through enquiry as a stance that we consider to be central to the re-professionalisation of teaching at the beginning of the twenty-first century.

Table 10.2 Characteristics of different models of professionalism

	Traditional professionalism	New professionalism	Involved professionalism
View of learning	Learning is an individual process	Learning is an individual process	Learning is a social process
Professional activity	Decision-making about the nature of professional activity belongs in the hands of professionals	Professional activity needs to be organised by professional managers	Professional activity is a set of relationships between self (professionals) and the products of professional practice (i.e. research/ theory). This makes up the context of professional practice
Quality measures	Quality is determined by professional knowledge	Competency can be measured through performance criteria	Quality through professional development by intentional engagement and dialogue with the social, historical and ethical context of professional practice
Organisation	Professions organised according to their own disciplinary structures	Increased specialisation and fragmentation sees professions organised by generic structures	Professions organised according to their own disciplinary structures, but open to influence from stakeholders and through dialogue with related disciplines

Notes

1 See www.teachernet.gov.uk/professionaldevelopment/
2 Available at: www.teachernet.gov.uk/
3 See www.tda.gov.uk/teachers/professionalstandards.aspx

References

Bell, B. and Gilbert, J. (1994) 'Teacher development as professional, personal, and social development'. *Teaching and Teacher Education,* 10, 5, 483–97.

Bentley, T. (2003) 'Foreword'. In D. Hargreaves (ed.), *Education Epidemic. Transforming secondary schools through innovative networks.* London: DEMOS, pp. 9–16.

Boyask, D., Boyask, R. and Wilkinson, T. (2004) 'Pathways to "involved professionalism": making processes of professional acculturation intentional and transparent'. *Medical Education Online 9.*

Bruner, J. (1986) *Actual Minds, Possible Worlds.* Cambridge, MA: Harvard University Press.

Butler, D., Lauscher, H., Jarvis-Selinger, S. and Beckingham, B. (2004) 'Collaboration and self-regulation in teachers' professional development'. *Teaching and Teacher Education,* 20, 5, 435–55.

Clarke, C. (2004) 'Clarke sets out plans for high quality professional development for teachers'. Available at: www.dfes.gov.uk/pns/DisplayPN.cgi?pn_id=2004_0154

Cochran-Smith, M. (2003) 'Learning and unlearning: the education of teacher educators'. *Teaching and Teacher Education,* 19, 5–28.

Cochran-Smith, M. and Lytle, S. (2001) 'Beyond certainty: taking an inquiry stance on practice'. In A. Lieberman and L. Miller (eds), *Teachers Caught in the Action. Professional development that matters.* New York: Teachers College, Columbia University, pp. 45–58.

Daly, C., Pachler, N. and Lambert, D. (2004) 'Teacher learning: towards a professional academy'. *Teaching in Higher Education,* 9, 1, 99–111.

Department for Education and Employment (DfEE) (2001) *Learning and Teaching. A strategy for professional development.* London: TSO.

Department for Education and Skills (DfES) (2004) *Five year strategy for children and learners. Putting people at the heart of public services.* London: DfES. Available at: www.dfes.gov.uk/publications/5yearstrategy/

Edge, J. and Richards, K. (1998) 'Why best practice is not good enough'. *TESOL Quarterly,* 32, 3, 569–76.

Evans, L. (2002) 'What is teacher development?' *Oxford Review of Education,* 28, 1, 123–37.

Furlong, J., Barton, L., Miles, S., Whiting, C. and Whitty, G. (2000) *Teacher Education in Transition. Re-forming professionalism?* Buckingham: Open University Press.

Goldman, S. (2001) 'Professional development in a digital age: issues and challenges for standards-based reform'. In D. Boesel (ed.), *Continuing Professional Development. Improving teacher quality: imperative for education reform.* National Library of Education: Office of Educational Research and Improvement, US Department of Education, pp. 117–43.

Gore, J., Griffiths, T. and Ladwig, J. (2004) 'Towards better teaching: productive pedagogy as a framework for teacher education'. *Teaching and Teacher Development,* 20, 4, 375–87.

Hanlon, G. (1998) 'Professionalism as enterprise: service class politics and the redefinition of professionalism'. *Sociology,* 32, 1, 43–63.

Hargreaves, A. (1994) *Changing Teachers, Changing Times: Teachers' work and culture in the postmodern age.* London: Cassell.

Hargreaves, D. (2003) *Education Epidemic. Transforming secondary schools through innovation networks.* London: Demos.

Hoban, G. (2002) *Teacher Learning for Educational Change.* Buckingham: Open University Press.

Hoyle, E. (1974) 'Professionality, professionalism and control in teaching'. *London Education Review,* 3, 2, 13–19.

Hoyle, E. and John, P. (1995) *Professional Knowledge and Professional Practice.* London: Cassell.

Lambert, D. and Pachler, N. (2002) 'Teacher education in the United Kingdom'. *Metodika,* 3, 5, 221–33.

Lieberman, A. and Miller, L. (1994) 'Problems and possibilities of institutionalizing teacher research'. In S. Hollingsworth and H. Socket (eds), *Teacher Research and Educational Reform*. Chicago: University of Chicago Press, pp. 204–20.

McGregor, J., Holmes, D and Temperley, J. (2004) 'Collaborative enquiry in networked learning communities'. Paper presented at the British Educational Research Association Annual Conference, Manchester.

National College for School Leadership (NCSL) (no date) *Networked Learning Communities*. Cranfield.

O'Neill, O. (2002) 'Called to account'. Reith Lectures 2002. Available at: www.bbc.co.uk/radio4/reith2002.

Pachler, N., Daly, C. and Lambert, D. (2003) 'Teacher learning: reconceptualising the relationship between theory and practical teaching in Masters level course development'. In Proceedings *Forum Quality Assurance in Distance-Learning and E-learning: International Quality Benchmarks in Postgraduate Education*. Krems, Austria, May 2002, pp. 7–25.

Patrick, F., Forde, C. and McPhee, A. (2003) 'Challenging the "new professionalism": from managerialism to pedagogy?' *Journal of In-service Education*, 29, 2, 237–53.

Queensland School Reform Longitudinal Study (QSRLS) (2001) *School Reform Longitudinal Study*. Brisbane: The State of Queensland (Department of Education).

Reid, A. and O'Donoghue, M. (2004) 'Revisiting enquiry-based teacher education in neo-liberal times'. *Teaching and Teacher Education*, 20, 6, 559–70.

Sachs, J. (2003) *The Activist Teaching Profession*. Buckingham: Open University Press.

Scardamalia, M. and Bereiter, C. (1999) 'Schools as knowledge-building organizations'. In D. Keating and C. Hertzman (eds), *Today's Children, Tomorrow's Society: The developmental health and wealth of nations*. New York: Guilford, pp. 274–89.

Shulman, L. (1996) 'Just in case: reflections on learning from experience'. In J. Colbert, K. Trimble and P. Desberg (eds), *The Case for Education. Contemporary approaches for using case methods*. Boston: Allyn and Bacon, pp. 197–217.

Wenger, E. (1998) *Communities of Practice. Learning, meaning and identity.* Cambridge: Cambridge University Press.

Whitty, G. (2002) 'Teacher professionalism in new times'. In W. Chyuan Hsieh and S.M. Lee-Wen (eds), *School Management and Leadership.* Taiwan: Hung Yeh Publishing.

Conclusion

Jon Pickering, Caroline Daly and Norbert Pachler
Institute of Education, University of London

The chapters in this book point to a concept of professional learning that is based on the belief systems of teachers. Developing beliefs about learning and teaching involves inevitable struggle for teachers whose practice is located within existing frameworks. The teachers we discuss in these chapters reflect both the potential conflicts and generative synergies between the different types of knowledge they encounter – between 'academic' and 'workplace' knowledge, and between the informal and formal professional discourses on which they draw in a Master's-level online environment. Our focus has been to analyse the transformative effects of new designs for continuing professional development (CPD) which oppose false dichotomies between 'theory' and 'practice', but this is a learning process for all involved. Through our practitioner research, it is possible to have a dialogue with fellow CPD providers and more fully understand the 'newness' of these ways of working. Together we have begun to address new concepts of teachers' knowledge and to identify new CPD pedagogies, which include harnessing the affordances of technologies and collaborative networks for learning. This is a learning process for higher education (HE) and other CPD practitioners as well as teachers – together we are exploring what these new designs have to offer teachers and how to develop courses that meet their needs in contemporary contexts.

A newly designed approach to CPD should focus on three key

themes which have emerged from the research findings and research-informed practice of contributors to this book. They work in combination, not as discrete elements, and reflect the broader shift towards co-constructed teacher knowledge which is at the centre of a range of research in CPD, both in the UK and abroad (e.g. Sachs, 2003a, b; Street and Temperley, 2005). These are:

- shared practice;

- collaborative learning networks; and

- scholarly reflection on practice.

Running through these key themes are the affordances of new technologies to bring about a new kind of learning.

These new designs might appear self-evident and simplistic; nothing new in fact. Indeed, governments and CPD providers might say that they do all this already. However, the evidence of the authors in the different chapters suggests that saying is not the same as enacting, particularly with regard to the third point above, scholarly reflection, an area in which HE has a considerable input and interest. The authors in this book are not alone in thinking that HE is being marginalised from the development of CPD in the UK, particularly in England. This view is supported in the recent position paper put together by the CPD committee of the Universities Council for the Education of Teachers (UCET, 2006).

This marginalisation is based essentially on a backward-looking delivery model of CPD, in which CPD in England particularly is being given the same central government direction as, in turn, the curriculum, assessment, inspection, teacher education and pedagogy have been. The UCET position paper confirms the marginalisation of the HE contribution to CPD in England and Wales in recent years. It reflects the need to recover from the hitherto centralist and managerialist focus on teachers' professional learning. This focus has resulted in what Lingard *et al.* (2003) have termed a 'hollowed-out depthlessness' in education, in which there has been a collapse of 'consensus about the purposes of schooling and the constitution of citizens and the nation' (2003: 13). The need for a values framework is evident in how Hugh Kearns and Maureen Thatcher (Chapter 1) highlight the ways in which teachers write about their practice and in the emphasis in the portfolios on the detectable changes in the teachers' philosophical statements about their beliefs.

For teachers in England and Wales, there may be an argument that the extended remit of the Training and Development Agency (TDA) in relation to CPD will itself provide a new design for teachers' professional learning that is more collaborative and non-hierarchical. Less best practice and top-down, in other words! However, the draft document resulting from the consultation (TDA, 2006) suggests that the new design, whilst advocating collaboration through a coaching and mentoring strand, remains standards-driven and top-down. For example, critical engagement with research does not begin until teachers reach the 'excellent' stage. The concept of 'teacher leadership' is still premised on a dissemination or cascade model, centred on the responsibilities of identified 'expert' teachers (or Excellent, or Advanced Skills Teachers (ASTs)) to model practice and monitor others. There is no sense that teachers who are not yet at these stages may be able to initiate and sustain excellent practice in collaborative ways. This has not been the experience with many of the newly qualified teachers (NQTs) on the Master of Teaching (MTeach) course at the Institute of Education, University of London.

The standards do now include more of the right language, e.g. a focus on 'collective responsibility', but the different roles allocated to teachers make it difficult to know how they can be equipped to contribute throughout their careers – or before some of the talented ones have left. It is still a hierarchical design for CPD, underpinning this understanding of leadership, still with a greater emphasis on 'informed' practice for Excellent Teachers and ASTs. This is as problematic as it is promising. We must ask: Informed by whom? For what educational purposes? According to what values or belief system? There is insufficient focus on a critical stance towards working with 'information' on which to develop teaching, whether it be 'research' or statistics/data types.

Taking into account the current CPD landscape in the UK and the position taken by the TDA consultation paper, the UCET paper highlights, rightly in our view, the need for HE to be proactive in forging links with the range of stakeholders in CPD and to seek to bring them together rather than competing within different models for professional learning. This book aims to make a significant contribution to such a call, but at the same time warns that HE needs to go further than entering into a spirit of collaboration with other providers. We should also lead a review of the importance of independent criticality in teachers' learning and how it is to be achieved. To this end, the UCET paper begins to address the need for different countries within the UK to learn from each other and acknowledges the gap between the role of HE in the English/Welsh and other systems. This is a way forward that we deem to be of central importance.

The transformative nature of the new designs

The newness of what is being suggested lies in the transformative aspects of the three key themes that this book has identified – shared practice, collaborative learning networks and scholarly reflection on practice.

Shared practice

Professional learning through shared practice, for example, transforms teachers through the mutuality of learning that comes from authentic exchanges about practice that lead into changes in practice. This professional learning needs to be much more like Fielding *et al.*'s (2005) joint practice development, in which teachers have more choice about their professional learning, and who contributes to it. This may be at times a best practice model delivered by experts. However, it may also be a more constructivist or co-constructivist form of learning, which has the potential for teachers to be agents for change through mutuality of learning, rather than invariably being passive recipients of change. This balance is noted by authors in different national contexts within the UK. In their chapter based on the Northern Ireland context, Hugh Kearns and Maureen Thatcher (Chapter 1) advocated a balance in CPD provision, with a greater focus on sustainable, transformative, contextualised and self-regulated learning. This would offer teachers more of Lingard *et al.*'s 'positive thesis' (2003) for professional learning in contexts of continual change, as Caroline Daly and Norbert Pachler (Chapter 2) propose from an English context. And Jim O'Brien (Chapter 9), in Scotland, ends his chapter considering that the 'jury is still out' on whether the Scottish Chartered Teacher model of CPD will result in the enhanced pedagogy it seeks. Or, as he questions, will it actually lead to a reification of the dominant 'best practice' model, which is not necessarily informed by research, debate and experimentation, the importance of which for teachers is highlighted by Anne Turvey and Hilary Kemeny in Chapter 5?

Collaborative learning networks

The book's second theme is the strength of collaborative networks in providing effective professional learning, which includes, as with shared practice, an element of choice about who, when and why teachers join networks. A network can be subject-, phase- or experience-based, as most are currently, but they can also be non-hierarchical, cross-phase, cross-subject or cross-experience. Whatever the focus of the professional learning is, the experience should not always be a lone activity, as Karen Turner and Shirley Simon (Chapter 3) discuss in relation to portfolios. Collaboration, they say, is needed for enhancing reflective processes, but a good balance, enabling both individual and collective reflection, is currently dependent entirely on circumstance, not choice. Louise Johns-Shepherd and Elizabeth Gowing (Chapter 4) discussed the benefits of interest-based, collaborative networks that seek to transfer and disseminate evidenced practice, not the more seductive, simplistic one-way best practice approach currently in existence. This would be a truly transformative approach to networks, as teachers draw on their own and others' practice-based evidence to change their and others' practice. As with their fellow authors, they see networks as complex and organic. A new design for professional learning would, they say, need to acknowledge the multilayered and connected nature of networked learning as well as the tremendous variety of networks, be they large, small, local, national, face-to-face or virtual. We are arguing in this book that the teaching profession needs structure for professional learning that is genuinely network-based, built less on creating new, organised networks and more focused on providing time and opportunities for the fostering of collaborative ones. The tension then is, as Jon Pickering (Chapter 8) discusses, between teacher networks that are solely exclusive by reflecting group interests and hierarchies, and those that offer inclusivity by encouraging mutuality of interest and contribution. It is a collaboration that is co-operatively grounded, not ring-fenced by compliance. As Norbert Pachler (Chapter 10) concludes in his end piece, teachers' professional learning needs to sit in democratic and discursive, i.e. collaborative, notions of professionalism.

Scholarly reflection on practice

The third key theme advocating new designs for professional learning focuses on the benefits of scholarly reflection on practice. As noted in the Introduction, this concept sees the fusion of theory and practice as being at the heart of teachers' professionalism. The tendency to see the theory and practice of teaching as separate entities or, at best, complementary strands misses the point for the

Index